Invest Like a Girl

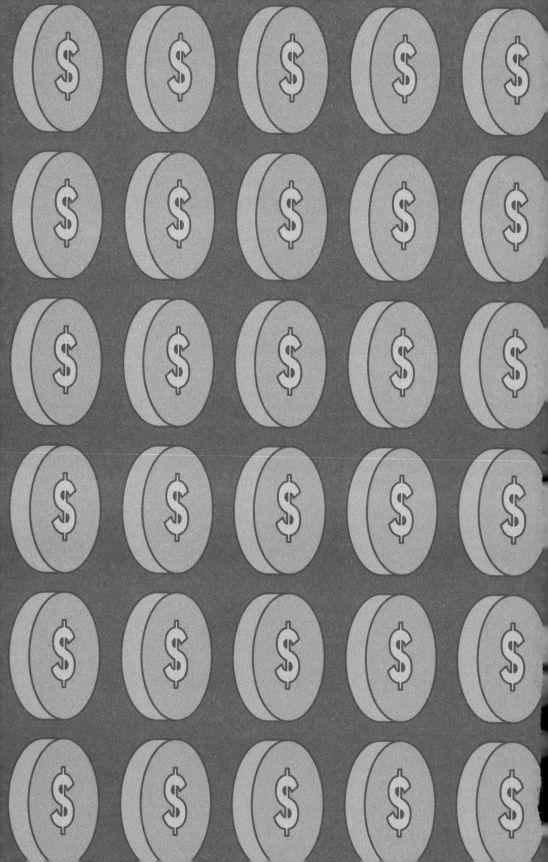

Invest Like a Girl

Jump into the Stock Market, Reach Your Money Goals, and Build Wealth

Jessica Spangler

RODALE
NEW YORK

Copyright © 2024 by Jessica Spangler

Published in the United States by Rodale Books, an imprint of Random House,
a division of Penguin Random House LLC, New York.
RodaleBooks.com | RandomHouseBooks.com

RODALE and the Plant colophon are registered trademarks of Penguin Random
House LLC.

This book is designed to provide general information about personal finance for
educational purposes only. The author is not a licensed financial advisor, and
neither the author nor the publisher are engaged in rendering legal, financial, or
other professional services by publishing this book. Readers are encouraged to
consult an appropriate professional to answer their questions specific to their
unique personal financial situations. The author and publisher specifically disclaim
any liability, loss, or risk incurred as a result of the use and application of any of
the information contained in this book.

Library of Congress Cataloging-in-Publiction Data is available upon request.

ISBN 978-0-593-58172-8
Ebook ISBN 978-0-593-58173-5

Printed in the United States of America

Book design by Andrea Lau
Interior art: Molibdenis-Studio/Shutterstock
Jacket design by Anna Bauer Carr
Jacket art: Simple Line/Shutterstock

10 9 8 7 6 5 4 3 2 1

First Edition

To my mom, who taught me everything I know about
courage, resilience, and power

Contents

Invest Like a Girl

Introduction

I'll admit, it took me a little while to understand that women aren't treated like men when it comes to money. I attribute this to the fact that I grew up surrounded by powerhouse women. For the better part of my adult life, and certainly by the time my brain's critical thinking center was fully formed, the primary breadwinners in my family were all women. But it didn't start out that way.

I was seven years old when I first began to learn the immeasurable value of financial independence and the powers of choice, opportunity, and flexibility that come with it. At the time, I thought the most exciting part of my day would be my childhood friend's birthday party at Santini's, the pizza place down the road. And it was, until my next-door neighbor instead of my mom arrived to pick me up. Everyone was hush-hush, as if this were perfectly normal, but I knew it wasn't. Kids aren't stupid. Where were my parents?

The gnawing feeling that something was gravely wrong sat in the pit of my stomach as if it lived there—heavy as the weight of all the basketballs I had just spent the last several hours shooting and missing (mind you, I've never been a star athlete). I made small talk on the car ride home, for reasons I didn't understand. Confusion turned into tension, and the tension grew for what seemed like days. No one was telling me anything. Just when I felt that I might explode, I finally learned the news: My dad had suffered a massive heart attack at work. The doctors think he died before he even reached the hospital. They did everything they could. He didn't make it.

My world was flipped upside down, second only to my mother's. In an instant, she had been thrust into the role of single mother and all that came with it. At the time, she didn't have a "job" per se, though her stay-at-home-parent duties could have earned her a six-figure salary if she had been paid for them. She had no college degree. She had no income. What she did have was me and my little brother, sheer willpower, and a measure of determination that I've spent my entire life learning to replicate.

Newly widowed with two kids in tow, my mom had many jobs to do, but most pressing was to find one that paid her. She started as a real estate appraiser. As it turned out, that first required 2,500 hours of unpaid (or barely paid) apprenticeship. Ultimately, the apprenticeship paycheck didn't quite cut it, so my mom turned to real estate sales as a financial cushion while she continued working on her appraiser license.

As for me, I learned by osmosis, and I learned *all kinds of things.* Aside from learning to cook fish sticks in the toaster oven and convince my brother they were chicken nuggets on her workdays, I went on listing appointments, tagged along to open houses, and watched (and watched, and watched) my mom draft contracts. By thirteen, I could spot a house with bad energy from a mile away. By sixteen, I knew what foreclosures were and how they happened. By the skin of our teeth, we survived the housing bubble of 2007 and the housing crash of 2008 that followed, and I watched it all from the passenger seat.

But I also learned about the perceptions people have about women and money, and the very real sexism and gender bias that take place surrounding it. Real estate appraisal was a male-dominated field back then and still is now. I remember how many of the more experienced men talked down to my mom, though I didn't (and couldn't) fully understand why at the time. I was too young to interpret such chauvinistic behavior, which I would see over and over again. My mom used to half-joke that if she were just a few inches taller, perhaps they would take her more seriously. She felt more powerful on the phone than she did in person, when the guy on the other end would need to "man up" and face the music: that she was, in fact, a woman, and that he would need to deal with it. I picked up on these patriarchal signals even as a child (and I still remember them more than twenty years later), but I didn't recognize them as blatant discrimination until I was much, much older.

After everything I've told you, you might describe my mother as courageous. Resilient. Powerful. And yet, my mom describes herself during this time in her life, the period after my dad's passing, as "feeling like an egg." She felt so fragile. At any moment, she worried that something might happen to her, and her kids would be left with nothing. For both of us (and for a long time), the prevailing thought process of our shared experience became fear: It was a day like any other, until it wasn't. At any given moment, I could be minutes away from having no source of reliable income. Minutes away from having no way to pay the bills, or to buy groceries. A blessing and a curse, my dad's death forced us to see the world through the lens of three guiding principles: that I cannot rely on another person for income, that I will not rely on another person for income, and that one source of income is only one step away from no source of income.

You might be thinking my three tenets sound more like evidence of textbook scarcity mindset, and you'd be right. It took time and many more life and money lessons to shake the feeling, and I'm not certain

I'll ever shake it completely. But, for all of its shortcomings, this simple framework (and more challenging shift in mindset) did lead me on a lifelong quest to achieve complete financial independence—and, eventually, though I didn't know it at the time, to compile the most important bits I've learned and share them here with you.

From where I sat then and from where I sit now, it would be impossible for me to ever describe my mother as an egg. Through every financial pitfall, I learned courage. Through every struggle, I learned resilience. What might have at first pass instilled scarcity in time evolved into empowerment—for both of us. In retrospect and in due time, I built my own custom-crafted library of financial know-how. I soon realized that I knew enough about money to never need to rely on another person for income (if I don't want to). If I ever lost my source(s) of income, I knew I could always find another one. And, most important, my financial knowledge afforded me the enormous privilege of choice—and no one could ever take that away from me.

But, alas, for everything my life experiences taught me about money, it wasn't enough to build real wealth. I knew that if I wanted to do something substantial with my money knowledge, to really change my future, I needed to put it to good use. I needed to learn how to invest.

You see, I knew that knowing more about the life-changing tool called investing could open endless financial doors, but it hasn't been easy for women to gain access to the key. Until a short while ago, women couldn't even open the most basic of bank accounts. Credit cards for unmarried women didn't come into the picture until much later, in 1974 (as if marital status should dictate your ability to repay debt). And even with the new laws, Black women still struggle to be approved for the standard financial products, like loans and mortgages, that the legislation had promised them.

To make matters worse, financial education can be hard to come by. In 2022, less than 25 percent of high schools offered formal personal finance education to their students. Without a clear structure in place to transfer financial knowledge, many women often wind up internalizing the bad messaging they receive about money from society at large. The media we consume, the world we live in, and the stereotypes we take as given become our textbook.

Instead of being encouraged to take calculated risks, women are told to play it safe. (Why invest when you could save?) Instead of being shown the tools we need to grow our money, we're advised to make our meals at home and clip coupons. (You'll never buy a house if you don't buy things on sale.) Instead of being taught how to spend our money according to our values, we're asked if we really need that mascara or why we're going to Starbucks again. (You spent *how much* on a purse?) Instead of being trusted to make the best financial decisions for ourselves, the unsolicited questions, comments, and concerns about our choices somehow manage to squeeze through. Feeling bad about spending money is like a rite of passage into womanhood.

But it doesn't stop there. We're supposed to feel bad about making money, too. A woman who pursues career over family is materialistic (but a man is driven). A woman who seeks a partner with strong financial footing is a gold digger (but a man is wise). Women who strive to make more money are greedy (but men are ambitious), and women who negotiate their salary are aggressive and pushy (but men are assertive and confident). I saw it firsthand: the road to becoming a powerhouse woman earns you a lot of dirty looks before it ever earns you praise.

Unsurprisingly, this bias has consequences. Among other things, it contributes to gaps, and there are gaps aplenty. First, there's the gender wage gap; even now, on average, women continue to be paid less than men for doing the same work. Making 82 cents to every man's dollar can equate to hundreds of thousands of dollars in lost wages and investment assets over the course of our working lifetimes, and that's before you factor in the career breaks that women are more likely to take if they choose to have children or care for their elderly parents or in-laws.

Next, we've got the gender financial literacy gap, which persists well beyond our working years. More than 80 percent of women between the ages of sixty and seventy-five could not pass a financial literacy quiz designed to test their knowledge on retirement, which nearly *twice* as many men were able to pass.

Then, there's the gender wealth gap: Families headed by women own roughly half of the wealth owned by families headed by men. And, for the record, people tend to assume that anyway, even if they've never heard the statistic. When we eventually relocated to a new town, many perplexed parents made my mom feel like an outcast. How could a single parent, a single mom no less, afford to buy a home?

And last, but certainly not least, the gender investing gap: Women keep most of their money in the bank, while men invest it. Whether or not you were the intended recipient, you've likely encountered the resounding message that investing is of utmost importance. Despite what we've been told (and told, and told again) about saving, it is investing that helps you grow your money much faster than letting it sit in your bank account. (We'll learn why in chapter 2).

But for women, investing is especially important. As we've seen (example: my father), women tend to outlive men, which means we need more money to sustain us after we retire. In part because we live longer, we also tend to face higher health-care costs as we age. Investing not only means that you can eventually stop working, it also allows you to actually enjoy your time off, build a financial cushion, and comfortably take care of yourself should any health concerns arise. You can more easily survive an unexpected expense, exit a relationship that makes you feel unsafe, or leave a job that makes you dread waking up in the morning. There's real power in financial independence, and investing helps you achieve it.

And, as it turns out, when given the opportunity to do so, surprising no one, we're *great* at it. In Fidelity's 2021 Women and Investing Study, only a third of women said they consider themselves to be an investor at all, but even without the up-front confidence, women *still* had stronger returns, outperforming men by forty basis points or 0.4 percent on average, which could equate to tens of thousands of dollars in additional gains over time. In short, investing is awesome, but it's even better when you invest like a girl. In fact, it's one of the most efficient ways to get ahead.

So how do we unlearn generations of bad bias and replace it with real financial knowledge? The same way rich white dudes have been boosting each other up for all of eternity: We teach ourselves, and then we teach each other. Women are incredible at smashing down barriers. We've been doing it for so long it might as well be our middle name. Make it harder, and we'll still do it better.

I'm not an investment banker or a billionaire CEO, but that's exactly my point. You don't need to be any of those things to be a great investor. You don't need to have a trust fund or work on Wall Street to start building wealth, nor do you need a formal education in finance, a custodial investment account, or a generational wealth funnel. There are actionable steps that all of us can take to improve our financial footing, and I've spent the last decade of my life dedicated to figuring them out.

To set myself up for financial success, I needed more than just my memories. I needed to learn how to invest: in both myself and in the stock market. And that, I can proudly say, I've taught myself. I've leveled up from investing just $5 each month to sometimes more like five *figures* each month. I went from full-time student to full-time clinical pharmacist, annihilated my student loans, and, eventually, I built a six-figure business. Now, I share money knowledge online to more than a million people each day, with the goal of making financial literacy easy to understand and accessible to all.

What's the most important lesson I learned along the way? Knowledge really is power. If there's one thing sharing money info with the masses has taught me, it's that the force that holds so many back from making strides with their finances isn't lack of interest but lack of knowledge. If you're picking up this book, there's a good chance you want to have more money and you want to start investing, but you don't know how or where to start. That sounds like a complex problem, and the good news is that this book has answers.

Invest Like a Girl is for *all* women: women who have money but lack financial freedom, women without money who want to level up their finances, women with life goals and retirement goals that they reeeeally need to start funding, women who have already started investing but want to enhance their existing knowledge, women who have no desire to start investing but have lots of desire to stop working one day, and everyone in between.

Think of this book as your beginner's guide, your jumping-off point to achieving your money goals and kick-starting your financial independence with the help of investing. A handbook of practical tips and tricks, data-driven tools, and everything I've learned over the years of doing it myself, plus a handful of mistakes I wish someone would have told me about so that I didn't have to make them. Everything I share comes from getting my own hands dirty, learning the ropes, and doing the work. And with all the worksheets, checklists, and exercises I've included in the chapters that follow, you can dive right in and do the same.

Once upon a time, the loudest voice in my head told me that I must make enough money to survive, that I must not rely on anyone else for income, and that I must have multiple streams of income to do so. Now, every day, the even louder voice in my head tells me I can do all that *and more*. I can reach my money goals, splurge every once in a while, buy the damn pumpkin spice latte, and still retire on my terms. Because I gave myself the tools, the time, and the knowledge—because I trust *myself* to take care of me—I have no need to worry. I know that, no matter what happens financially, *I* will help me and carry me through. And I hope that, by the end of this book, you'll know that you can, too.

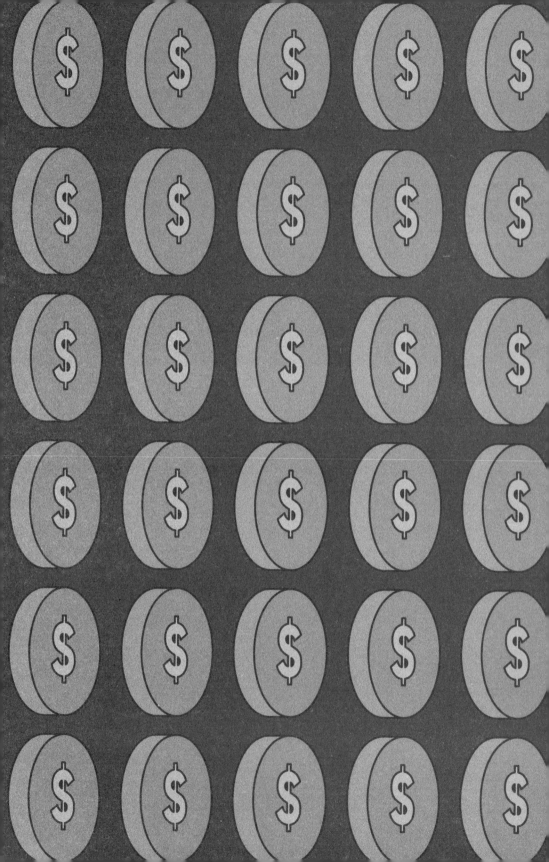

PART I

Building a Solid Foundation

Let's be real—the gender investing gap is no joke. Male investors may have had a head start, but that doesn't mean we can't catch up. In fact, we're more likely to surpass them in the process.

Time and time again, women have proven that we're not just good, but great at money. Despite having far fewer years to accumulate it, women now hold more than 30 percent of global wealth, amounting to tens of trillions of dollars in assets, and this number is only expected to rise in the coming decades. Women-owned businesses generate $1.9 trillion in revenue and employ over nine million people, companies with at least 30 percent women in leadership positions add 6 percent to their net profit margins, and during the 2008 financial crisis, women-led companies in the S&P 500 index outperformed male-led companies by 18 percent. But just in case that wasn't enough to convince your meathead uncle of our investing prowess, direct him to the study I mentioned earlier. You know, the one that analyzed more than five million Fidelity customers over the last ten years and found that when comparing the investing returns of men and women, it was women who walked away the clear winners.

The overall implication is even clearer: Women know exactly what they're doing, once they know how to do it. This section will level the playing field and provide you with the tools you need to make your own informed investment decisions. You'll find resources and exercises designed to boost your knowledge about investing and your financial literacy as a whole, plus some added tips and tricks to help you take actionable steps toward building wealth along the way.

Women have lots of money (though there's always more to be had), we spend lots of money (though there's always more to be spent), we make lots of money (though there's always more to be made), and we can learn to *invest* lots of money, too. And, boy, when we do, we are very, very good at it. We have all the power we need to overcome the gender investing gap for good and build lasting generational wealth, and there's more for the taking. So let's get started.

Chapter 1

Make Your Money Work for You

Have you ever tried to bake a pizza without first preheating the oven? (Please tell me I'm not the only one cursed with this degree of impatience. I chose to work in the *emergency* department for a reason.) You might have satisfied your pizza craving, sure, but the dough was probably weird and soggy, and I know some of that cheese in the middle was still frozen. Or what about painting your nails without the base coat and top coat? Mission accomplished, your nails are painted, but your tips will be chipped by the end of the next business day, for sure. I may or may not be speaking from personal experience here, too. Okay, fine, I am.

My mom has a saying: "If you're not going to do a job right, you might as well not do it at all." Doing a job right doesn't mean doing a job *perfectly*, but it does mean doing it in a way that'll save you from unnecessary headaches later.

All good things need a primer—including investing. To build wealth that lasts a long time, not just a good time, you'll need to set yourself up with systems that can carry you well beyond the short term. This chapter will help you do just that.

Your Investing Prep Work

So, I heard you want to turn your hard-earned cash into a money-making machine. I do, too, and I love the enthusiasm, but before you dive headfirst into the world of stocks and bonds, there are five crucial steps you must conquer to set the stage. Think of them as your investing prep work. Once you have a solid foundation in place, you'll be ready to advance to the next level.

FYI, there's no need to rush any of these five steps. Naturally, some of them—such as paying off high-interest debt and building an emergency fund—may take some time, so feel free to go at your own pace. Likewise, if you've already completed some (or all) of these checklist items, feel free to fast-forward. At the end of the day, taking any one of these five steps will put you leaps and bounds ahead financially, so don't get caught up in analysis paralysis. There's no need to worry about the perfect order or "doing the wrong thing." If you're looking to improve your financial future, the only wrong thing would be not preparing to invest at all.

Step #1: Get a Clear Picture of Your Net Worth—What You OWN and What You OWE

I have only experienced two things in life so scary that they nearly ruined my ability to sleep forever. The first was watching *The Ring* in sixth grade (never again), and the second was meeting my six-figure student loan balance for the very first time. Throughout college, I avoided my student loans like the plague, and I was damn good at it. I endured eight years of higher education earning a doctorate, and, let me tell you, I made it all eight without even so much as glancing at that federal student aid website. Why bother? I already kept a running tally of my loan balance (plus interest) in my head . . . or so I thought.

Mental math, I said. All I needed to do was carry the one . . . add another several thousand dollars in interest over there . . . I knew what my balance was, right?

Wrong. To say I was off by thousands of dollars would be an understatement. Tens of thousands of dollars was more like it. As much as I love compound interest when it comes to investing, I can confirm that it really *does* work the same way in reverse with student loans. (We'll discuss compound interest in more detail on page 63.)

The first thing I felt was shock, and then that old familiar feeling came around: fear. How the hell was I ever going to pay this off?

The anger came later. How could I have ever possibly understood the enormity of a six-figure loan burden at age seventeen?!

I took a break. I ate a snack. I went to bed. And then I made a plan. What came afterward, I can't say I fully expected.

I felt *better* knowing the balance. I felt empowered. Once I actually knew the number, I could actually make a plan. I could prioritize paying off my private student loans first, since they had higher interest rates. Meanwhile, I could arrange for income-based repayment on the rest of my federal loans so that I wouldn't get slammed with both payments at the same time.

And it worked. My *very* expensive diploma now sits in a not nearly as expensive frame. Taped to its glass is my favorite letter of all time. The one telling me my private student loan balance is officially zero.

You can't know how much you stand to win or lose with investing if you have no idea what's going on with your money. No matter how scary it might be to crunch the numbers, you need to look your money in the face. Instead of being frozen in fear, running the numbers allows you to light your inner fire and take action. And once you do, you might just find yourself feeling *so* much better about your finances.

The first place to start is with your net worth, which offers a generalized view of your overall financial picture at a specific moment in time. The easiest way to calculate your net worth—if you're nerdy like me—is to create a spreadsheet. Drawing a table on a piece of paper or using the worksheet on page 18 will work great, too. Create two columns, one titled *assets* and the other titled *liabilities*.

An asset is anything that you own that has monetary value. In general, this means something that you can sell for cash or something that holds some kind of underlying cash value. This can be a physical object like a house, a car, jewelry, expensive machinery, or equipment, but it can also be less tangible things, like all the money in your bank accounts and all your investments.

A liability, on the other hand, is anything involving money that you owe. In short, liabilities are debts. These include credit card balances, car loans, medical debt, personal loans, mortgage loans, or student loan balances.

List your assets and liabilities in their respective columns and then tally up the total for each (see the table that follows for some examples). To find your net worth, simply subtract your total liabilities from your total assets.

Assets		Liabilities	
ITEM	VALUE	DEBT	AMOUNT
Cash	$13,000	Mortgage	$165,000
Furniture	$7,500	Car Loan	$7,000
Investments	$4,000	Student Loans	$27,000
House Value	$210,000	Credit Cards	$6,000
Car Value	$17,000		
Total:	$251,500	Total:	$205,000

Net Worth: $251,500—$205,000 = $46,500

Worksheet: Calculate Your Net Worth

I totally understand it can be daunting to see the numbers for what they are, but the sooner you know what you're working with, the sooner you can make a game plan. Your net worth doesn't change if you keep yourself in the dark, so it's best to turn the lights on and take it all in! Besides, it might turn out to be less scary than you think.

Assets		Liabilities	
ITEM	VALUE	DEBT	AMOUNT
Cash		Mortgage	
Furniture		Car Loan	
Investments		Student Loans	
House Value		Credit Cards	
Car Value			
Total:		Total:	

Net Worth (Assets minus Liabilites):

If you have a positive net worth, nice work! If you have a negative net worth, don't panic. At a glance, all your net worth says is that right now, today, you have more assets than you do liabilities, or vice versa.

In either case, this big-picture view of your finances can help you figure out your next steps to get investing-ready. For example, if the majority of your liabilities column is filled with high-interest credit card debt, you'll likely need to pay down your cards before moving on to investing, regardless of whether your net worth is positive or negative. If the majority of your liabilities come from low-interest debt, it might make more sense to spend the bulk of your time investing, especially if the potential return on your investment will be higher than the interest that you'll owe. (We'll talk about how to prioritize paying down debt on page 49.)

Step #2: Set a Budget and Understand Your Cash Flow

If you're going to start investing, there are some hard pills to swallow, if you will, before you begin. (I'm a pharmacist by trade. I'll let you decide what that says about my personality, but I *have* been known to get a little punny on occasion.) The first hard pill to swallow is that there are only two ways to have more money available for investing. You either need to spend less, or you need to make more.

That said, we don't need to make grand sweeping changes to our lifestyle, cut our spending in half, or deprive ourselves of everything in life that brings us joy. We just need to take a hard look at our budget.

What budget? Okay, fair. I don't fantasize about making one in my spare time either, but keeping track of our income and expenses lets us know how much we can afford to set aside for investing, and the amount we designate can quite literally change our lives financially. If investing is one of the most effective ways to grow our money, we've got to figure out how to dedicate some of our money to it.

To create a good budget, one that you like and will actually stick to, you'll first need to track your income and expenses. This will require the help of another good spreadsheet, or a list on a piece of paper, or the worksheet I've included on page 20, and the best way to fill it out is to be obsessive and meticulous. Just kidding (sort of), but the more detailed here the better. If your net worth is the big picture, your income and expenses are all the teeny-tiny little pixels that make up the final snapshot of your finances. The more pixels you add, the better the resolution, and the clearer the snapshot becomes.

Create two separate columns, *income* and *expenses*, or use the worksheet provided for you, and start writing. Channel your inner spreadsheet extraordinaire and document every single source of income and every single expense you have to your name on a *monthly* basis.

For income, this means anything that reliably makes you money each and every month, even if the precise amount isn't always the same. For most people, this means your paycheck after taxes. If you have any additional income sources, like a side hustle or a small business, write down those earnings, too. If you work a commission job, receive tips for wages, or your income is variable from month to month, take all your income for the year, and then divide that number by twelve to average it out on a monthly basis.

Your expense list might be quite a bit longer than your income column. Don't feel bad; that's normal. Most people don't have thirty-seven different income streams the way we have thirty-seven different bills. Cell phone bill, car payment, rent, credit card bills, student loan payments. If it's a bill that you might only pay once a year, or once every six months (think car insurance or homeowner's insurance), divide that bill by twelve (or by six if it's an expense you pay every six months) so that you can account for it on a—you guessed it—monthly basis.

Worksheet: Track Your Monthly Income and Expenses

The idea here is to get a clear picture of all your money coming in and going out for a thirty-day period. Write down all your income, and every bill you can think of.

MONTHLY INCOME

Income Source	Amount
TOTAL	

MONTHLY EXPENSES

Expense	Amount
TOTAL	

Once you know where your money is coming from and where it's going, now it's time to budget.

If you're anything like me, you might have a hard time deeply connecting (or surface-level connecting, or connecting at all) with any one budgeting method, because your personal finances are always changing. Budgets often seem so rigid, and anything I want to use consistently needs to feel flexible. A super-effective budget method that works for me—and has been praised by both rookies and veterans alike—is the 50/30/20 rule. It's simple enough to get you going, and adaptable enough to adjust as needed. Best of all, it doesn't ask you to deprive yourself. (As you'll see, you'll still be able to spend almost a third of your income on things you want but don't need, which seems pretty darn reasonable, if you ask me.)

To start, you'll designate a fixed percentage of your income to three easy-to-remember categories:

- 50 percent toward needs (think food and groceries, rent or mortgage, and minimum payments toward credit card bills)
- 30 percent toward wants (think nice-to-haves, like a new video game you've been eyeing, concert tickets, or a bucket list trip to Italy)
- 20 percent toward savings, additional debt repayment, and investing (think extra money to set aside for the future after all your needs and wants are accounted for)

To make your own 50/30/20 budget, head back to the detailed expense list you created on page 21. Using the bullet points above as a general guideline, categorize each listed expense as a need, want, or future. Then, add up all the expenses in each category, and divide it by your total monthly income to determine its percentage. Again, the beauty of this budget is that it's flexible. Don't worry if the percentages you prefer to use aren't *exactly* in line with the numbers listed here, but do use them as a point of reference, and compare what you've outlined in your income and expense lists to what you see above.

Here's an example of what this might look like in practice:

Monthly Income: $5,000

Category	Expense	Amount	Budget
Needs	Mortgage or Rent	$1,300	50%: $2,500
	Groceries	$350	
	Credit Card	$400	
	Utilities	$200	
	Transportation	$250	
	TOTAL:	**$2,500**	
Wants	Shopping	$500	30%: $1,500
	Travel	$500	
	Experiences	$500	
	TOTAL:	**$1,500**	
Future	Savings	$250	20%: $1,000
	Investments	$750	
	TOTAL:	**$1,000**	

Worksheet: Budget Your Expenses

Monthly Income: _____

Category	Expense	Amount	Budget
Needs			50%: _____
	TOTAL:		
Wants			30%: _____
	TOTAL:		
Future			20%: _____
	TOTAL:		

So, how's your table looking? Does your rent alone make up more than 50 percent of your expenses? Yikes, not ideal, but not totally uncommon in a high cost-of-living area. If you're having a treat-yourself day, or a treat-yourself month, does your wants column add up to 35 percent instead of 30 percent right now? I won't judge you for living your best life every once in a while, as long as it isn't keeping you from achieving your overall goals.

At the same time, the closer we can get our numbers to the targets above, the better shot we have at finding some leftover money. If half of all your streaming subscriptions disappeared overnight and $50 landed in your pocket, would you even notice they were gone? If your food delivery app spend was reduced from $700 to $400, plus a $200 grocery list, could you still eat all your favorite foods and find some extra cash to move toward the future category?

The reason I ask is because the 20 percent you designate for your future includes money to set aside for investing, and investing is the name of the game here. This should not imply that you must eliminate your morning coffee to start investing. (My five-dollar medium iced caramel latte with oat milk pre–twelve-hour shift is nonnegotiable on a twice-weekly basis.) But if too many of our present-day needs and wants are taking up too much space in our budget, we should try to knock *some of them* down a notch to make room for our financial future. Even better if, during our meticulous budgeting efforts, we can identify and eliminate the "financial fluff" expenses we all accumulate and that we don't value that much anyway. Remember that *you* are your most important bill. Your money goals are there for you to reach them, and if you can do this by making small changes that have big impacts, why not go for it?

TIP: The more you can afford to set aside for investing, the better, but you should never ever feel that you *can't* start investing until you can set aside an arbitrary amount of money (in this case, 20 percent). Investing is not a gatekeeping restaurant: There is no minimum spend required. Any amount invested is better than no amount invested, whether that's $5 a month or $500 a month, and the sooner you get started the better.

Step #3: Build an Emergency Fund That Covers Three to Six Months of Basics and Necessities

What's that saying? Life's what happens when we're busy making other plans? Or another personal favorite: When one light goes out they all go out? As much as we would love to waltz through life with no interruptions, that is simply not how this thing goes. Sometimes (and often when we least expect it) we are confronted with an emergency expense—your dog finds a rogue grape and eats it, two weeks later your car battery dies in the freezing cold, and then you lock your keys inside your car with no spare in sight. Oddly specific? Well, I've been there, and I've learned from it. An emergency fund is an essential player in *anyone's* financial game plan, and for good reason. It's specifically designed to hold money for the times that would financially devastate you otherwise. It allows you to financially expect the unexpected. (Take that, universe.)

The classic rule of thumb for an emergency fund is that it should hold enough money to cover three to six months' worth of living expenses. Reason being, in the hopefully never-event that you lose all your sources of income and simultaneously face an unexpected expense like an emergency medical bill, veterinary care for a beloved pet, or last-minute car troubles, the emergency fund will be there to keep you afloat and pay your bills while you hunt for a new source of cash. Emergency funds are best kept in a high-yield savings account (HYSA) where they can earn higher interest than what you would typically see in a traditional savings account.

What's the catch? There isn't one. Banks that offer high-yield savings accounts usually do not have physical buildings, so they save big money on costs like electricity and rent, and can pass those savings on to you in the form of higher interest rates. You could also consider using a credit union and take advantage of their unique business structure, which operates on a not-for-profit basis to offer competitive interest rates to their members.

Why create an emergency fund before you start investing? Because the money you invest isn't as readily accessible as the money you keep in a high-yield savings account. An emergency fund, aptly named, is designed for an emergency. It's simply holding cash, and it allows you to access that cash quickly if you need it in a pinch. On the other hand, an investment account is holding stocks, bonds, and a whole bunch of other financial instruments. These financial instruments have cash value, sure, but to turn them into cash, they will first need to be sold. If the market is having a particularly bad day, the cash value of your investments might be struggling. Since we can't predict how the market will behave on any given day (let alone the day of an emergency), it would be a real shame to convert your investments into cash only to take a loss out of necessity. For that reason, an emergency fund is best kept within the safe and cozy confines of a high-yield savings account, where it can't fall victim to fluctuations on short notice.

TIP: While saving three to six months' worth of living expenses is the general recommendation, it's a good idea to customize the amount you save to fit your situation. For example, if you work in a super-niche field—say, I don't know, wildlife conservation for a very particular species of insect (hey, I have a friend who does this; don't knock it)—it might take a lot longer than six months to find a new job. In this case, it might be better to dedicate a little extra money to your emergency fund. If, instead, you're a retail store manager and you'd say your skill set is easily transferable to a wide variety of roles, you might be able to find a new position in no time. In that case, your emergency fund might need to hold only one to two months' worth of living expenses. Personal finance is personal. The point is this: After you've set up your emergency fund and you feel comfortable that you've saved enough, investing becomes much more doable, even with any financial hiccups you might sustain along the way.

Worksheet: Calculate the
Amount for Your Emergency Fund

Using your monthly expense worksheet from page 23, multiply your total in the Needs column by the number of months you estimate it would take you to find a new job. This number will be your general savings goal for your emergency fund.

_____ × _____ = _____

Total monthly amount for Needs   Number of months   Emergency fund amount

Step #4: Eliminate Any High-Interest Debt

There is a story from Greek mythology about a guy named Sisyphus who was punished by the gods. Basically, the gods were pretty ticked off at Sisyphus for all his trickery, so they condemned him to an eternity of rolling a giant boulder up a hill, only to have it roll back down again as soon as he reached the top. Sisyphus was doomed to repeat this task forever, over and over again, without ever being able to complete it. If you're a checklist kind of gal, this probably sounds like your personal nightmare.

Philosophers often use the story of Sisyphus as a metaphor for the absurdity of human existence. I have no desire to get all existential on you right now, so I'd like to use it as an *investing* metaphor instead. If you're trying to invest while carrying around high-interest debt, you might as well be Sisyphus rolling that gigantic boulder. Talk about fighting an uphill battle.

Not all debt is created equal, and high-interest debt deserves some special attention. Before you start investing, you'll want to seriously focus on reducing your high-interest debt burden. Why? Because for every financial step you take forward, high-interest debt will take you two steps back.

Interest can be good or bad. For your bank accounts, having a higher interest rate is great for you, because you're earning more money on your money: the money you keep in the bank. For your loans, however, a high-interest rate—anything around 7 percent or higher—can set you back big-time.

An example of high-interest debt that might jump out in your head immediately is credit card debt. Credit card interest rates are typically much higher than 7 percent. In fact, at the beginning of 2022, the average credit card interest rate was around 15 percent, and by the end of 2022, it was closer to 20 percent.

This also means that some debt obligations, like student loans and mortgages, are *not* considered high interest, as long as the interest rate is 7 percent or lower (see A Quick Note on Student Loans and Mortgage Payments below). For that reason, you do not need to feel the same sense of urgency in paying them down.

A Quick Note on Student Loans and Mortgage Payments

Many student loans, particularly federal loans, which tend to have lower interest rates than private loans, will not qualify as high-interest debt, under the 7 percent or higher definition. The same can be said for homeowners with a mortgage interest rate less than 7 percent, or any other loan holder with an interest rate below that threshold.

If you fall into any of these categories, you should not feel as though you *must* pay off your entire student loan balance, or your mortgage for that matter, before you can start investing. In fact, depending on your loan balance and projected annual returns, in some cases it would actually behoove you to start investing prior to total debt payoff. Ultimately, what you choose will come down to personal preference and your individual financial goals, but know that choosing to invest and pay off your loans at the same time is a totally viable option.

On the other hand, if you can't possibly imagine investing before making a significant dent in your loan balance, you do you. Not everyone can tolerate large amounts of debt for extended periods, and if you're looking to prioritize payoff so you don't need to worry about monthly payments, feel free to use the strategies I've outlined on page 49.

Although, ideally, all debt will be paid off in a reasonable amount of time, it's important to prioritize paying off high-interest debt before you start investing, because the average investment return will almost certainly not beat the percent APR your credit card is holding you up against. If you're investing in the total stock market, even with an excellent average return of 10 percent per year, that's still no match for your credit card with an interest rate of 16 percent. For example, let's say you have $10,000 in credit card debt with an APR of 16 percent. If you only make the minimum monthly payment of $200, it'll take you nearly seven years to pay it off, and you'll wind up paying more than $15,000, including interest.

Now, let's say you also have $10,000 to invest in the stock market. Historically, the average return on the total stock market over a thirty-year period has been around 10 percent per year. So, if you invest that $10,000 in the stock market, you might expect to earn a return of $1,000 per year (before the magic of compound interest).

But here's the thing: That $1,000 return is less than the nearly $1,600 you would be paying in credit card interest in your very first year. To stop hemorrhaging money and start building wealth, you've got to stop the bleeding at its source.

TIP: If you've already accumulated some credit card debt and had the pleasure of meeting those dreaded interest charges, don't panic. Unlike Sisyphus, you're not doomed to repeat the same task forever and ever. We'll chat soon about how to create an action plan to reduce your high-interest debt burden so that you can jump headfirst into the investing game and get rid of that pesky debt boulder once and for all. Flip to page 49 to learn more.

Worksheet: Classify Your Debts

Take a closer look at all your debt sources, make note of each of their outstanding balances and interest rates, and fill out the table below. You'll take this worksheet with you and put it to good use in a later section, "Out of Debt and into the Game," on page 47.

Debt Source	Outstanding Balance	Interest Rate

Step #5: Establish Your Retirement Accounts

Once you have all those boring pieces squared away, you can finally get to the fun part, right? Definitely, as long as you consider setting yourself up for retirement fun. And you should! The cool thing about retirement accounts is that they come with tax advantages. With a retirement account, you get rewarded for stashing away your money for later, in the form of tax breaks. Pretty cool, right?

These tax breaks differ mainly in when you get to receive them: Some reduce your taxes now, some reduce them later. Some retirement accounts, like a traditional IRA (individual retirement account) or an employer-sponsored 401(k), allow you to deduct your annual contributions from your annual income now (up to a maximum amount), effectively reducing your annual income tax. You get to grow your money over time *and* reduce your taxable income in the process. Because you contribute pre-tax money, your taxes are *deferred* until you start withdrawing money in retirement. On the other hand, a Roth IRA allows you to deposit post-tax dollars into the retirement account. In this account you get your tax break later, because when you withdraw your contributions *and* earnings in retirement, you can do so tax-free.

Of course, the most exciting part about establishing your retirement accounts is that it lets you dip your toes into investing. Saving for retirement has been advertised in the entirely wrong light. Everyone receives the same enthralling workplace pamphlet or the time-honored advice about "saving for retirement," but what we really need to be calling it is *investing* for retirement—because, truthfully, that's what it is! And because retirement accounts are tax-advantaged, they have a special edge over individual brokerage accounts, which is the type of account that most people think of when they hear the word *investing*. While it's easy to feel that you want to skip to the fun part of investing, take solace in knowing that setting up, funding, and investing in your retirement account actually *is* the fun part, because it is investing, and it comes with extra fun benefits in the long term.

 The Roth IRA Billionaire:
A Case Study

The reason tax-advantaged investment accounts are so great is that, without the added expense of taxes weighing you down, your investment has the potential for even higher returns. If you're having trouble visualizing quite how much this matters, take the cofounder of PayPal, Peter Thiel, for example. He invested $1,700 in his company back in 1999 through his Roth IRA.

By the time PayPal went public in 2002, Thiel's initial

investment had grown substantially. And because he had invested through his Roth IRA, he didn't have to pay a single penny in taxes on those gains. But Thiel didn't stop there. He continued to invest in once little-known companies through his Roth IRA, including Facebook in its early days. Today, his Roth IRA is estimated to be worth over $5 billion—all completely tax free.

Thiel's investment strategy faced its fair share of controversy and caused some to criticize the use of Roth IRAs to shelter such large investments for the already mega rich. But love it or hate it, there's no denying that the guy took full advantage of all the retirement account had to offer.

In the end, Peter Thiel saved himself millions of dollars in taxes—and that's just on his investment in PayPal alone. See what I mean by tax-advantaged?

There's no set amount of money that you *need* to have invested in your retirement accounts before moving on to the individual taxable ones, but, at bare minimum, you should *at least* get your match money. Many employers match contributions to their employees' retirement accounts, which is basically free money. I repeat: If you aren't contributing up to the match amount, you are leaving free money on the table. If your employer matches 50 percent of your 401(k)/403(b) contributions up to 6 percent of your salary, and you earn $50,000 per year, that's an extra $1,500 per year that you can invest in your retirement account for free without even touching your own cash. Your company is practically begging to give you a bonus, and that rarely happens in any other context. Please take it!

If you can set aside more than that, even better. A good rule of thumb is to allocate 10–15 percent of your annual salary toward your retirement. If you're making pre-tax contributions to your retirement account, it's hopefully money you won't miss, since it comes right out of your paycheck before it hits your bank account.

For women, there are a few additional factors to consider when calculating the amount you'll need to retire. First there are the unpredictables, like how long you'll live after you stop working. Women tend to live longer than men (talk about being naturally better at something), so we often need to set aside more money to carry us through our retirement years than the standard 10–15 percent. Then there are the slightly more predictables, like your current spending and saving habits and how much money you'll need each year to live comfortably without a paycheck. (You can estimate this number using the worksheet below.) Next comes the very real possibility that, as much as you'd love to sock away all of your money until you turn 59½, you might need to dig into those funds at some point (despite the penalties you may incur for doing so). All these things will influence how much money you should set aside, and you shouldn't feel bad about any of them.

Worksheet: Estimate Your Retirement Expenses

Using your completed expense list on page 21, identify which of these you expect to increase, decrease, or disappear altogether in retirement (think paid-off mortgage—a girl can dream), plus any additional expenses you anticipate in your elder years. Document them here in the table opposite to get an idea of your recurring expenses in retirement.

MONTHLY RETIREMENT EXPENSES

Recurring Expense	Amount

Total monthly expenses: _____

Multiply this total by 12 to calculate your rough annual

retirement income requirement: _____

This number will help you decide how much money you may need to withdraw from your retirement accounts each year to keep you comfy once you're no longer working (before accounting for social security), and, by proxy, it should give you a better idea about how much in total you should save.

The HSA's Triple-Tax Advantage

An HSA (health savings account) is a special type of savings account for health-care expenses, and you'll usually find them attached to a high-deductible health plan (HDHP), if you have one. What makes an HSA so awesome is that it's triple tax-advantaged under the right conditions, which means that you pay no taxes on your contributions, no taxes on your earnings in the account, *and* no taxes on your withdrawals when you spend the money on qualified health-care expenses.

When you contribute money to your HSA, you can deduct that amount from your taxable income for the year, up to the maximum. So, if you contribute $3,000 to your HSA, that's $3,000 less to pay taxes on. You can use the money in your HSA to pay for a wide range of health-care expenses on a tax-free basis, from doctor visits and prescription drugs to dental care and period products. Plus, your HSA balance rolls over from year to year, so you can keep contributing and saving for future health-care expenses.

But this is the best part: aside from the unimpressive interest rates these accounts usually offer, you can create even bigger earnings in your account by *investing* your HSA money. Typically, whoever manages your HSA will have a minimum amount needed in the account to start investing, and often that number is around $1,000. Once you meet that threshold, you can begin investing your HSA money, if you choose to, and it's done exactly the same way as a brokerage account.

Level Up Your Income

As I shared earlier, there are really only two ways to find some extra cash to start investing: spending less or making more. We already talked about the spending less part, so now let's focus on the making more.

For the last hundred years, women's participation in the workforce has grown steadily. In 2019, women hit a new milestone by surpassing men as the primary college degree holders in the United States. Even so, despite all our progress with working longer hours and earning higher degrees, the gender wage gap still has a lot to say about the extent of that progress, and it's speaking loud and clear.

Today, women of all races earn—on average—just 82 cents to every dollar earned by men, and this wage gap is even wider for women of color. When comparing the median earnings of full-time, year-round workers, women who identified as either Hispanic or Latina earned only 54 cents to every man's dollar, Native American women earned only 50 cents, and Black women earned only 57 cents. Notably, women who identified as Asian American earned a slightly higher average of 93 cents to every man's dollar, but this figure varied widely when broken down further. For example, while Indian American women earned $1.07 (a success that should be celebrated), Nepali American, Cambodian American, and Vietnamese American women earned only 54, 60, and 63 cents to every man's dollar, respectively. Migrant women, in particular, are more likely to work in various forms of informal employment, such as seasonal agriculture work, hospitality services, and care sectors, which creates an enormous barrier in finding access to livable wages, insurance, and health care.

Though transgender women were not included in this dataset (and are often left out of the broader conversation entirely), they, too, experience compounding financial barriers and societal bias, which can heavily impact their earnings. In the last year alone, half of LGBTQI+ Americans reported experiencing workplace harassment and discrimination in some form, including being fired unfairly, having their hours cut without cause, or being denied a well-deserved promotion.

So how do we *all* level up together in a world that feels like it's designed to hold us down? I recognize that not every tip that's worked for me—a young, able-bodied, cisgender white woman—will work the same for everyone. So, where possible, I've supplemented my privilege with inclusive data that help to tell a better, fuller story about the best things we can do to advance in our careers and make more money.*

Have the Conversation

It is *really* hard to know if you're being compensated fairly if you have absolutely no idea what your coworkers are making, and most companies aren't exactly shining beacons of hope in the pay-transparency department. We know that salary transparency in general improves women's wages. In fact, when women have more information about opportunities outside of their current job—especially when that information includes pay—we are much more likely to seek out promotions and raises, which helps boost wages and provide upward job mobility into more senior leadership roles.

The wide-ranging challenge of occupational discrimination is not an easy one to face, but the first step toward being paid what we're worth is to honestly communicate with each other about what we're being paid. If you've always had a hunch that your favorite coworker is making more than you, and you've always wanted to ask how much they're making but you're afraid of making things super awkward, don't let that stop you. Instead, say this:

> **You:** "Hey, I'm thinking about asking for a raise because I'm not sure I'm being compensated fairly. If you don't mind me asking, how much are you making in your current position?"

---

* While I've done my best to include knowledge from studies that evaluate outcomes in all identifying groups of people, it's not always possible. The overall inclusivity of science is improving, but marginalized groups have traditionally been left out of the picture. Recognizing these limitations in addition to my own, I've included additional resources you may find helpful on page 299.

Colleague: "Jeez, quiet down! Are we even allowed to be talking about this?"

You: Definitely. It's actually against the law for an employer to penalize their employees for talking about their wages. But, just to play it safe, I'm asking you off the clock, on my break. The more we talk about this stuff, the better opportunity we *both* have to make sure we're being paid fairly and that our wages are in line with the market rate.

Colleague: You know what? You're totally right. Thanks for clarifying, and now that you say that I appreciate you asking. I'm making $27 an hour.

You: No kidding! Thanks for sharing. I thought I was being underpaid, and turns out I'm right. I'm only making $25 an hour, and Jeff told me he's making $29 . . .

Colleague: Hang on, Jeff's making $29 an hour? He was *just* hired, and he has no experience! You know what? Say no more. Let me send a quick email: "Hey boss, I'd like to put 30 minutes on your calendar this week for a quick chat. Do you have some time on Friday?"

Know Your Worth

"OK, bossy pants, chill out. We'll get it taken care of. What are you, on your period or something?"

My ex-supervisor thought it was a good idea to say this after I politely explained to him that my pay stub was *still* missing the hours from the extra shift I picked up over a month prior. (There is nothing on this earth quite like working in the restaurant industry.)

Ring a bell? If it does, I wish it didn't, but I'm not surprised. Much to my dismay, just about every woman I know has a story with the same overarching message as this one. When a man is assertive, he's a boss, but when a woman is assertive? She's bossy. No matter how perfectly reasonable a request. And bossy is not okay.

There's a lot we can't control when it comes to earning our keep in the workplace, but there are some things we can, including mindset. While playing it cool to avoid looking "bossy" isn't the same as underestimating yourself, they both produce the same result. They make us undervalue our worth, and often lead us to accept positions, opportunities, and salaries that do not serve us in the long run.

Personally, I try to remain steadfast in demanding to be paid what I'm worth by taking responsibility for the downstream consequences if I don't. I think of it like this: The job and the pay rate I accept affects all women. If I choose to tolerate low pay, that sets a precedent, and lowers the salary for the next woman who applies for a similar position. We owe it to ourselves, and to one another, to accept nothing less than what we deserve.

A mindset shift alone *is* a powerful thing. But knowing precisely *if* what we're accepting is less than what we deserve requires research. It is absolutely critical, before accepting any position—ideally before even walking into the interview—that you have conducted thorough market research to understand how much you *should* be getting paid. A great place to start is a website like Glassdoor or Indeed, where you can search similar positions and get a solid idea about what the going rate is. Try to home in on where you live and work specifically, and make sure to note any major differences in geographic location, as the cost of living in a given area will impact wages.

Last but not least, print out the information you've found or save it as a tab ahead of time, and study it like a textbook. Commit it to memory. When you walk in for your interview, you will not accept whatever number they decide to throw at you. You will accept *only* what you're worth, and you'll know what that number is by heart. And that's that.

Always Negotiate

The first time I had the chance to negotiate a raise, I didn't, because I had no idea what I should be asking for. I showed up to the interview in my fancy blazer and must have charmed their socks off because they offered me the job on the spot. And then came my first mistake. Without another thought, I took it.

Men are taught their entire lives to negotiate, for the better lunch from the lunch lady and the higher salary at their very first job. And while it seems like they are hardwired to accept nothing but the best when it comes to pay, women more often hesitate to ask for the same.

A Harvard study found that men were twice as likely as women to negotiate their salary in a job interview *if their interviewer was a woman.* In the exact same scenario, only 23 percent of women negotiated.

Men are also four times more likely overall to ask for a salary raise. And our hesitation to negotiate has a *big* impact. Smaller periodic pay boosts snowball into larger percentage-based annual raises, possibly even larger percentage-based bonuses, and, of course, you can't forget about your percentage-based contributions to your retirement accounts. Not to mention that your future employer will almost *certainly* ask you at some point: What are your salary expectations for this position? When all is said and done, thirty years down the line, not negotiating your salary could quite literally cost you millions of dollars in lost wages and compound interest.

Negotiating early and often is important to accelerate your career *and* your salary, and the best time to do this is before you even accept the job.

For starters, be sure to always ask for the job offer *in writing* so that you can carefully review the terms. Reviewing the terms of a job offer is a lot like looking your money in the face: You have to know what is being offered before you can decide what more to ask for. If they call you with the good news on a Thursday or Friday, it's easy enough to ask for a copy in writing and take the time over the weekend to look everything over. During the week, asking to take until Friday is reasonable. If you have multiple offers (and even if you don't), don't be afraid to make this request. Asking for up to a week is typically acceptable. Taking the time to carefully review the terms will put you in a position of knowledge, and knowledge is power. You can take this power with you after your review, and present your demands to the employer's representative.

TIP: It's easy to get nervous at this part, but whatever you do, don't say "I'm looking to make X." Saying you're "looking to make" a specific amount totally blows your cover. If that's the salary you're looking for, that means you're probably not currently making it, and that's way too much information to give the person who's about to determine your new one. Instead, try saying: "I really appreciate the offer and I'm looking forward to working with the team. Based on my experience and the market rate for this position, I was expecting something in the range of X to Y." Or, if they have the gall to ask about your salary expectations during the interview process and try to put you on the spot, you can say: "I'm interviewing for positions that pay X."

See the difference? Now you're not only implying that your experience is worth the figures you provided, but you're also hinting that you're in demand. After all, you are interviewing with other companies, who could hire you at any moment. And even if you're not, it's all about creating the vibe.

If the salary negotiation doesn't quite land where you were hoping, don't be afraid to negotiate other benefits. Nothing is off the table here. Get creative and ask for what you think would make the most sense for you. Think additional vacation time, health insurance, or a once-weekly work-from-home day.

If you already have a job and are looking for a raise, *ask for one.* Send your boss an email or pop by their office for a quick chat. Let them know you'd like to have a conversation about compensation, and request some time on their calendar. Maintain your confidence here— there is *nothing unreasonable* about asking to be paid. No matter how strange it may feel, understand that requesting a raise is standard operating procedure, and totally normal.

To prep for this conversation, I like to create what I call a "Brag Box." In your work email, create a separate folder and label it the Brag Box. Throughout the year, any time you get an email about how you did a great job, a project that you worked on that was successful, or a metric you reached above all odds, move it into your Brag Box folder.

Next, in your company directory for job postings, find the description of your position. If you don't have this on hand (or you can't find it on your own), you can reach out to HR and they should be able to provide it to you. What we're looking for here is your position's "Roles and Responsibilities" column. The goal is to respond to each of these objectives with a specific example of how you met or *exceeded* these expectations, so for each of these points, make a bulleted list. Then, you can bring your list with you when you chat with your boss.

You can say something like:

Hi, [Boss's Name]. Thank you for meeting with me. I wanted to take some time to discuss my performance and accomplishments in my position. I've been reflecting on my responsibilities and how I've contributed to the team's success, and I've prepared a list of specific examples that I'd like to share with you.

As outlined in the job description, my responsibilities include:

[Insert Point 1 from Roles and Responsibilities]: [Insert specific example from your Brag Box].

[Insert Point 2 from Roles and Responsibilities]: [Insert specific example from your Brag Box].

[Insert Point 3 from Roles and Responsibilities]: [Insert specific example from your Brag Box].

Given the consistent positive feedback and achievements in my role, I would like to discuss the possibility of a raise. I would appreciate the opportunity to have a conversation about my compensation during our next one-on-one meeting.

If you're not looking for an impromptu chat and your annual review period is only a short while away, table this information for a more formalized sit-down where you'll have ample opportunity to negotiate.

Move On

Not to be mean, but in all likelihood, your company doesn't care about you. To be clear, when I say "your company," I do *not* mean the local convenience store owner who helped you get your first job, or the super nice couple who runs the humble bed-and-breakfast in your favorite ski town. I mean the faceless corporate entity staring only at the bottom line of its balance sheet. No matter how much your manager or your coworkers care about you, your paycheck doesn't come out of their pockets. At the end of the quarter, if their revenue isn't where it needs to be to maintain your salary, they are going to have to let you go. It's nothing personal, it's just business—but that works both ways. If you're not getting the money and respect that you deserve, do not hesitate to look for another position. Everyone, but especially women, benefit from changing jobs regularly. In fact, the *Wall Street Journal* reported that women who changed jobs in the last two years raised their earnings by more than 30 percent on average. So go forth and find new jobs without pause. After all, it's just business.

An easy and effective way to improve your job prospects is to update your résumé, and the key here is to use action words. Keep it clean and simple with bullet points that mean something. Give specific examples of how many people you oversaw, how many prescriptions you verified, how many offices you managed.

Describe these achievements in both quantitative and qualitative terms. Quantitative achievements speak in terms of *numbers*. This would be things like the number of locations you oversaw, the number of employees you trained, the number of sales you completed. Don't sell yourself short here—break it down and show off! Your marketing plan directly increased sales by 67 percent in your branch alone, a 31 percent increase year over year. Basically, you're a rock star.

Qualitative achievements speak to the *quality* of your work. Meaningful qualitative improvements can be just as—if not more—important than the numbers, depending on the setting. You analyzed the results of your employee engagement survey and took them to heart, implementing one work-from-home day per week to reduce burnout and improve employee morale. This change directly correlated to reduced callouts, improved productivity, and a noticeably more positive work environment overall. Naturally, if they're looking for the same results, the only logical conclusion would be to hire you.

Finally, always leverage your work experience when applying for a new job, no matter how similar or different this opportunity may be from what you've done in the past. You don't always need direct experience in the exact position you're applying for. If you're missing a few of the qualifications listed in the posting, but you know you'd be great for the job, *apply anyway*. Last time I checked, you're not getting paid to decide whether or not you qualify—that's the hiring person's job, so don't do it for them! Write down all transferable skills that would be useful in the role you're applying for, and go for it.

Start a Side Hustle or a Business

If you can't find a job that serves you, make your own! Better yet, start your side gig while you're still working full time so that you can pay the bills while you set yourself up with something new. The possibilities are endless, so don't limit yourself. Dog walking on the weekends, starting an Etsy print-on-demand store, freelance voice acting (yes, that's actually a thing). Use your strengths to your advantage. If you love to write, sell an ebook. If you love to draw, sell stickers. Even if the goal of your side hustle isn't to replace your main hustle completely, it can add some extra cash to your pockets to put toward investing, and that alone makes it all the more valuable.

Out of Debt and into the Game

Not all debt is bad debt. In fact, the mega rich know this better than anyone, and regularly leverage their debt to purchase assets as tools to make them more money. Beyoncé is one of the richest women in the United States. She didn't need to take out a loan to buy her multi-million-dollar mansion in Bel Air, but with a net worth, credit score, and interest rate like hers, it sure made sense to. If she could borrow the bank's money to pay for her home while keeping her own money free to invest in assets that produce a much higher rate of return, why wouldn't she? All the while, the underlying value of her home can increase over time, which she can later sell for a profit at the bank's expense. Perhaps there is good debt after all.

That aside, some debt definitely is bad debt, and having too much of it can hold you back from advancing toward your financial goals. The high-interest kind, in particular, is like a giant, money-sucking monster. It can be so easy to fall into its clutches, especially when you're just trying to make ends meet.

At first, it doesn't seem like a big deal. You'll just pay it off next month, right? But then life happens. Your car breaks down, your kid gets sick, or maybe you lose your job. Suddenly, that balance isn't so easy to pay off. Every month, you're shelling out more and more money just to cover the interest, and your bills don't disappear in the meantime. Your outstanding balance just keeps growing. Making the minimum payment winds up looking more like borrowing money from a loan shark—you end up paying back way more than you borrowed in the first place. Plus, it can be tough to break out of debt when you're living paycheck to paycheck. It's a vicious cycle—you need to borrow to make ends meet, but that just leaves you deeper in debt.

While credit card debt is one of the most common types of high-interest debt, there are other forms that can be just as costly. Here are a few examples:

- Payday loans: These short-term loans are often marketed as a quick and easy way to get cash, but they come with sky-high interest rates. In some cases, the interest rates on payday loans can be as high as 400 percent or more.
- Car title loans: If you own a car, you may be able to get a loan by using your car as collateral. But be warned—car title loans can come with interest rates that are just as high (if not higher) than payday loans.
- Personal loans, especially from predatory lenders: Some lenders specifically target people with bad credit or those who are in financial distress, offering them loans with exorbitant interest rates and fees.

If all this sounds scary, fear not! There are ways to escape the clutches of high-interest debt. It does take a bit of discipline and a lot of determination, but with a solid plan and some hard work, you can break free from the monster that's been holding you back.† As we learned in step #4 of Your Investing Prep Work, "Eliminate Any High-Interest Debt" (see page 28), you'll want to first tackle any debt with an interest rate above 7 percent.

---

† In all seriousness, if the monster that's been holding you back from your money goals feels more like a person and less like a theoretical concept, please know that 99 percent of domestic violence cases involve financial abuse, and that there is help available. It is possible to regain control of your safety and security, and I've included resources to help you on page 302.

Step #1: Create a Payoff Plan

High-interest debt payments eat into your investment profits, so it's absolutely worthwhile to take the time to reduce your debt in this category before investing. In practice, this usually looks like grabbing the table you created on page 17 and noting the interest rate assigned to each liability line by line. Once we know what the interest rate is for each of our debts, we can begin to prioritize payoff. There are two main strategies for doing this.

The Avalanche Method: This involves arranging all your debts in order of descending interest rate, and then prioritizing paying off those with the highest interest rates first, regardless of the balance. For example, let's say your high-interest debt is spread across four credit cards. Each of your credit cards has a different interest rate:

- Credit card A: 14 percent with a $3,000 balance
- Credit card B: 11 percent with a $600 balance
- Credit card C: 16 percent with a $200 balance
- Credit card D: 17 percent with a $1,000 balance.

Using this strategy, we would first pay off credit card D, then credit card C, then credit card A, and finally credit card B. The Avalanche Method is my favorite debt-repayment strategy because it'll save you the most amount of money in interest overall.

The Snowball Method: Here, you pay off your debts in order of lowest to highest balance. That way, you eliminate the smaller debt sources sooner, which provides some motivation to keep going. Using the Snowball Method, you would first focus on paying off credit card C, then credit card B, then credit card D, and finally credit card A. Admittedly, using this method will not save you the most amount of money in interest. However, it might motivate you to continue the process of debt payoff, which for some people is more important. In the end, the method you find to be most sustainable for you is the right choice.

Overall, how much you can afford to set aside each month toward debt repayment will depend on your personal budget, so check back with the 50/30/20 plan you created earlier to find your magic number. If this number changes each month, that's okay. Whatever extra you can afford to put toward high-interest debt payoff will only help you move closer to the finish line.

Step #2: Lower the Interest Rates

Talk to your lenders about lowering your interest rates. Securing a lower interest rate reduces the overall amount you'll need to pay back and saves you money in the long run.

Credit card companies have a large amount of control over what they charge you in interest, and they often run promotions where they'll lower the interest rate for an extended period. Explain to your credit card company that you're looking to get serious about paying off the balance, and fighting against a higher interest rate is making it super difficult. Many credit card companies will find a way to accommodate your request, either in the form of a voucher, lower interest payments, or granting you a lower interest rate altogether.

 TIP: To get started, call the customer service number on the back of your card and say something like this:

You: Hi there, I'm a long-time customer and I love this credit card, but I've noticed that my interest rate is higher than what other companies offer. Would it be possible to lower it? I'm looking to get serious about paying down my balance.

Representative: I would be happy to look into that for you. Based on your history, I see that you've been making payments consistently and on time. I'll submit a request to lower your interest rate. The final decision will depend on factors like your overall credit profile and the going rate.

You: That's great to hear! Lowering the rate would really help me pay this off and continue enjoying your services. Thank you for your help!

For credit cards specifically, another option is to open a balance transfer card, which could allow you to consolidate some or all of your credit card debt onto a new credit card with a 0 percent interest rate for a set period of time. This will allow you to make payments that bypass the interest and go straight to the principal. There are plenty of cards that offer this service, but just be mindful of the total balance that you'll be allowed to transfer. Also make sure to keep track of the expiration date for the promotional interest rate so that you don't get hit with a large interest charge at the final billing cycle. There is one caveat: You will need a good credit score to do this, usually 670 or higher, so keep that in mind when considering this option or applying for a card in this category.

With personal loans and other high-interest debt, lowering your interest rate isn't usually as simple as a quick phone call, but it certainly can't hurt to ask. If you don't ask, the answer is always no, and if the answer is no anyway, you can always look into refinancing. A loan re-finance lets you replace your existing loan with a new one (ideally with a lower interest rate). This option might be great if interest rates have dropped significantly, are lower than your current rate, or if your credit score has improved since you applied the first time.

Step #3: Boost Your Credit Score

The best way to secure great interest rates, and possibly refinance to a lower one, is to have a kick-ass credit score. The best way to have a kick-ass credit score is to know the components that make up a kick-ass credit score.

- **Payment history:** Payment history is by far the most important component of a credit score, because it tells the lender how good you are at paying them back. Late payments or missed payments can really drag your score down, so if you haven't already, set up that autopay ASAP.
- **Credit utilization:** This is the percentage of your total available credit that you are currently using. Keeping credit utilization low, at least below 30 percent, is super important to keep your score strong.
- **Length of credit history:** The longer your credit history, the more the lenders think you can handle the whole "borrowing money" thing, and the higher your credit score. This is why you should *never* close your first credit card if you can help it. Put a soda on there every once in a while, set up a recurring subscription, and if the annual fee still outweighs the benefit, ask to downgrade to a no-annual-fee card instead of closing it altogether. Keep that longest line open.

- **Credit mix:** *Credit mix* refers to the different *types* of credit accounts you have open, such as credit cards, auto loans, student loans, and mortgages. Having a mix of credit accounts tells the lender that you can handle different types of debt, which brings your score up.

- **New accounts:** This is the number of recent credit inquiries and new accounts opened. Any time you take out a new loan of any kind, you've earned yourself a new account. Opening too many new accounts in a short period can bring your score down, so be mindful of what you're opening and when. Perfect example? Never open a new credit card right before applying for a mortgage (or right after preapproval, or right before closing). Google it and thank me later.

 TIP: A good rule of thumb is to treat your credit card like a debit card: Never put more on the credit card than you can afford to pay off in cash right away. The myth that the only way to build credit is to run a balance is totally false, and it might actually hurt you in the long run. One of the best and most effective ways to have a great credit score is to pay your statement balance off—in full and on time— each and every month.

Step #4: Manage Lifestyle Creep

Lifestyle creep is the slow and sneaky process of making more money and gradually inflating your lifestyle in tandem. Instead of pocketing the newfound income from a raise at work, you spend it on lifestyle upgrades. This might mean moving to a nicer apartment with more amenities or buying a fancy car with a higher monthly car payment. It can also look like upgrading from instant coffee to an artisanal roast. This seems like a small upgrade at first, and that's all well and good. But the next thing you know, you're buying a $200 coffee maker and signing up for a monthly coffee subscription service that's delivering coffee faster than you and all your family members can drink it. That escalated quickly!

As pharmacy students, many of my friends and I grew accustomed to making very little money for a very long time. After our undergrad years, we paid even more money to progress into our graduate years, and then we paid *even more money* to move on to our advanced practice rotations, where we learned how to practice working for free. (I am assured an unpaid internship is somehow still legal in the name of learning, but I digress.)

For me, remaining a full-time student while many of my peers from high school had already started full-time jobs meant seeing them start to buy houses and cars while I was stuck living in the dorms, plus working as an RA because I sure as hell could not afford Boston housing.

Thankfully, our years of hard work did eventually pay off, and, after graduation, many of my friends from pharmacy school and I began earning six-figure salaries. Slowly but surely, I watched my friends shift comfortably into two distinct spending categories, and in the beginning I wiggled my way in between them. Half of my friends spent their new paychecks on brand-new cars, expensive handbags, and fancy vacations. The other half continued to live just as we had been all along, albeit perhaps for too long, in hindsight.

For my friends in the increased spending group, this, of course, was a long time coming. I, too, felt it in my bones. We had just worked our butts off for many, many years, and we *all* wanted to treat ourselves. I, for one, was going shopping.

Pre-graduation days, I had a friend several years my senior, who was already working as a pharmacist when I was still in school. I remember the shock on my face watching her walk into her favorite store, pick up any sweater she wanted, and buy it. At the time, she said to me, "One day, you'll be able to do this, too!" and I barely believed it. When I landed my first job as a pharmacist, you know exactly where I went.

I bought the sweater. I also bought what I *thought* was a very nice couch—it sure was expensive enough. (For the record, it didn't hold up at all; the fabric pilled everywhere.) And, fine, I did buy a fancy bag (or two). *But!* I knew I didn't want to treat myself out of my future money goals, so I had to check myself before I wrecked myself. To save for a down payment on a house, I continued to drive my paid-off 2013 Honda Civic (The Little Engine That Could, as I call her). The COVID-19 pandemic destroyed the temptation of fine dining for me, so I continued to buy groceries and incorporate my weekly ramen noodles into my dinner rotation (sriracha is a transformative condiment). And, minus the addition of my newly beloved sweater, I continued to wear the same gently worn, recycled clothing that I always had.

Keeping your wants in check as your salary advances will ensure that you don't lose sight of your long-term goals, and prevent you from winding up in worse financial shape than you were before the boost. When you live below your means, you reduce your everyday financial stressors and increase your financial security, giving yourself a larger cushion to fall back on in case of emergencies or unexpected expenses. And while that peace of mind is priceless, it also earns you added flexibility and freedom not just to invest, but to pursue your passions, travel, retire early, or do anything you value most.

Avoiding lifestyle creep doesn't mean everyone should follow the same boring blueprint and never indulge in anything they actually enjoy. We all have different personal preferences and financial goals. (Remember how I said personal finance is personal?) Some people value having a nice car, even though I don't, and some people have no desire to own real estate, even though I do. Instead of worrying about the "right move," you should spend money on things *you* value in moderation, reevaluate those things and how much you're spending on them regularly, and make sure you reserve *some* funds for things you'll value later on in life as well.

Step #5: Think Like an Investor

Thinking like a consumer is easy. We are born into a world of endless things to buy. Our dopamine reward system is inundated with stuff on a near-constant basis, and most people, myself included, crave instant gratification whether we like it or not. In fact, from a biological standpoint, we're hardwired to seek out things that bring us immediate pleasure and avoid things that don't. When forced to choose between an instantaneous reward, like shopping, or a delayed reward, like investing, most people are inclined to choose the former because it feels good right now.

But long-term goals, like investing, have bigger payoffs that feel even better later, despite the work it takes to wait for them. Instead of solely focusing on cost, consider your possible return on investment. Anyone can shell out money on liabilities that empty their pockets, but investors know that buying stocks, bonds, and other assets will make their money work for them and create a steady stream of cash flow in the future.

It's hard to eliminate our consumerist tendencies altogether, but challenge yourself to look at brands you buy time and time again, and consider whether it makes sense to invest in them as a company—not just as a customer buying their products, but as an investor who purchases their stock and becomes a stockholder. Not only will this give you both bragging rights and voting rights in their shareholder meetings, but you can also gain confidence by investing in products you truly feel will be with you (and others) for the long haul.

How do you do that? We'll learn all about it in the next chapter.

Chapter 2

Investing 101

You've got your personal finances in order—or you've got a very solid plan for doing so—and you're ready to move on to the good stuff. The investing stuff.

There's a good chance that if you've looked into investing before, you might've been overwhelmed by the sheer *amount* of information that's out there. For some people, it's enough to make them close their laptop, say, "Nope. Never again. Not for me," and mistakenly believe that investing is an ultra-complex mystery. But for the adventurer, the person who loves a good challenge, or anyone who suspects it can't possibly be that complicated, I have good news for you: Investing is so much easier than you think. This chapter will cut right through the noise and show you all the big-picture principles that you need to know to get started investing right away.

How Investing Works

You may have heard that investing makes you money, but you might not be entirely sure *how*. Investing is all about buying things that are worth more money as you hold on to them. In financial lingo, we say that our goal is to buy assets that appreciate in value over time. We call these appreciating assets.

Imagine a world where lemons get more and more expensive by the year. Some people will just continue to buy lemons, no matter what the price is, paying more and more for the same fruit with each passing day. Not you, though. You have a better idea.

You decide to buy a seed to plant a lemon tree. That way, you can grow your own lemons. Sure, this takes some work, but by the time your tree is full grown and producing lemons, your one tree alone is worth a lot—much more than what you bought the seeds for. With all the lemons that your tree produced, you've got yourself a small fortune. But why stop at a small fortune when you could keep going and have a big one? You decide to plant another lemon tree. And another lemon tree. And now, you have so many lemons, you're rich. Or more accurately, you could be rich if you decide to *sell* some lemons. So you sell some of your lemons, a few bushels at a time, to generate some extra income. Every once in a while you come across a bad tree that grows lousy lemons, but most of your lemons taste great. You repeat this process over, and over, and over again, and after thirty years, you have an entire lemon orchard. At this point, you have so many lemon trees, you could live comfortably off selling lemons for the rest of your life.

That's exactly what we're doing with investing, but with different types of appreciating assets. We've got stocks and bonds, commodities, and real estate, and a whole bunch of other options that you'll learn about in the coming pages. And we'll pick and choose different assets to create our own custom fruit basket of investments—your portfolio. Your fruit basket might not look exactly like my fruit basket, and that's okay. There is no perfect combination. Building your portfolio can take as much or as little effort as you want it to. Ultimately, the goal is to create the fruit basket that best aligns with your own personal time horizon, risk tolerance, and financial goals (and I'll explain these concepts more in chapter 4, page 136).

The Case for Investing Versus Just Saving

On the corner of my family's kitchen counter sat the change jar, and every day after work, I'd watch my dad empty his pockets into it. Closely. My prime directive? Get a Gameboy Color. As a kid, I tried my best to reach down into the change jar to snatch a quarter or two, but always to no avail. The neck was too narrow, and my arm was too short. I was out of luck. There had to be another way.

My parents and I made a plan. If I could score some goals in soccer, we could set aside some change to buy the Gameboy. Despite my total lack of foot-eye coordination and the fact that I played defense (good one, kid Jess), the mere *thought* of getting to play Pokémon Yellow was all it took to make me a soccer superstar. I scored three goals in a week (and was almost certainly offsides for all of them).

We took the change jar to the bank. You know, the place with the magical money machine that turns little cents into big dollars. I watched the coins fall into the machine's grate, counting, waiting. I had no idea how much I even needed for the Gameboy Color, but on that day I had a good feeling about my chances.

Spoiler alert: I got the Gameboy Color, and I eventually got Pokémon Yellow *and* Super Mario Brothers, too. The whole experience felt like a revelation to my six-year-old brain. If I worked hard at something, I could set aside some money, and when enough of that money added up, I could buy something amazing with it.

But, as I got older, the novelty of the change jar wore off. I had been putting pennies, nickels, dimes, and quarters into this jar for *years*, and you're telling me it only adds up to $50? The magic money machine in the bank didn't seem so magical anymore. There had to be a better way to make more money. And there was. I just didn't know it yet.

Inflation: Why Saving Doesn't Cut It

There's a good reason (or reasons, if you take my next suggestion) why many people turn to savings accounts to store their money. For starters, everyone needs somewhere safe to store the cash they need to regularly access—and thanks to the Banking Act of 1933 passed in the midst of the Great Depression, we no longer need to resort to our mattresses. So long as your savings live in an FDIC-insured bank account, saving money has virtually zero risk. FDIC insurance essentially means that in the highly unlikely (but not totally impossible) event that your bank were to go, well, bankrupt, your money would be protected by the federal government to the tune of $250,000. And while this might feel super safe and comfortable, it's no way to make your money grow.

Keeping all your money in a savings account is the financial equivalent of putting pennies into a change jar, and then cashing in that change jar for $40 or $50. It's nice to find a small amount of money lying around that you wouldn't have had otherwise, but it is most certainly not going to pay your bills in retirement.

Why? Because this nasty bug, inflation, is eating away at your money each and every day, and it doesn't feel bad about it. Here's the deal: When the prices of goods and services go up over time, a concept with which we are all too familiar, the value of your money goes down. The result? You can't buy as much with the same amount of money as you could before. In the good ol' days of the early '90s (shout-out to my fellow millennials), the average loaf of bread cost 75 cents. You know what it costs today? In 1980, the median home value was

$47,200. In 1970, the average cost of tuition and fees for one year at a private four-year college was $1,794. I'm going to stop talking about this now before I upset myself.

What I'm getting at here is, if your money is just sitting in the bank, you're probably on the receiving end of a bogus low-interest rate—one that is much lower than the rate of inflation. According to the FDIC, in 2021, the national average interest rate on a savings account in the United States was around 0.06 percent. Yes, that is a zero POINT zero six percent. If you have $100 today, but inflation is running at 3 percent, that means the haircut you bought today for $100 will cost you $103 next year. But if you gave $100 to the bank, you would *still* have $100 one year later—not enough for that haircut. As your money sat in the bank for 365 days, you actually *lost* three bucks in spending power.

Even in a high-yield savings account with a much better interest rate, you *might* have kept pace with inflation, but you almost certainly didn't beat it. And if the inflation rates were even higher than the average 3 percent, like the 7–9 percent they were in 2022, your savings account would have never stood a chance. Not to mention, as most banks are for-profit institutions, they're selling a variety of financial products, like loans and mortgages, to a variety of people. They're loaning the money kept in bank accounts, yours included, and collecting interest on the (other people's) money they lend. And what are you getting in return? Quite literally pennies on the dollar.

Because of inflation, and because banks tend to pay pretty lousy interest, you will never save yourself rich. But you may well *invest* yourself rich by using a different kind of account—an investment account. Investing helps you beat inflation by providing the potential for higher returns than any form of savings account could offer. Have you ever met a savings account with a 10 percent return? Me neither, but I have met the stock market (we quite like each other, actually), and it's averaged nearly 10 percent per year since its inception. Which is great, because that's exactly the kind of return you'll need to kick inflation to the curb and build your wealth for good.

Don't Close That Account!

All this talk about inflation is important, but it doesn't mean that your savings account serves no purpose. Everyone needs an account or two (or five) to keep their money in, whether it's for paying bills, saving for a summer vacation or a down payment on a house, or storing your emergency fund.

While we all need a good, safe spot to access our funds at a moment's notice, we don't need to fill our accounts to the brim. Instead of stockpiling cash, most investors keep *just enough* in their bank accounts for an emergency fund, a short-term financial goal or two, and all their regular expenses—and move the rest into investments, where their money can get to work.

The Magic of Compound Interest

Investing takes your money and multiplies it exponentially—instead of just adding it together. We call this compounding. This means that the amount of money you earn grows over time, even if you never add another dollar to your initial investment. But I *strongly* encourage you to do so. The longer your money stays invested, and the more money you tack on, the more powerful compounding becomes. No more watching your money creep along a linear path. With investing, your money takes on a remarkable upward curve.

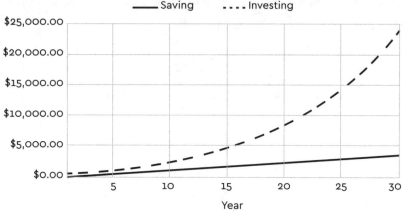

To give you an example, let's say, at present, you prefer stashing your money into a trusty savings account. You're nervous about investing. You're worried about losing your hard-earned money in the stock market because right now it seems confusing and scary. Totally fair. You decide to save $10 a month, every single month, for thirty years. You plunk this money into your savings account with a 0.06 percent interest rate, shut the door, close your eyes, and wait. After thirty consecutive years of saving, you've saved $3,600, plus some chump change in interest—around $32 dollars, to be exact.

Future you, on the other hand, has read this book cover to cover and knows that investing your money will make it go way further than it will in a savings account. So you decide to invest the same amount, $10 a month, into a low-cost index fund or ETF that tracks the S&P 500 (if these words still sound like gibberish, don't worry, they won't for long). With an average annual *investment* return of 10 percent over thirty years, you earned nearly $23,000, even with the ups and downs that happened in the interim.

SAVINGS VS. INVESTING $10 A MONTH

Year	Saving	Investing
1	$120	$125
2	$240	$265
3	$360	$419
4	$480	$590
5	$600	$778
10	$1,203	$2,061
15	$1,808	$4,176
20	$2,414	$7,664
25	$3,022	$13,413
30	$3,632	$22,892

But how? Both saver-you and investor-you put in the same amount of money for the same amount of time. What accounts for the difference? Just that magical thing called compound interest.

Compound interest is the interest you earn on both the initial amount that you've invested *and* the accumulated interest at the end of every compounding period, which could be daily, monthly, quarterly, or annually. In other words, compound interest is interest that's earned not only on the initial principal, but also on the interest. It's interest you earn on interest. As your money grows, that extra amount is reinvested, and compounds into even more money.

Let's return to the investments that future-you decided to make. This time, you invested $120 all at once with no recurring investment, and the stock market had an annual rate of return of 10 percent. After your first year, you'll have earned $12 in interest. In the next year, you'll earn 10 percent on $132: the $120 that you initially invested, plus 10 percent on the $12 of interest that you've accrued. Even though you've added no additional money, you're still earning additional money, thanks to the magic of compound interest.

SAVING VS. INVESTING $120 ONCE

Year	Saving	Investing
1	$120	$132
2	$120	$146
3	$120	$161
4	$120	$178
5	$120	$197
10	$121	$324
15	$121	$534
20	$122	$879
25	$123	$1,446
30	$123	$2,380

Compound interest creates a snowball effect: The initial amount you invested *and* the interest you earn grow together. Eventually, the amount you earn from interest outpaces the amount that you've put in. In both of the examples above, you contributed the *same amount of money toward your investment and savings*: $3,600 over thirty years, or $120 all at once. In either case, the difference in outcome came from *the rate of return*: in the savings account, your 0.06 percent earned you peanuts, but in the investment account, your 10 percent earned you thousands of dollars in *interest alone*! It's not that savings accounts don't provide compound interest, because they do—it's just that it amounts to virtually nothing. Interest on interest is useless when the rates are so low that the amount accumulated is negligible. With the stock market averaging around 10 percent per year for almost a hundred years, your money skyrockets past a traditional savings account.

The Sooner, the Better

Simone Biles began gymnastics at the age of six. By sixteen, she was a world champion. By nineteen, she was a four-time Olympic gold medalist.

Much like the kids who start honing their skills early and go on to the big leagues (and, ignoring the enormous innate talent component, because I could never do a flip like that after any amount of practice), investing earlier allows you to leverage the power of compound interest sooner. Because of the way that compound interest works, the longer your money is invested, the more time compound interest has to do its thing, which results in a higher overall return on your investment. In short, compound interest works better the longer you let it work.

Great results become much easier to achieve the sooner you get started. As an example, imagine this scenario: You've finally finished school and landed your first full-time job in your field. Starting at age thirty, you set aside $100 each month to invest in an index fund tracking the broader market. Assuming a 10 percent annual return averaged over thirty years (which historically is not unreasonable for a fund of this kind), you would earn a total of approximately $190,000 in compound interest alone, bringing your total investment balance to approximately $226,000 at age sixty.

Age	Total Investment	Total Earnings	Total Value
30	$1,200	$61	$1,261
40	$12,000	$8,614	$20,614
50	$24,000	$52,644	$76,644
60	$36,000	$192,927	$228,927

On the other hand, let's consider an alternate universe, where you do not invest. After finishing school and landing your first job, lifestyle creep got the better of you and, as your income increased, so did your expenses in lockstep. By age forty, you realize you need to get started investing if you want to retire. You do the same thing: Set aside $100 each month for investing in the same exact index fund with the same exact annual return. In this scenario, you would only earn around $52,000 in compound interest, bringing your total balance to $76,000 at age sixty. By starting ten years later, you missed out on ten additional years of compound interest, *to the tune of more than $150,000.* If you wanted to catch up to this number, at age forty, you would need to begin investing more than double each month to achieve the same balance in twenty years.

Age	Total Investment	Total Earnings	Total Value
40	$1,200	$61	$1,261
50	$12,000	$8,614	$20,614
60	$24,000	$52,644	$76,644

But the final numbers aren't the only reason to start investing early. Investing as early as possible can help you build wealth over time. If you're just starting out in your career and may not have a lot of savings or other sources of income, investing *any amount* has the potential to completely change the way your financial future plays out. Investing just $25 a month starting at age twenty grants you the same amount of money as someone who starts investing $200 a month at age forty—which is more than $150,000, by the way. So please, whether that means $5 a month or $50, invest *any amount you can* as soon as it makes sense to.

Starting earlier can also help you diversify your investment portfolio and manage risk. As you move through life, your investment goals and priorities might change, just as your lifestyle, social, and career goals might change. Investing when you're young gives you the opportunity to experiment with different investment strategies and assets to figure out what works best for you, and the flexibility to withstand any losses or temporary downturns in the meantime. Over time and with experience, you'll build a well-balanced and diversified portfolio that can stand up to market volatility, personal volatility, and all the unexpected twists and turns of life, while still achieving your long-term financial goals.

Catch-Up Investing

If you're a catch-up investor, you may need to adopt a more aggressive approach and set aside a larger portion of your income for your investments, but one of the many great things about getting older is that we're usually making more money than we used to. This can come in handy big-time when making "catch-up contributions," which are designed to accelerate your nest egg and make up for lost time. The IRS allows anyone age fifty or older to make investment contributions above the standard limits to most retirement accounts, which can help you boost your retirement savings. Even if you can't live entirely off your investment returns alone, any amount you earn from investing can help you reduce your working hours and live a more comfortable life.

Balancing Risk and Returns

Everything good in life comes with risk, including many of our everyday routines. Traveling on a plane carries a small but measurable risk of crashing, but, of course, we still fly, because we understand that the risk is low and the benefits of air travel are significant. Driving a car carries the even greater risk of getting into an accident, but that doesn't mean we all stop driving. Instead, we take precautions, like wearing a seat belt and following traffic rules to minimize the risk while still enjoying the benefits of being able to travel quickly and efficiently. Even going to the gym carries the risk of "accidental injury or death," according to the yellow warning stickers, but that doesn't stop us from working out to clear our minds, move our bodies, and improve our mental and physical well-being.

We can't let fear of risk hold us back from living our best lives. In fact, taking risks can often lead to some of the greatest rewards, and this is especially true with investing. Investing in the stock market comes with the potential to lose money, yes, but it also comes with the potential to change your life with significant returns. By understanding the relationship between risk and reward and knowing how to take calculated risks, we can use risk to our advantage.

Get to Know Risk and Reward

Investment risk is the uncertainty and potential for loss that comes with investing in anything. All investments carry some varying level of risk, and, as a trade-off, some varying level of reward. You cannot have one without the other. Some investments, like stocks (page 81), are generally considered to be higher risk while simultaneously having the potential for higher returns, while others, like government bonds (page 89), are considered to be lower risk and therefore have the potential for lower returns overall.

There are several different types of investment risk:

- **Market risk:** This is the risk that the value of an investment will decline due to changes in the overall market or economic conditions. For example, if you buy a house at the height of the market when housing prices are very high, and several years later the market is doing poorly, your house might be worth less than what you bought it for.

- **Credit risk:** This is the risk that a borrower will default on a loan or bond, causing the value of the investment to decline. This risk generally affects lenders and those on the providing end of financial instruments, but it can affect investors, too. For example, when a company issues a bond, it is effectively taking out a loan and promising to repay the bondholder—the investor—with interest. If the company is unable to make the required payments, the bondholder will be at risk of losing some or all of their investment.

- **Interest rate risk:** This is the risk that changes in interest rates will affect the value of an investment, like bonds. An increase in interest rates will decrease bond prices. Conversely, if interest rates fall, bond prices increase.

- **Inflation risk:** This is the risk that the value of an investment will be eroded over time by rising prices, also known as inflation. If your investments are earning less than the rate of inflation, your money will not be able to buy as much in the future as it does today. For example, if the inflation rate is 7 percent and your investment account is earning only 6 percent, then the purchasing power of your investment is actually *decreasing* by 1 percent.

- **Liquidity risk:** In the context of investing, this refers to the risk that an investor will not be able to sell their investment and convert it into cash when they need to. This scenario happens when there is no market for the investment or because the value of the investment has declined significantly. It's important to consider liquidity when choosing your investments, especially if you may need to access the funds on relatively short notice. In general, investments that are more liquid, such as larger stocks, index funds, and ETFs that track the broader markets, are considered to be lower risk than investments that are less liquid and "harder to get rid of," such as real estate.

Remember: Many of these risks are a normal part of life *and* investing, and some of them, like market risk, are largely unavoidable unless you can repeatedly and successfully predict the market (which we know most people cannot). Though, at first glance, risk might seem scary because we can't always control and predict it, we can control how we react to it. Ultimately, a great investor will spend less time worrying about how to avoid risk completely and more time deciding how to manage it.

Investing Is Not Gambling

One of the biggest myths about investing is that it's some kind of ultra-risky game, akin to a form of gambling, and that there's nothing you can do to reduce your risk. But there are many things that separate investing in the stock market from trying your luck at a slot machine.

For starters, investing is based on a principle of *ownership*. As an investor, you're in the driver's seat, and you have the autonomy to choose your financial destiny, make informed decisions, and strategically steer your investments toward long-term growth. When you invest in a company's stock, you're buying something that has real value and can generate real cash. This means that the value of your investments is based on the quality of the underlying assets, not luck. By contrast, gambling is typically based on random chance. You have little to no control over the outcome. In most forms of gambling, the odds are actually stacked *against* the player, and the chances of winning anything are typically very low. Casinos are designed to generate profit from people losing money, hence the saying "The house always wins."

Another key difference is the *level* of risk. While there's always some level of risk involved in investing, you can manage and minimize this risk with different investment strategies. We'll talk about those strategies, such as diversification (see page 74), in detail later in this chapter. Gambling, on the other hand, often involves much higher levels of risk, and you have little or no ability to manage it. There is no strategy to luck.

Finally, the best investing is typically done with a long-term view in mind, while gambling is often focused solely on short-term gains. Investing for the long term helps to reduce risk by allowing investments to ride out short-term market fluctuations, which makes them way more likely to have positive returns over time. Gambling is more likely to result in sporadic wins and losses.

But if you're still not convinced, take a look at the data. Historically, investing in the stock market has been a reliable way to grow wealth in the long run. The stock market has returned an average of roughly 10 percent per year since its inception nearly a century ago, even after accounting for intermittent market crashes.

By taking a measured approach to investing and understanding how to manage risk, you can build a portfolio that generates significant returns over time with a comparatively low level of risk—no casino required.

Don't Put All Your Eggs in One Basket

Variety is the spice of life, and when it comes to investing (and protecting your investments against risk), the more variety, the better.

For example, imagine it's a sunny summer day, and you're heading to the grocery store to pick out ingredients for a fruit salad. I personally like my fruit salad to have blueberries, strawberries, and red grapes, but I would really prefer to skip the pineapple and green grapes. (Is there anyone out there who genuinely enjoys sour grapes?) You, on the other hand, might love pineapple in your fruit salad, and kiwi, and banana. You can build your portfolio in the same way you build a fruit salad. You might have some apples (stocks) for a potential sweet return; some bananas (bonds) for a more stable, steady return; and maybe some oranges (REITs) for a little bit of added diversity. You can mix and match these fruits any way you like—and use any amounts you prefer—to create something that meets your investing wants and needs.

This mix-and-match approach is such a staple in investing that we have a special name for it—diversification. *Diversification* refers to the practice of holding a mix of different assets in a portfolio, rather than investing in a single asset or a narrow range of them. The goal in diversifying your portfolio is to spread out risk across a wide range of investments, in the hope that any losses in one investment will be offset by gains in the others. In other words, it helps us avoid keeping all our eggs in one basket.

Having a diversified portfolio is important because it can help to reduce the overall risk of your portfolio. To be clear, diversification doesn't guarantee against losses, but it *can* help to smooth out the ups and downs of the market. By maintaining a mix of different asset types, you become less exposed to (and less affected by) the risks associated with a particular type of asset. For example, if your investment portfolio contains only stocks and the stock market takes a nosedive, the value of your portfolio will most certainly feel it. On the other hand, if you instead are holding a mix of different assets, the impact of a lousy stock market will hurt much less in the short term.

This is not to say that your mix of assets must be elaborate and complicated to be successful. Often, the best and most diversified portfolios are also the simplest (you'll see this later in part II).

The Conventional Wisdom of Portfolio Diversification

You might be wondering what a diversified portfolio actually looks like. A super-common guideline that many people have traditionally used is the 60/40 allocation, in which you assign 60 percent of your portfolio to stocks and 40 percent to bonds. In recent years, this has begun to fall somewhat out of favor with investors in search of higher returns. In the current environment, people tend to lean closer to an 80/20 allocation, with 80 percent in stocks and 20 percent in bonds.

There are a handful of other recommendations that most people might find useful when diversifying their portfolios. For example, if you're young and looking for long-term growth, you might want to have more stocks in your basket, as they come with higher levels of risk but tend to offer higher potential returns over the long term. If you're closer to retirement and looking to preserve your wealth, you might want to have more bonds, as they tend to offer more stability.

But, ultimately, the choice is yours. In the end, the goal of your investment portfolio is to create a mix of assets that helps *you* achieve *your* personal financial goals while also managing risk at an acceptable level—and that can look different for everyone. Your portfolio doesn't have to fit neatly into any one-size-fits-all box, or even resemble most people's portfolios. (I'll show you how to make decisions about asset allocation in chapter 5, page 172, and we'll cover plenty of sample portfolios that'll help you build your own in part II.)

Play the Long Game

The Tortoise and the Hare is a well-known fable that has been passed down for centuries. You know, the one where the total show-off speedy hare challenged the unbothered tortoise to a race (and lost)? We have no idea who originally wrote the story or when it was first told, but I'd be willing to bet that if the tortoise were around today, they'd make a kick-ass investor.

The moral of the story is that slow and steady wins the race. It's not always about being the fastest or the most talented; sometimes, it's just about being persistent and consistent in your efforts. In truth, investing shouldn't be that exciting, and I mean that in the best way possible.

There are two overarching schools of thought when it comes to investing. The first (and worst, in my opinion) is short-term investing, which involves making financial moves with the intention of profiting from rapid market fluctuations or short-lived opportunities. This typically means holding investments for a few days to a few months (and definitely less than a year), before selling them to cash in on quick gains.

Long-term investing takes a more patient approach and is exciting in a *good way*. It allows you to focus on holding investments for an extended period, spanning several years or even decades, with the goal of benefiting from the overall growth of your investments over time, enduring market fluctuations and staying committed to your financial objectives. It allows you to take full advantage of compound interest and withstand short-term volatility for significant gains in the future.

Plus, speaking of gains, the long-term investor gets a special discount on their capital gains. *Capital gains* are the profits you make when you sell an investment (like a stock) for more than what you originally bought it for. Uncle Sam wants a portion of those proceeds, and he'll take them from you in the form of capital gains tax. For short-term investors, who hold investments for *a year or less* before selling them, that means they're on the hook for short-term capital gains tax, which is taxed the same as your regular salary or wages. As a reward for holding on to their investments for *longer than a year*, long-term investors get to pay a flat tax rate that is lower than their rate for short-term gains, providing an incentive to hold investments for the long haul.

Short-term investing is time-consuming, risky, and exciting in a *bad way*. Short-term investors have to closely monitor market trends and news on a daily basis in order to make timely decisions and maximize profits—that is, if they make any profits at all. While movies and TV shows may have given you the impression that playing the stock market is hectic, fast-paced, and requires lots of last-minute strategizing, you don't need to do any of that to get the most out of investing. In fact, you'd be much better off doing the opposite. Statistically speaking, that is.

For starters, historical data shows that the stock market tends to provide higher returns over the long term than over the short term. For example, according to Morningstar, the S&P 500 index returned an average of roughly 10 percent per year over the thirty-year period from 1992 to 2022. However, when you look at the returns by the year, the index sank by almost 20 percent in 2022 alone. Those other twenty-nine years clearly made a big difference in the overall average. Just as a bad day doesn't erase the progress we make as people, a bad year in the stock market doesn't erase decades worth of strong returns.

But it doesn't stop there. Looking at data going back to 1930, Bank of America found that if an investor tried (and failed) to time the market and subsequently wound up missing the S&P 500's ten best days each decade, their total return would land somewhere around 28 percent. If, on the other hand, the investor held steady during all the ups and downs—as a true long-term investor would—their total return would have been closer to 17,000 percent. Your eyes do not deceive you. Seventeen thousand.

And if that wasn't enough to convince you, studies in the field of behavioral finance have shown that short-term traders tend to make decisions based on emotions, such as fear, greed, and overconfidence (cough, cough, like the hare), which can lead to poor investment decisions overall. A study published in the *Journal of Finance* found that investors who traded frequently underperformed investors who bought and held on to their investments to the tune of 6.5 percent per year. Yikes. Trading too frequently is expensive, and it doesn't usually end well. If you're constantly reacting to short-term fluctuations in the stock market, you might rack up unnecessary trading fees, taxes, and, most likely, losses. For most people, short-term trading will do nothing but eat into your returns over time, and make it harder to achieve your long-term goals.

The good news is that women are natural experts at the slow-and-steady-wins-the-race approach to investing. The same study by Fidelity that found women investors outperformed men also found that women were more likely to stay invested during market downturns and less likely to make impulsive investment decisions. Research at Warwick Business School found that female fund managers outperformed their male counterparts by nearly 2 percent per year on average over a fifteen-year period, and attributed this outperformance to women's tendency to take a long-term view, avoid overconfidence, and better manage risk. And a study by the University of California, Davis, analyzed over 35,000 investment accounts and found that women were less likely to panic-sell their investments during market downturns, which allowed them to benefit from market recoveries over time.

In summary, the next time some guy makes the *classic* remark, you know, the one that goes something like "I wouldn't want a woman to manage my investments because they can't even manage their emotions," remember these numbers and feel free to share them. We do just fine, thank you, and we'll take our thousands of additional investment dollars with us.

Chapter 3

Know Your Investments

To be a great investor, you first gotta know what it is you're investing in. Fair enough, right? Investing, like anything else, is a skill that can be learned, and that requires you to dive into some details. A great painter is going to want to know a thing or two about brushstrokes and canvas. A great gardener is going to want to know a thing or two about plants and soil. Naturally, a great investor is going to want to know a thing or two about the different types of investments—and there are a whole bunch of them to choose from, each with their own identifying characteristics, pros, and cons.

In this section, we'll break down the investments you're most likely to encounter when building your portfolio, so that you can have a better understanding of each of them and how they fit into the bigger picture.

The Mainstays

First up are your portfolio's heavy hitters, the tried-and-trues, the financial ride-or-dies, if you will. It would be wild for me to so much as *mention* any other investments before these, like pouring your milk into the bowl before your cereal. Excuse me? You do *what?* Nope, don't even tell me. I already know you're better than that.

Stocks

Stocks are "securities that represent an ownership share in a company." I know that's blah, blah boring speak. Allow me to translate.

A security is a financial asset that you can trade in for money. There are three main types of securities: equities that provide rights of ownership, debts like loans with repayment, and hybrids of both. Stocks are equities.

Why are they equities? Because stocks involve *ownership*, meaning you get *equity* when you buy stock. When you invest in a stock, you are purchasing a piece of ownership in that company, and your purchase immediately grants you the fancy title of "shareholder." As a fancy shareholder, you, of course, earn yourself some fancy perks, like the right to vote on certain company decisions. For some stocks, shareholders even receive a portion of the company's profits, known as dividends. Pretty sweet.

The concept of buying a piece of a company for a hopeful chunk of its profits dates back to the 1600s. At the time, the coolest things since sliced bread were the maritime trade routes to the East Indies. Everybody and their mother—but especially the Netherlands, England, and France—wanted a ship to send east so that they could bring back all the goodies and sell them for a hefty profit.

But medieval ships weren't exactly luxury cruise lines. Voyages like these were risky with a capital *R* and had to face all kinds of obstacles. Think pirates, poor weather, and worst of all, no GPS.

To improve their chances of success and make the journey worthwhile, the ship owners did what any savvy medieval business owner would eventually do. They sought investors to front them some cash, enough to buy safety upgrades, a capable crew, and, I would imagine, the best compass money could possibly buy, pre–Industrial Revolution, that is. In exchange, the sailors would offer up a percentage of their profits to investors from selling wares collected on their successful voyage.

As it turns out, each one of these adventurous ships became, more or less, a company. In the beginning, each "company" would shut down at the end of every voyage after paying out its proceeds. But eventually, the East India companies became so successful that they began selling "stock" in their ships. Owning a stock meant earning proceeds on *all* the voyages the ship took, in the present and in the future.

So where do you buy and sell stocks anyway? The answer is the same now as it was back in the 1600s (though technology has streamlined the process quite a bit). You buy and sell stocks at a stock exchange, more conversationally known as the "stock market." Stock exchanges function like big marketplaces where buyers and sellers come together to make trades (originally in person but now mostly online). Back in the day, stock shares were issued on pieces of paper, and you had to sell your physical piece of paper with the help of a broker to transfer ownership. Now, we mostly do this digitally, from the comfort of our couch, with the help of the internet. Physical buildings to trade stocks do still exist and are still used regularly—the most famous example being the New York Stock Exchange (NYSE)—but they also exist virtually, and there are many, many exchanges all around the world.

When a company wants to raise big money (or, to use the financial term, raise capital) to expand their business, invest in research, or even pay off debts, they can split themselves into shares and sell those shares of stock to the public, aka investors, on a stock exchange. This is called going public. These investors can either hold on to their shares for dear life or sell them to other investors on the exchange. The price of the stock goes up or down, based on supply and demand. If a lot of people want to buy a particular stock, the price will go up, and if a lot of people want to sell it, the price will go down.

When you invest in stocks, you're taking on some level of risk, as the value of your investment can (and will) fluctuate due to a number of reasons (we'll cover this in more detail in "Riding the Ups and Downs of the Market" in chapter 5, page 191). However, stocks have historically outperformed *all other types of investments* over the last century, so it's pretty much a nonnegotiable to include them in your portfolio in some capacity.

Pros

- **A greater chance for higher returns:** Because stocks have the potential to yield higher returns, they can be a great way to grow your wealth over time.
- **A way to get in on the ground floor:** You have the opportunity to participate in the growth and success of a company. If your stock choice turns out to be the next tech giant, you're in for a more than pleasant ride.
- **Easy access:** It's easy to buy and sell stocks online through a brokerage account (see page 160), which can be opened with as little as a few dollars in as little as ten minutes.
- **Part ownership:** When you buy stocks, you become a partial owner of a company. This can provide a sense of pride and satisfaction in supporting a business whose values align with your own.
- **The ability to generate income:** Some stocks pay dividends, which are a portion of the company's profits that are paid out to shareholders (and, yes, that includes you!).

With enough money invested, these payouts can provide a steady stream of income and possibly pay your bills.

Cons

- **Increased volatility:** Stocks can be volatile, meaning their value can go up and down rapidly and unpredictably. This can result in significant losses, especially if you need to sell your shares during a market downturn.
- **The temptation to look (and look again):** The more often you check your portfolio, the more likely you are to notice intermittent and often temporary losses. This is called "myopic loss aversion," and it can lead to overly negative reactions, and a nagging (detrimental) urge to sell. Anyone can get caught up in the ups and downs of the stock market every once in a while, which can lead to impulsive decisions that harm your portfolio.
- **Risk of loss:** Investing in stocks always comes with the risk of losing money, even if you invest in well-established companies. There is no guarantee of returns, and stock prices can go down as well as up.
- **Research required:** To invest in individual stocks successfully, you need to understand the companies you're investing in. This can be incredibly time-consuming and requires a level of expertise that not everyone wants to acquire.
- **Fees:** Buying and selling stocks often comes with fees, such as commissions and other transaction costs. These fees can eat into your returns and make it harder to achieve your investment goals.

Stocks Might Be a Good Choice If

- You're looking for long-term growth with hefty historical returns. You're interested in "blue-chip stocks" with a history of strong earnings and a solid reputation.
- You're comfortable with taking on more risk. You're considering investing in high-growth stocks with more volatility but also the potential for higher returns.
- You enjoy looking into a company's financials, growth potential, and industry trends.
- You are patient and willing to hold on to your stocks for the long term, even during market downturns or fluctuations.

How Do I Pick the Right Stocks for Me?

When researching a company as a potential investment, there are a few handy tips and tricks (plus some minor calculations) to use as a jumping-off point. Not one of these alone will be enough to figure out if purchasing a share of a company's stock makes sense—they should all be used *together*.

- **Determine the company's market capitalization:** Market capitalization, also known as "market cap," is a metric that represents the total value of a company's outstanding shares of stock in the stock market. It's calculated by multiplying the current share price by the total number of shares owned by shareholders. In other words, when we say Apple is *valued* at $2.47 trillion, we're talking about its market cap, and Apple at the time of this writing has the largest market cap in the *world*. Companies with a higher market capitalization are generally considered to be more established and therefore less risky, while companies with a lower market capitalization might be a bit more volatile.

- **Check the price-to-earnings (P/E) ratio:** The P/E ratio is an easy way to help evaluate whether a stock is overvalued or undervalued. To calculate the P/E ratio, divide the current price of the stock by its annual earnings per share (EPS). Or, since we live in the internet era, you can also simply google WHAT IS [A COMPANY'S] P/E RATIO. In theory, a lower P/E ratio is better, as it suggests that the stock is undervalued and has more potential for growth, and a P/E ratio of around twenty is considered to be the market average. However, some industries might have higher or lower average P/E ratios, due to their growth potential and projected future earnings. A high P/E ratio might not always be a bad thing if the company has strong growth potential and is in a growing industry, while a low P/E ratio may not always be a good thing if the company is struggling financially.

- **Investigate the company's financial health:** Look at the company's financial statements for signs of financial health, like a reasonable debt-to-equity ratio, profitability, and positive cash flow. After the stock market crash of 1929 (and during the Great Depression), the Securities and Exchange Commission (SEC) was created to protect investors, regulate the stock market, and maintain order. Today, public companies have a whole bunch of documents that they are required to hand over to both the SEC and their investors. Most people who are not full-time stock analysts are not reading all of them cover to cover. (That includes me.) Here are three that will likely help you evaluate a company's financial health:

1. The **annual report** is a once-yearly comprehensive document with detailed information about the company's operations and financial performance over the past year, plus a bit about its future plans. It typically includes the company's financial statements (audited by an independent accountant), products and services, and market outlook, as well as information about the company's management. Leadership isn't everything, but it can say a lot. Look for experienced executives with a proven track record of success.

2. The **quarterly earnings report** provides information about the company's financial performance during the previous quarter. For many long-term investors, this information might be a little more zoomed in than they need it to be. Paying attention to regular earnings updates is important if you're looking for trends, but remember that short-term earnings can change without impacting long-term results.

3. The **prospectus** is a document that is given to any person seeking to buy a company's securities, like stocks or bonds, and is designed to help potential investors make informed decisions about whether to invest in what's being offered. This typically includes information about the company, the terms of the offering, and the risks and potential rewards of investing in the company. It will also include information about their business operations, management, and financial performance in the form of two main documents: the balance sheet and the income statement. The balance sheet provides a snapshot of the company's financial position. It's like

the assets and liabilities worksheet you made for yourself earlier, on page 17, and it can help you understand the company's financial strength and ability to pay its debts. The income statement is like the income and expenses worksheet you made on pages 20 and 21, and includes information about the company's revenue, expenses, and net profits (or losses). This can help you understand the company's overall profitability and its ability to generate income.

- **Take a quick glance at analyst recommendations:** Expert opinion isn't everything, but if the company you want to invest in doesn't have a single expert supporter, that's probably a red flag. Look for consensus recommendations that are positive and not hype-driven, indicating that the stock is, according to most people, a pretty good investment. The overall expert sentiment about a particular stock might change over time as companies release all the documents we just went over, so it can't hurt to pop back periodically to make sure you're still on the right path.

Fractional Shares

Fractional shares are pieces of stock that make up a portion of a whole share, and they can make it easier to invest in expensive stocks or to diversify your portfolio with smaller amounts of money. For example, if a stock is trading at $100 per share and you only have $50 to invest, you can purchase just half a share (0.5 shares) for half the price. Fractional shares also make it easier to participate in dividend reinvestment programs (DRIPs). With DRIPs, companies reinvest dividends paid to shareholders into additional shares of the company's stock, and fractional shares allow investors to reinvest *all* of their dividends, regardless of whether they have enough to buy a whole share.

Fractional shares have become more popular in recent years with the rise of investing apps and online brokers. Nowadays, most platforms will allow you to buy and sell fractional shares in real time, often without any fees or minimum investment requirements.

Overall, fractional shares are pretty sweet, adding both flexibility and accessibility to the stock market. However, it's important to note that fractional shares might not be available for *all* stocks or in *all* brokerages, so make sure to check if your platform offers this feature. And even though fractional shares are mostly a big win for retail investors, meaning investors who don't professionally trade stocks for a living, they do have some small limitations of their own. For example, you won't be able to vote in shareholder meetings without a full share.

Bonds

Government bonds, also known as US Treasuries here in America, are what most people tend to think of when they hear the word *bond* (unless they're thinking of Bond, James Bond). Treasury bonds are debt securities handed out by the federal government to raise money. Unlike an equity security, like a stock that gives you ownership, debt securities give you the ability to collect debt repayment. (Yes, for once the government gets to owe *you* money and not vice versa. Isn't that fun?) Treasury bonds are sometimes called "sovereign bonds" to emphasize the fact that the federal government issuing the bond has the power and authority to guarantee repayment, which makes them a relatively low-risk investment.

When you buy a Treasury bond, you're lending money to the government in exchange for a promise that they'll:

1. Pay you interest on the loan for the borrowing period (the time to maturity), *and*
2. Give you back the full amount you loaned them (the principal amount) once the bond matures.

The terms of a Treasury, like the interest rate, maturity date, and principal amount, are typically set at the time of the bond issuance, aka when you buy the bond. They come in a variety of maturities, ranging from short-term bonds with maturities of a few months (called Treasury bills) to medium-term bonds with maturities of two to ten years (called Treasury notes) to long-term bonds with maturities of twenty or thirty years (the true Treasury bonds). You can buy Treasuries directly from the government, but many investors often do it through their online brokerage account (because, let's be honest, the government website, TreasuryDirect, is clunky).

Treasuries are mainstays of many people's investment portfolios, as they can provide relatively low-risk returns in the form of guaranteed interest payments and a source of stable income. However, it's important to note that the value of a bond can fluctuate due to changes in interest rates (see "interest rate risk," page 71), and there's still some risk involved in investing in Treasuries (especially if you have plans to sell them early, which we'll cover in the sidebar "You Gotta See It Through," opposite).

While Treasury bonds might be the first type of government bond that comes to mind, they're not the *only* bonds out there. There are also municipal bonds, lovingly referred to as "munis." These are issued by state and local governments to fund public infrastructure projects, like building schools, highways, and bridges. Municipal bonds are usually tax-exempt at the federal level and might also be exempt from state and local taxes, depending on where you live and which state you bought them from. This makes them a popular choice for investors seeking tax-advantaged income.

And then—totally separate from government bonds—there are corporate bonds, issued by corporations, to raise capital for their businesses. Corporate bonds are generally riskier than government or municipal bonds because a corporation's ability to repay you is tied to its financial performance, but the risk associated with *any* bond depends on the specific characteristics of the issuer and the terms of the bond. For example, a highly rated corporate bond issued by a stable, profitable company might be less risky than a municipal bond issued by a financially struggling local government. On the other hand, a municipal bond issued by a state or local government with a history of strong fiscal management will be much less risky than a corporate bond issued by a questionable company with a rocky financial outlook.

When you invest in bonds, your level of risk depends heavily on the terms of the underlying agreement. By choosing strong bonds with stable returns and reputable sources, you can set yourself up for added stability and steady returns.

 You Gotta See It Through

One of the coolest things about bonds is that you get all your initial money back. That is, *if* you hold the bond until maturity. If you don't, the price you get when you sell is anyone's guess, and subject to the going market rate, courtesy of interest rate risk.

Bond prices and interest rates have an inverse relationship. When interest rates rise, newly issued bonds tend to offer higher interest payments, making the existing bonds with lower interest rates less attractive. As a result, the market value of the existing bonds goes down. If you try to sell a bond before it matures in a rising interest-rate environment, you might have to sell it at a lower price than what you originally bought it for, leading to a loss.

On the opposite side of the coin, if you decide to sell a bond in a low interest-rate environment, you might actually make some money on your bond, but that's not typically the point of buying bonds. Holding a bond until the date of maturity is the only way to ensure that you will receive your entire principal amount back, plus all the interest payments in the meantime, so keep that in mind when choosing between your short, medium, and long-term options.

Pros

- **Steady income:** Investing in bonds can provide a steady stream of income, received through regular interest payments. These payments are typically a fixed amount, which can make it easier to budget and plan your finances.
- **Stability for your portfolio:** Bonds are generally considered to be relatively stable and predictable, especially compared to stocks. They can help to insulate your portfolio from the ups and downs of the market, and can act like a

counterbalance to stocks during market downturns. When stock prices are falling, bond prices might rise as investors flock to the relative safety of fixed-income investments.

- **You'll (usually) get out what you put in:** Bonds give you a measure of protection that not many other investments can, because the principal amount of the bond—what you put in—is typically repaid when a bond matures. If you play by the rules and with the right players, you get your initial investment back (and then some, plus interest).

- **Potential tax benefits:** Certain types of bonds, like municipal bonds, can offer tax advantages for investors. Because these bonds are used to fund public projects, the interest income is generally exempt from federal income tax, and in some cases might also be exempt from state and local taxes, depending on where you live and the state the bond was issued in. Treasuries, on the other hand, are taxable at the federal level, but usually exempt from state and local taxes.

Cons

- **Lower returns:** Bonds tend to have lower returns, compared to other types of investments like stocks. This means that you might have to save and invest more money (or look outside of bonds alone) to achieve your financial goals.

- **Nothing's risk-free:** Bonds, though often referred to as "safer," are not immune to risk. Bonds are prone to interest rate risk (see page 71), which means that the value of a bond is directly related to the prevailing interest rates. If interest rates are increased to combat inflation, the value of existing bonds tends to fall, which means you run the risk of losses if you sell the bond before maturity.

- **Not everyone's trustworthy:** There is always the risk that the issuer of a bond will default on its payments and won't pay you back. (This is an example of credit risk, see page 71.) So far, the US government has *never* defaulted on its payments (a Lannister always pays his debts), but the same can't be said for everyone else. While a bad outcome is more common for bonds issued by lower-rated companies, all bonds technically carry some level of credit risk.

- **Damned if you do, damned if you don't:** If you decide to sell your bonds early, you might find yourself in a pickle if interest rates are high and bond values have plummeted (see "You Gotta See It Through," page 91). On the other hand, if you do hold your bonds until maturity, and enough time passes, the initial investment you get back will almost certainly be worth less money than when you bought the bond initially, thanks to inflation.

Bonds Might Be a Good Choice If

- You're seeking a steady source of income and are willing to accept potentially lower returns in exchange for lower risk.
- You're heavily invested in stocks and are looking to add diversity to your portfolio.
- You're nearing retirement, and you might be more concerned with preserving your wealth and generating a steady stream of income than seeking higher returns.

How Do I Pick the Right Bonds for Me?

When researching a bond as a potential investment, there are some important factors to look out for.

- **Check the bond's credit rating:** A bond's credit rating is an assessment of the issuer's ability to pay back the principal and interest on the bond. If you're not in the mood to gauge a company's ability to pay you back, your safest bet is lending money to the US government with Treasuries. But if you're interested in exploring other types of bonds, credit rating agencies, such as Moody's or Standard & Poor's, assign letter grades to bonds based on their creditworthiness. A solid credit rating for a bond is typically at or above what's known as "investment-grade" quality, meaning that the bond has a credit rating of BBB— or higher by Standard & Poor's and Baa or higher by Moody's (AAA and Aaa are the max score on both scales, respectively). Bonds with lower credit ratings are often referred to as "junk" bonds, a term that I think speaks for itself. It's also useful to look at the bond's credit rating outlook, which indicates whether the credit rating is likely to change in the near future. A positive outlook suggests that the bond's credit rating may be upgraded, while a negative outlook suggests that the bond's credit rating may be downgraded. Last but not least, check the bond's credit rating history to see if there have been any recent changes in the bond's credit rating. A history of upgrades or downgrades may provide insights into the issuer's creditworthiness and financial stability.
- **Assess the coupon rate:** The coupon rate is the fixed

interest rate that the bond issuer pays you each year—this is your annual income from holding the bond. The coupon rate is expressed as a percentage of the bond's face value, and is determined when you buy the bond. Most bonds come with a coupon rate that remains fixed for the life of the bond. Bonds with higher coupon rates will pay you more interest, but they may have lower yields if their market price rises above their face value. Unlike long-term Treasury bonds and medium-term Treasury notes, short-term Treasury bills do not pay a regular coupon.

- **Note the bond's yield to maturity (YTM):** Bonds have a fixed coupon rate, but yields can change. That said, most beginner investors focus on the yield to maturity (YTM), shown as an annual percentage rate. A YTM of 5 percent means that the bond, so long as it's held until maturity, should give you an annual return of 5 percent.

- **Keep your goals in mind:** What are you trying to achieve by investing in bonds? Long-term bonds typically have a higher yield to maturity, but also come with greater risk than short-term bonds because they're more sensitive to both interest-rate changes and inflation. Short-term bonds, on the other hand, offer lower yields, but are much less sensitive to these two factors.

 A Quick Note on I Bonds

I bonds, or series I savings bonds, are a type of savings bond issued by the US government, and they offer some unique advantages—especially when inflation is high. The beauty of I bonds is that they are inflation-protected (hence the *I* in

I bonds), which means that their interest rates adjust to keep pace with inflation, helping to protect your purchasing power over time. The interest rate on I bonds comes from a combination of a fixed rate and an adjustable inflation rate. While the inflation rate adjusts every six months, the fixed rate remains the same for the life of the bond.

You can buy up to $10,000 worth of I bonds per calendar year. Unfortunately, you can't buy them through your regular online brokerage, and you'll need to use the TreasuryDirect website. Like all bonds, I bonds come with their own set of rules, and these come with a minimum holding period of one year. This means you can't redeem them until you've held them for at least twelve months. If you wind up redeeming them before five years, you'll lose the last three months of interest.

All things considered, because I bonds are backed by the US government, they're relatively low-risk, and they can be a great way to save for the future while protecting your money from inflation in the process.

The Funds

The degree to which index funds, ETFs, and mutual funds are truly the crème de la crème of modern-day investing cannot be overstated. These are the metaphorical meat and potatoes of your portfolio, the bread and butter, *and* the dessert that comes afterward.

An investment fund is like a giant piggy bank that collects money from a bunch of different investors, and then invests that money *for them* in a wide variety of assets. And when I say "wide variety of assets," I'm not talking about just a few rinky-dink securities, like a handful of stocks or bonds here and there. I'm talking about a giant basket of them. Many funds will spread your money over *hundreds* or even *thousands* of different investments. And all you have to do is select a fund and add your money to the piggy bank.

Far and away, the biggest advantage of using a fund is the fact that you get instant diversification into a vast assortment of financial products, and you don't even have to pick them. Quite possibly, the fund will select more investments in an instant than you would ever have the time to in your entire working life. Unless, of course, on your days off, your definition of *fun* involves individually researching, analyzing, selecting, and subsequently purchasing literally *thousands* of different securities. Oh, that's *not* what you feel like doing in your spare time? No kidding. Me neither.

There are three main types of funds—mutual funds, exchange-traded funds (better known as ETFs), and index funds—and truthfully, each of them are important enough in their own right to warrant their own chapter. Instead, despite my desire to sing their praises for all of eternity (and in a concerted effort to avoid talking your head off), I've condensed the most important information about them so that you can spend less time reading and more time doing the thing that actually makes you money: investing.

Mutual Funds

Mutual funds are the esteemed elders of the funds, and they deserve your respect, because despite all their shortcomings, they're the ones that started it all. Historians estimate that people have been pooling together their investing money to reduce risk and maximize returns for hundreds of years now, but the first "modern-day" mutual fund began in 1924. And for a long time, nobody knew how great they were.

In the 1960s, people started to catch on. This time period, referred to as the Wonder Years, saw a steep rise in what were known as go-go funds: aggressive mutual funds focused on investing in high-risk, high-reward assets. The funds boasted above-average returns and reeled in an unprecedented number of new investors, fueling an already enthusiastic market sentiment. Because of their success, one mutual fund manager in particular, Gerald Tsai Jr., evolved into more than just an investor—he became a celebrity. A *Newsweek* article described Tsai, who helped forge Fidelity Investments into what it is today, as "radiat[ing] total cool." Which brings me to my next point about mutual funds: They tend to be managed by real, live people.

You see, there are two main drawbacks about relying on people when it comes to managing investments. The first is that investments managed by real live people tend to be very expensive, because real live people require real live salaries. For that reason, the fees associated with keeping your money in a mutual fund are often *much* higher than what you will find in the other funds covered in this chapter. Fees hurt, and they hurt bad, because the more money you pay in fees to the fund, the more money gets taken away from your returns. For two funds that invest in the exact same basket of assets, the fund that costs more money will earn you less.

The other problem with people is that, for better or for worse, humans tend to make mistakes. And mistakes were made. Right after the Wonder Years of the 1960s came the 1970s. And what's the name for those? Ah, yes: the Woeful Years. And I'm not joking. After reaching its peak in 1972, the market crashed, and the go-go mutual funds crashed alongside it. Account values dropped between 40 and 50 percent, and the mutual fund industry's losses were not made up for until more than fifteen years later.

This experience was shocking enough to scare some people away from investing in mutual funds forever—until safer, less risky products were created—and, slowly but surely, the investors started coming back. But, for others, it was a catalyst to create something even better. And so, they did.

Pros

- **Pooled money:** Mutual funds combine money from many different investors, which gives you added buying power.
- **Instant diversification:** Mutual funds spread their holdings across a wide range of securities to help reduce risk.
- **Access to different investment products:** Mutual funds can give you access to a variety of investments that you might not be able to access on your own.

Cons

- **Hefty fees:** Mutual funds charge big fees, which can eat into your returns over time.
- **Lack of control:** Investing in mutual funds means your investment decisions are made by the fund manager, which could be frustrating for anyone who is looking for more control.
- **Less than impressive performance:** Not all mutual funds perform well. Some mutual funds perform below their benchmarks or the broader market, as you'll learn in the next section.
- **Minimum investment requirements:** Mutual funds will often require you to invest an initial amount, usually somewhere between $500 and $5,000, to take part in the

fund, which might raise the barrier of entry for new
investors.

- **Strict schedule:** Mutual funds can be traded only once a
day, and not until *after* the market closes at 4 p.m. ET. If
you try to buy or sell shares of a mutual fund before then, it
will only go through after the market closes and at the next
available price.

Index Funds

Mutual fund manager and founder of Vanguard Group John Bogle
had a theory. He believed that most *actively* managed funds, those that
were run by real live people, actually performed *worse* than the broader
market average, and that most people would be much better off by
investing more *passively*. He also knew that funds could get expensive,
and were sometimes riddled with fees that were eating into investor
returns.

But it was more than that. Bogle had studied the history of the
stock market, and took particular interest in what's called a *market
index*. One of the first and best-known market indexes, the Dow Jones
Industrial Average (named for its creators, Charles Dow and Edward
Jones), was born in 1896: a collection (often referred to as a basket)
of the once twelve, now thirty largest and most influential companies in
the United States. And then, in the 1950s, came the glorious S&P 500.
The S&P 500 tracks the performance of the 500 largest and most successful companies in the United States, and it's weighted by market
capitalization (see page 85). Market capitalization represents the total
value of a company, which means that larger companies (aka large-cap
companies) have a greater impact on the performance of the index. In
no time, the S&P 500 index became one of the best and most widely

used benchmarks to track the performance of the broader US stock market.

Bogle wanted to create a fund that would allow investors to achieve better market returns than mutual funds at an even lower cost. To do this, he came up with the concept of the low-cost index fund, which would simply track a market index, like the S&P 500, without the need for real live human fund managers. Because of this, they could charge fees that were a fraction of the cost charged by actively managed mutual funds.

By investing in an index fund, you're investing in *all* the companies that its corresponding index is tracking. For example, if you invest in an index fund that tracks the S&P 500 index, you're investing in a fund that contains five hundred stocks from the top five hundred companies in the United States, all with the click of a button.

Bogle's idea turned out to be revolutionary. Just as he predicted, index funds *have* beaten most actively managed mutual funds over the long term and by a long shot. A report by S&P Dow Jones Indices found that over the fifteen-year period ending in December 2020, fewer than 8 percent of large-cap fund managers outperformed the S&P 500 index. If you, like Bogle, were looking for a low-effort way to outperform the majority of mutual funds with impressive historic returns at a fraction of the cost . . . voilà. It doesn't get much better than this.

Pros

- **Convenience factor:** You don't have to pick any stocks yourself, and the ones the fund picks for you are well-diversified. Easy peasy.
- **Much lower fees:** Passively managed index funds have *much* lower fees than their actively managed counterparts, which means more of your earnings stay in your pocket.

- **Easy to invest:** Index funds are super easy to buy and sell, and you can do so with just a few clicks of a button on your computer or phone.
- **Impressive performance:** Index funds (and the indexes they track) have a long history of impressive performance, with the data to prove it.

Cons

- **Lack of control:** Investing in an index fund means that your investment decisions mirror the index it follows. If you want to choose your investments one by one, you can't do that here.
- **Market fluctuations:** While index funds tend to perform consistently over time, like anything else, they are still subject to short-term market fluctuations.

 An Important Distinction

Index fund is an umbrella term used to describe *any* fund that tracks a market index. For that reason, the phrase *index fund* alone doesn't tell you whether or not it's actually a passively managed *mutual* fund. If it is, it will be subject to some of the same cons listed in the Mutual Funds section, including minimum investment requirements and strict trading schedules. (Revisit page 100 to learn more.) If an index fund is *not* a mutual fund, it's probably an exchange-traded fund (ETF), which we'll cover next.

Exchange-Traded Funds (ETFs)

And then, along came ETFs. In the early 1990s—when *most* of the best things were born if you'd ask me (1993 represent!)—a physicist and financial pioneer named Nathan Most had an idea for a new type of investment product: one that would smash together the benefits of mutual funds, index funds, and individual stocks all into one neatly wrapped package. Most wanted to create a fund that not only could be traded throughout the day on a regular stock exchange (like a stock), but was also relatively cheap and designed to track a specific index (like an index fund).

To bring his idea to life, Most teamed up with a financial firm called State Street Global Advisors, and in 1993, ahem, they launched the first ETF: the SPDR S&P 500 ETF (ticker symbol SPY). SPY was designed to track the performance of the S&P 500 index.

Today, there are thousands of affordable ETFs traded all throughout the day. They cover most asset classes and sectors, are designed for just about any investment strategy you can think of, and are available for anyone to buy as much or as little as they want.

Pros

- **The diversification we know and love:** Containing hundreds or thousands of different securities, ETFs give you the same benefits of instant diversification that come with mutual funds and index funds.
- **Flexible trading:** Like a stock (and unlike mutual funds), ETFs can be bought and sold at any time during regular market hours, and there is usually no minimum investment.
- **Low fees:** Like an index fund, ETFs are typically designed to track a market index or another passively managed basket of securities, so the management fees are usually

much lower than those of an actively managed mutual fund.

Cons

- **Risky behavior:** Some passively managed mutual fund enthusiasts worry that ETFs might encourage frequent trading, which could create a bad habit for a long-term investor.

The Funds Might Be a Good Choice If

- You have no interest in cherry-picking individual stocks.
- You're an investor who likes to have options.
- You are any investor at all. The easier question to ask is who might funds *not* be good for, and to that I have no answer because I've never met them.

How Do I Pick the Right Funds for Me?

If there is any category of anything that you know you want to invest in, you can pick a fund that will do that for you. If you want a fund that tracks the entire stock market or just the top companies in the United States, there's a fund for that. If you want a fund that tracks travel stocks, hotel stocks, international stocks, medical stocks, health-care stocks, car stocks, robot stocks, technology stocks, energy stocks, real estate stocks, food stocks, farming stocks, hell—even bonds: Yep, there's a fund for that, too! If you can imagine it, it probably already exists. Your choices are damn near limitless and instantly diversified, and you've got data on your side to tell you the full story about their historical returns. Chef's kiss.

With so many options to choose from, there can be many things to consider when deciding which fund is right for you. Start here:

- **Decide if you want humans to manage your fund:** First, ask yourself whether you're on board to work with human fund managers. In case you couldn't tell, I'm not on board to work with human fund managers because I don't like their odds of beating the market (thanks, data), so I prefer passively managed index funds or ETFs instead.
- **Choose your flexibility:** Next, decide whether you can tolerate a minimum investment amount and the once-daily-trading schedule that you might encounter in a mutual fund, or if you would be better off with the added flexibility of an ETF. If this tempts you to trade more frequently, perhaps think twice.
- **Pick your flavor:** Decide what index or industry you're looking to invest in. If you're interested in funds that track the S&P 500, for example, you can do a quick online search for BEST INDEX FUNDS THAT TRACK THE S&P 500 and the internet will give you a *ton* of different options. If a fund you're interested in doesn't track an index, or even if it does, you can always take a look at the fund's holdings to see what underlying stocks, bonds, and other securities it's invested in. This is typically listed on the main overview page of the fund.
- **Check out the returns:** In most cases it's best to zoom out here, so look at the returns over the long term—ideally, ten years or longer. Not all funds will be ten years old, but the older the better. We know the broader market has averaged a return of around 10 percent in the long run, so anything around that is excellent. That said, don't forget what happened during the Woeful Years. The stock market naturally goes up and down, so make sure you're investing

in something you can commit to holding even when times get tough.

- **Don't forget about the fees:** When we talk about actively managed mutual funds being more *expensive* than index funds or ETFs, we're talking about their expense ratios. Expense ratios tell you about the money paid in fees as a percentage of the money you have invested in the fund. Actively managed mutual funds tend to have much higher expense ratios than passively managed index funds and ETFs. We'll talk more about expense ratios and how to interpret them in chapter 5, in a section titled "Understanding Your Investing Costs" (page 184).

The Runner-Ups

Now that we got the main players out of the way, we can move on to the benchwarmers, and fair warning: Some of these are better than others. We've got a motley crew of financial products coming up—some of which you may choose to never even use—so, to make things simple, I've included only a basic, bite-sized overview of each of them. Feel free to run (or not run) with any one of these after doing some additional research of your own, or skip to the next chapter if you're feeling eager to put what you've learned so far into practice. You can always revisit this section later, and the Mainstays are more than enough to get you started.

Certificates of Deposit (CDs)

Certificates of deposit are the responsible, reliable friends you can always count on. They'll hold on to your money for a set amount of time—one year, three years, five years—and, in return, they'll pay you a little extra in the form of interest. Just don't expect them to be super flexible—they're sticklers for schedules.

Technically, a certificate of deposit (CD) is a special type of savings account offered by banks and credit unions. However, it's considered an investment because you're still putting money in and expecting money out, plus a bonus in the form of interest payments on your deposit. When you open a CD, you're essentially lending money to the bank for a fixed period of time, in exchange for receiving a higher interest rate than a traditional savings account would give you. Here's how it works in four simple steps:

1. You choose the amount of money you want to deposit (above the minimum, if there is one) and the term length, which can range from six months to several years. The longer the term, the higher the interest rate typically is.

2. You agree not to withdraw the money until the term length is up. If you do, you may have to pay a penalty.

3. You receive a higher interest rate on your deposit than you would get in a traditional savings account. It's usually even slightly higher than the interest rate of many high-yield savings accounts.

4. Once the term is up, you can either withdraw your money (plus the interest) or renew the CD for another term. Some renew automatically, so keep an eye out for the grace period to withdraw your money, and ask about the interest rate if you choose to stay put.

One key consideration for investing with CDs is that they're not as liquid as your traditional and high-yield savings accounts. For this reason, they're probably not the best place to keep money you might need on short notice.

Pros

- **Higher interest rates:** CDs typically offer higher interest rates than traditional and high-yield savings accounts, especially if you choose a CD with a longer term length.
- **Low risk:** CDs aren't super-impressive *investments*; they're super-impressive *savings* accounts, and they're safe. Plus, as long as you choose a CD with a reputable bank, they're FDIC-insured up to $250,000, so you don't have to worry about any sketchy stuff going on behind the scenes. Outside of backing out early and paying penalty fees or utter apocalypse, there's no real money to lose here.
- **Fixed term:** A CD has a fixed term length, which can help you plan and save for specific goals and avoid cashing out early.
- **Built-in discipline:** CDs can help you save money and avoid spending it impulsively, since you can't withdraw the money without penalty until the term is up.

Cons

- **Limited access to funds:** Because you can't withdraw the money until the term is up, CDs are not the best option for a chunk of money you might need to access on short notice.
- **Early withdrawal penalties:** If you do need to withdraw the money before the term is up, you might have to pay a penalty. There are *some* CDs that will let you withdraw after a certain period of time with minimal penalties, but those are the exception, not the rule.

- **Lower overall liquidity:** Because you're promising to lock your money away, CDs are less liquid than traditional and high-yield savings accounts, which means it may take longer to access your money.
- **Lack of flexibility:** Since you lock into a fixed interest rate when you open a CD, you won't be able to take advantage of higher interest rates if they come along during the term of your CD.

CDs Might Be a Good Choice If

- You have a lump sum of money to save and want to earn a higher interest rate than most savings accounts can offer.
- You can agree to lock your money away for a while (and possibly pay a penalty if you change your mind).
- You want to save money for a specific goal for a set time, like a down payment on a house or education costs, without the risk of loss.

A Quick Note on Life Insurance

If you've ever been on the internet, you've probably seen a commercial for someone selling life insurance. You might have heard it refer to life insurance as an investment vehicle. So, is it a good investment? My answer is no—and maybe. Life insurance is good *insurance*, and it can be critical to have if there's anyone in your life who depends on you financially (and you don't yet have a substantial amount of money squirreled away to leave for them). However, for most people without a small fortune, it's not a great *investment*.

There are two main types of life insurance products: whole

life insurance, which is often pitched as an investment vehicle by salespeople, and term life insurance, which is not. While there's a myriad of products in between, the super-brief general overview is this: Whole life insurance means paying a monthly or yearly premium. The policy's cash value rises as the years go on, and when you die, your beneficiary gets the payout (minus whatever money you borrowed from it, plus interest). The big catch here is that when you pay your premiums, part of the money goes toward the insurance, part toward overhead and profits for the insurance company, and another part (50 to 100 percent of your first year's premiums, in fact) toward *commission to the salesperson* who sold you the policy. Any money left over goes toward the cash value. This is the part sometimes referred to as an "investment" because it earns interest or other investment gains and grows on a tax-deferred basis.

The average whole life insurance salesperson will sound very excited about offering a steady 4 percent per year return on cash value (before accounting for their commission, mind you, because your payments are literally their paycheck). In fact, these long-term commissions can add up so substantially, they might amount to more than the 4 percent you earn. Some people never get back the money they put in, even after thirty to forty years. By comparison, the total stock market has had a *much* more impressive average return of 10 percent per year over the last thirty years. Hell, a CD with a solid interest rate might even provide better "investment" returns than a whole life insurance policy.

If you have kids or anyone who depends on you financially, you have other options to protect yourself and your loved ones financially. A term life insurance policy will cover your beneficiary for a time period of your choice, and the premiums are generally much less expensive. At the same time, you can continue to invest in your retirement accounts—like a 401(k), a traditional IRA, or a Roth IRA—all of which allow you to choose a beneficiary who will receive the earnings in your account if you were to pass away. Statistically speaking, most people have better returns investing in this way, which might earn you more money that you can eventually pass on.

Annuities

Annuities, like whole life insurance policies, are another way to mix together insurance and investing (for better or, more likely, worse). They're categorized as insurance products rather than investments because they're primarily designed to provide a guaranteed stream of income to the annuitant (the person who purchases the annuity) for a certain period of time—typically for the remainder of the annuitant's life. And of course, because they're a contract between you and an insurance company.

An annuity works like this: You make a lump-sum payment or a series of payments to an insurance company in exchange for the guarantee of a future income stream. The insurance company then invests the funds and makes regular payments to you according to the terms of the annuity contract.

Unlike investments, such as stocks, and funds, and even bonds under the right circumstances, annuities typically do not provide the potential for significant growth or returns. Instead, they're designed to provide a steady and predictable source of income for the annuitant. Annuities are insurance products, and they provide protection, aka *insurance*, against the risk of running out of money in retirement. Annuities also tend to offer features that are similar to other insurance products, like the ability to provide a death benefit to beneficiaries in the event that the annuitant passes away before the end of the annuity contract.

There are several different types of annuities, including fixed annuities, variable annuities, and indexed annuities. Each type of annuity has its own set of features and corresponding risks.

- **Fixed annuities** provide a guaranteed stream of income for a set period. The income payments are based on a fixed interest rate, and the annuity issuer is contractually obligated to make the required payments to the annuitant.
- **Variable annuities** invest in mutual fund knockoffs called sub accounts. Their value is based on the performance of the underlying investments, so it's possible to lose money. To be frank, most variable annuities are not great because the investment options are subpar and the fees are enormous.
- **Indexed annuities** pay an interest rate that is linked to the performance of a market index, such as the S&P 500, with the *major* caveat of certain limitations and caps. You can read more in the Cons list on page 114, but to be brief, if you're looking for index fund-like returns, you're looking for an index fund, not an annuity.

If CDs are like the reliable friends who always show up to the party, annuities are like the creepy salespeople who are only there to try to sell you something. Certain types of annuities, particularly fixed annuities, *might* be a useful investment product for someone looking to supplement other sources of income in retirement. However, it's very important to carefully consider the specific terms and features of any annuity before deciding to invest in one. Annuities are highly complex insurance products with heavy drawbacks and a wide variety of risks, many of which often favor the insurance company over your best interests. Unlike stocks and bonds and funds that are designed to be *bought by investors*, annuities, like whole life insurance policies, are products that are designed to be *sold by salespeople*, so it won't be hard to find someone who will recommend them to you. Do your research carefully, and make sure you know exactly what you're getting into before you agree to one. Insurance products don't usually make the best investments.

Pros

- **Guaranteed income:** Annuities provide a guaranteed stream of income.
- **Potential for tax-deferred growth:** Some types of annuities allow for tax-deferred growth of your investment, which can potentially increase your savings over time.
- **Death benefit:** Some annuities offer a death benefit, which means your beneficiary can receive the remaining payments if you kick the bucket before receiving all your payouts.

Cons

- **High fees aplenty:** Annuities often have a lengthy list of significant and costly fees, including sales charges, surrender charges, and ongoing management fees, which can eat into your returns substantially.
- **Lack of flexibility:** Once you purchase an annuity, you may not be able to access your money or change the terms of the contract without paying significant fees or penalties.
- **The insurance company (usually) wins:** Some annuities will stop payments as soon as the owner dies. If your annuity

contract doesn't offer a death benefit, the insurance company keeps the remainder of the money you paid forever.

- **Complexity:** Annuities are complex financial products, with intentionally long and wordy contracts. It can be difficult to fully understand the terms and conditions before you purchase one, and even harder to know if you're getting a good deal.
- **Mediocre tax perks:** Your regular ol' retirement accounts, like your 401(k), traditional IRA, and Roth IRA, have *much* better tax benefits than an annuity. Unlike a Roth IRA, which provides tax-free growth and withdrawals in retirement, you have to pay taxes on the earnings from an annuity. Unlike a regular taxable investing account where you can at least take advantage of the long-term capital gains rates, annuity earnings are also taxed at your regular marginal tax rate, which can totally negate the benefit of even decades of tax-protected growth.
- **Inferior returns:** Indexed annuities claim to tie the annuity earnings to a stock market index, but the rules and limitations sprinkled into the annuity contract make this a less likely reality. You will almost certainly end up with a much smaller amount of earnings than if you had just invested in the same index fund—via the stock market, not an insurance product—all by yourself.

Annuities Might Be a Good Choice If

- You want a guaranteed source of income in retirement, value peace of mind above all else, and are worried about outliving your savings. Even still, you should be aware of their many, many drawbacks and consider talking to financial experts (and not salespeople) before deciding whether they are right for you.

Options

Imagine that you're planning a party and you want to make sure you have enough cake for everyone. You know that you'll need a certain amount of cake, but you're not sure exactly how many people are going to show up. So, you decide to buy a coupon, called an option, for $10.

The option gives you the right, but not the obligation, to buy 100 cake slices at a certain price within a certain time frame. This one prices each slice at $2, and it expires in one week. This means that you can buy 100 cake slices for $200 within the next week, if you want to.

If, during the week, the price of cake goes down to $1.70 per slice, you definitely wouldn't want to pay $2 per slice anymore, and since your option doesn't obligate you to make the purchase, you can let it expire. You lose the $10 you paid to buy the option in the first place, but you don't *have* to buy the cake with your now-crappy coupon. You can pay $1.70 per slice like everyone else

On the other hand, if the price of cake goes up to $2.50 next week, you can use your coupon (option) to buy that cake for $2 per slice as promised, and you'll save some serious cash.

Buying 100 slices of cake for $200 is already a pretty sweet deal when most people are paying $250, but if you're thinking like an options trader, you can get more bang for your buck by turning right around and *selling* that cake for $250. You spent $200 on the cake and $10 on the option, so you pocket $40 in profit.

Options work in a similar, albeit *much* less simple way. When you buy an option, you're buying a contract that gives you the right, but not the obligation, to buy or sell an underlying stock at a predetermined price (known as the strike price) within a certain time frame (the expiration date). When you "exercise" an option, you are choosing to buy or sell the underlying stock at the strike price specified in the option contract. Option contracts are agreements between two parties, and these contracts come with enough jargon to make up their own dictionary. Here's a quick breakdown of some of the more important terms:

- **Call option:** A contract that gives the holder the right, but not the obligation, to buy the underlying stock at the strike price by a certain date in the future.
- **Put option:** A contract that gives the holder the right, but not the obligation, to sell the underlying stock at the strike price by a certain date in the future.
- **Expiration date:** The date on which the option contract expires, and the holder can no longer exercise the option.
- **Premium:** The price paid to buy the option.

Without an in-depth overview, you might be struggling to understand the real-world use case for options contracts, and I don't blame you. People have different reasons for buying and selling options. Some people use options to hedge their current positions in the stock market for stocks they already own, while others use them to speculate on the movement of the underlying stock without needing to own it outright (which is quite risky). Either way, the general goal of options trading is, like most other forms of investing, to generate profit.

Options can be pretty complex financial instruments, much more complicated than stocks alone. They also involve a higher level of risk. They're not suitable for all or even most beginner investors, and they require a *super*-thorough understanding of how they work before getting started. Otherwise, you're almost guaranteed to lose some money.

One of the most important distinctions between stocks and options is that it's possible to lose *more than your initial investment* when selling options. This is due to the concept of leverage, which allows you to control a much larger investment using a smaller amount of money. Here's an example to help illustrate it: Imagine you want to buy shares of a well-known company, but you only have $100 to invest. With that amount, you can buy maybe one or two shares, depending on the share price. However, if you use options and leverage, you can control a larger number of shares, typically 100, with that same $100. This is because instead of buying the shares directly, you're buying an options contract, which gives you the right (but not the obligation) to buy or sell that larger number of shares at a predetermined price. So, by investing a much smaller amount, you get control over a much larger investment. Because your one option controls many shares, if the share price goes up, the value of the option will increase significantly. This means your investment can grow at a faster rate than if you had bought the shares directly. And, since there's no ceiling to how high stock prices can climb, your potential profits are limitless.

But the thing is, leverage works both ways. The lowest a stock price can drop to is zero, so you know you've got a floor for your losses. If you're caught selling a poorly timed call option without owning the underlying shares, there is *no limit* to how high a stock price can climb, meaning that your potential losses are limitless. When selling stocks, your worst-case scenario is losing what you put in; when selling options, it's possible for your account balance to go negative.

If you're seriously interested in exploring options, you're going to need way more than I could ever give you in a quick summary. There are entire books dedicated solely to investing in options and all the different strategies to use. Options trading can be powerful, but only after gaining a careful understanding of the process. Plenty of investors will lead perfectly fulfilling lives with perfectly fulfilling investment portfolios without *ever* having traded options. However, for the particularly savvy investor who thinks they would enjoy learning about the process of trading them, options are another tool in your investing toolkit (but please be careful—it's sharp).

Pros

- **Customizable versatility:** Options trading is super versatile and can be used to achieve a variety of investing goals. With options, you can tinker with the amount of risk you're willing to take by selecting the strike price and expiration date that best fit your objective.
- **Pretty cheap leverage:** Options allow you to leverage your money by controlling a larger position in the underlying asset with a smaller up-front cost. Want to make a big bet on a stock without having to *actually own* it, or double down on a stock you do own without another large payment? Options can help you do that.
- **Added income:** Options can be used to generate income through the sale of options premiums, which can bring in some extra cash flow if you know what you're doing.

Cons

- **Big swings:** The value of an option can change significantly in a short period of time. Because *one* option typically represents *one hundred* underlying stocks, big swings in the underlying stock price can lead to major losses, particularly if you're new to options—and the stock market is unpredictable at baseline.
- **A race against the clock:** Options have an expiration date. You only have a limited amount of time to make your move, so you'd better make it count. To really make you sweat, options come with "time decay," which means that as

an option gets closer to expiration, its value decreases at an accelerating rate. This makes it harder for an option to be profitable as time goes on.

- **Risky business:** Trading options means trying to accurately forecast the movement of the underlying asset within a relatively short time frame to profit from your position. This is inherently much riskier than, say, "safely" investing in government bonds with guaranteed returns. With options, if you guess wrong, you're losing money.

- **Mega complex:** Options are complex and require a thorough understanding of the underlying asset, market conditions, and options strategies before buying them. There are a ton of important points you'll need to understand, like the concept of implied volatility, and the entire gamut of the Greeks, the terms used to quantify the sensitivity of an option's value to changes.

Options Might Be a Good Choice If

- You're looking to leverage your position in stocks that you already own *and* believe in for the long term (only after extensive research and practice, of course).

Cryptocurrency

These days, it would be impossible *not* to talk about crypto. Cryptocurrency is a digital or virtual currency that relies on two foundations: (1) the use of cryptography, the science of using mathematical algorithms to create secure and anonymous transactions, and (2) decentralization, meaning it's not controlled by a central authority like a bank or government. Cryptocurrencies are created through a process called mining, where a vast network of computers verify transactions.

Transactions are recorded in a public ledger using blocks, which are cryptographically secured and linked together in a chain. This public ledger is called a blockchain. Once a block is added to the chain, it can't be altered or deleted, providing a theoretically tamperproof record of all transactions. This whole process was designed for the best-known cryptocurrency, Bitcoin, but now there are many other cryptocurrencies available, like Ethereum, Litecoin, XRP, and, of course, the one and only Dogecoin.

Cryptocurrencies can be bought and sold via online exchanges and stored in digital wallets, or you can buy and transfer crypto to physical hardware wallets. A hardware wallet is a physical device that's designed to securely store your crypto. Disguised as a super-fancy flash drive, the hardware wallet stores the private keys for your cryptocurrency in a secure offline environment, protecting them from hacking and other forms of cyberattacks. Hardware wallets are one of the most secure ways to store cryptocurrency, because they provide a physical layer of protection beyond just a software app assuring you that "Your crypto is safe with us, we promise" (which, as we've seen with FTX, is not always the case). If you can't commit to using a hardware wallet, I would not commit to investing in crypto.

Cryptocurrency has gained a ton of attention in recent years for several reasons. First, this was due to its decentralized nature, anonymity, and potential for high returns, but as time went on, it gained notoriety for its associated volatility *and* criminal activity, including money laundering and fraud. As an investment, cryptocurrency is still relatively new, so it lacks the long-term data available for more traditional investments.

In short, cryptocurrency can be a fun and exciting investment, but it's important to keep it in perspective and not go all-in. If you weigh the pros and cons, risks and benefits, and still decide to invest in crypto, my rule of thumb is to keep it around 5 percent (or less) of your overall portfolio, consider it strictly as a speculative investment, and never invest any more than you would be willing to lose.

Pros

- **Potential for high returns:** Cryptocurrencies are known for their volatility, which means that prices can fluctuate rapidly in a short amount of time. While this can be bigtime risky, there's no denying the potential for high returns if you invest at the right time.
- **An alternative asset class:** Cryptocurrency is often considered an "alternative asset class," meaning it doesn't necessarily move in the same direction as traditional investments, like stocks or bonds. This could make it a valuable addition to a diversified investment portfolio, at least in theory.
- **An accessible asset:** Anyone with an internet connection can invest in cryptocurrency, regardless of their location or financial status.
- **Room for innovation:** Cryptocurrencies are still a relatively new technology and are constantly evolving. This means they still have the potential for new features and applications that might increase their value.

Cons

- **Super volatile:** Cryptocurrencies are *highly* volatile, which means that their prices can fluctuate significantly in a short period. While a traditional stock chart displays bullet points for price changes on a daily, monthly, and yearly basis, the cryptocurrency charts assess changes on a second-by-second, minute-by-minute, hour-by-hour basis. This volatility can increase the risk of loss, particularly if you don't have a long-term investment horizon (or "diamond hands," in Cryptospeak). If you buy Bitcoin at a very high price, and its value cuts in half in a matter of hours, you can lose a lot of money very quickly if you decide to sell.

- **Lack of regulation:** Cryptocurrency regulations are still relatively unclear, which means less oversight and protection for investors. You're on your own if something goes wrong. Cryptocurrency pioneers founded the financial instrument for the purpose of keeping currency out of the hands of the government. However, this lack of regulation can make it difficult or even impossible to resolve disputes or seek recourse if you run into any issues with your investment (and, as we've seen in recent years, there are issues aplenty).

- **Major security risks:** Cryptocurrencies are initially stored in digital wallets, which can be vulnerable to hacking and cyberattacks. If your wallet is hacked, you might lose your whole investment. But our memory might be even more dangerous. It's estimated that the value of Bitcoin money lost, due to forgotten login info, is more than $24 billion. So, yeah. Take all the necessary steps to secure your wallet, like enabling two-factor authentication, purchasing a hardware wallet, and for the love of all things holy, using strong passwords that you actually remember.

- **Scammers galore:** There are more than a few scammers out there trying to take advantage of the hype, so be careful not to get burned. Unfortunately, in large part due to the lack of regulation and security risks previously mentioned, there have been countless cases of cryptocurrency scams, such as fraudulent initial coin offerings (ICOs), "rug-pull" scenarios (when a crypto creator promotes a new project to attract investors only to suddenly shut down, disappear, and abscond with your money), or Ponzi schemes that promise high returns with little or no risk. Be wary of any offers that seem too good to be true.

- **Limited acceptance:** Even if you're a huge fan of crypto, not everyone else is. Cryptocurrencies are not widely accepted as a form of payment (not yet, anyway). This limited acceptance can make it difficult to use your cryptocurrency for practical purposes, like paying your bills and making everyday purchases, leaving the overall utility of crypto less obvious.

Cryptocurrency Might Be a Good Choice If

- You're comfortable with increased risk and volatility, and are interested in the potential for decentralized technology and the possibility of significant returns.

Real Estate Investment Trusts (REITs)

If you've always wanted to invest in property outside of your personal dwelling, but you have absolutely no desire to be a landlord, enter stage left: REITs. A REIT (real estate investment trust) is a type of investment that allows you to invest in real estate without owning physical property. REITs are companies that own and operate income-generating real estate assets. Think office buildings, shopping centers, apartments, and hotels that collect rent from the people, businesses, and corporations that use them. And while all those people, businesses, and corporations are paying rent to their landlords, when you buy shares of a REIT, you become entitled to a portion of that rental income. REITs are required to distribute at least 90 percent of their taxable income back to their investors in the form of dividends, which makes them a popular choice for investors seeking to generate cash flow.

Most investors buy REITs on public stock exchanges. Publicly traded REITs are bought and sold like stocks and can be easily traded through a brokerage account.

There are three main types of REITS:

- **Equity REITs** invest in and own physical properties, such as apartments, office buildings, retail centers, and hotels. They generate income by renting out these properties to tenants and distributing rental income to shareholders. Some equity REITs specialize in owning and operating commercial properties, such as office buildings, shopping centers, and industrial parks, while others specialize in owning and operating residential properties, such as apartments, single-family homes, and student housing. In addition to commercial and residential REITs, there are also REITs that focus on specialized real estate sectors, such as health care (think hospitals) and self-storage.
- **Mortgage REITs** invest in mortgages or mortgage-backed securities, rather than physical properties. They generate income by earning interest on the mortgages they own or hold. As people or companies pay back their mortgages, mortgage REITs collect the money and distribute it back to you.
- **Hybrid REITs** combine aspects of both equity and mortgage REITs by investing in both physical properties

and mortgages, with the goal of generating income from both sources.

REITs offer a way to take advantage of the many benefits of the real estate market without the need to directly own and manage properties. Having said that, REITs also carry many of the same risks as homeownership, like the risk of declining property values, changing interest rates, the possibility of past-due payments, and the risk of default on the mortgages that REITs may hold. Same as with any other type of investment, it's important to carefully consider the risks and potential returns of REITs before investing in them.

Pros

- **Portfolio diversification:** REITs offer an easy way to diversify a portfolio. Plus, they act like a one-stop shop for real estate investing, enabling you to invest in lots of different properties without the responsibility (or up-front cost) of finding, owning, and managing them yourself.
- **Income generation:** Since REITs are required to distribute at least 90 percent of their taxable income to their shareholders in the form of dividends, they're a popular choice for investors looking for a reliable stream of income from alternative assets.
- **Professional management:** REITs are managed by professional teams who are responsible for the day-to-day operations and maintenance of the properties, so you don't have to worry about fixing the leaky roof or finding any tenants.
- **Liquidity and flexibility:** Unlike a physical house, which can take months or even years to sell in a tumultuous real

estate market, publicly traded REITs can be easily bought and sold through a brokerage account.

Cons

- **Limited control:** As a shareholder, you don't get to call the shots—the management team is in charge. You have limited control over the properties and operations of the REIT itself. The performance of a REIT can depend on the effectiveness of the management team, so choose wisely.
- **Risk of default:** REITs may hold mortgages on the properties they own, which can be risky if the borrower is unable to make payments and subsequently defaults.
- **Ethical implications:** There are ethical implications for all investments (see page 130 for more on social impact investments), but when it comes to investing in housing, a basic human need, some pretty major ones come into play. REITs have a responsibility to ensure that their properties are well-maintained and safe, and that they're not engaging in discriminatory or unethical practices. When you're choosing a REIT, you should consider whether the management team has a strong track record of ethical conduct toward the communities they serve. Are strong governance practices in place? Is the REIT transparent about its operations and financial reporting? There are also environmental impacts to consider. What steps has the REIT taken to promote energy efficiency in its properties? Are there initiatives in place to reduce energy consumption, utilize renewable energy sources, or implement energy-efficient technologies?

REITs Might Be a Good Choice If

- You love the idea of investing in real estate and having another source of income, but don't love the idea of putting down lots of cash, fixing properties, or finding tenants.

International Investments

The United States is home to the largest stock market exchange on earth, and for that we get a lot of attention (among other things). But there are plenty of other countries with highly profitable economies and impressive stock markets of their own, and investing in them in the form of international stocks can be another great way to diversify an investment portfolio.

If there's one thing international investors know about America, it's that US stocks have been known to perform very, very well, especially over the long term. However, even though the United States has more financial assets than any other country in the world, our international friends and their respective stocks have come out on top in the returns department every so often. For example, from 2002 to 2007, the MSCI EAFE Index, which tracks developed international markets outside of North America, outperformed the S&P 500 index every year, sometimes by a large margin. But just a few short years later the tides had turned, and from 2010 to 2020, the trusty American S&P 500 index was back in the lead eight years out of ten.

Looking at the trend lines, what this has equated to historically is that when US stocks have performed *very* poorly, I'm talking returns less than 4 percent annually, international stocks have usually fared better—with a few notable exceptions. For example, when the pandemic came along, global markets everywhere tumbled: ours, theirs, and everybody else's included.

By holding stocks in companies located in different countries, you can gain access to a wider range of economic and political environments, which can help to reduce the overall risk of your portfolio under the right circumstances. International stocks will come with their own set of risks and uncertainties, which can be extra difficult to assess because they're taking place in a foreign financial climate. That said, there's always the possibility that the international market will outperform the US market in any given year, and if you're not invested in international stocks, you won't be able to find out.

Pros

- **Portfolio passport:** International stocks and index funds can help to diversify a portfolio beyond the US market, broaden your horizons, and give you exposure to a wider range of economic and political environments.
- **Potential for higher returns:** International stocks and index funds can offer the potential for higher returns than domestic investments when the US market is performing ultra-poorly.
- **Emerging markets:** Investing in international stocks and index funds can allow you to tap into opportunities for global growth and development.

Cons

- **Currency fluctuations:** Exchange rates are constantly changing, and these changes can affect the value of international stocks and index funds.
- **Political problems can wreak havoc:** Same as at home, economic or political instability in a foreign country can impact the performance of international investments.
- **Increased volatility:** International stocks and index funds

may at times be more volatile than domestic investments in countries with fewer government regulations, heightened political tensions, and frequent or devastating environmental disasters.

International Investments Might Be a Good Choice If

- You believe in the growth potential of companies in foreign markets, and you're willing to navigate the unique risks and considerations associated with investing in global economies in order to diversify your portfolio and tap into international gains.

Social Impact Investments

A lot of people feel kind of weird about investing because they don't want to invest in companies that are actively making the earth worse. And that's both a totally legitimate concern and a very popular one, which is how social impact investing came into vogue. Social impact investing is the practice of investing in companies, organizations, and funds with the intention of generating a positive social and environmental impact on top of the standard expectation of financial return. These investments can take various forms, including:

- Direct investments in companies or organizations that are focused on solving social or environmental problems, like renewable energy, affordable housing, or universal education.
- Investing in funds that focus on specific impact areas, like clean technology or microfinance.
- Investing in stocks from publicly traded companies that have a positive social or environmental impact, like those that prioritize sustainability or diversity in their operations.

- Investing in bonds issued by governments or organizations to finance projects that have a positive social or environmental impact, like equitable infrastructure projects or renewable energy sources.

In theory, social impact investing can be a cool way to sync up your values with your investments, and to have a positive impact on the world while also potentially making some money, but this type of investing has come under its fair share of scrutiny. It's difficult to measure and quantify the impact of investments, which makes it challenging to determine whether an investment is having a positive social or environmental impact or if it's just a marketing ploy. There's also often a lack of transparency surrounding social impact investments, so it can be difficult to determine whether they're actually aligned with social or environmental goals at all. Plus, for all that effort, the returns of social impact investments have shown mixed results, which prompts some people to question how much money they're willing to sacrifice in support of (hopefully) yielding some positive social or environmental change.

In brief, social impact investing is still a relatively new field, and there's concern that its benefits may not be reaching the most vulnerable populations or addressing the root causes of social and environmental issues. While there's nothing wrong with wanting your money to go toward something good, it might not be possible to know what kind of an impact your contribution is truly making (at least right now), and you will almost certainly need to do some extra research to confirm the social impact companies you're funding are actually putting their money where their mouths are.

A Quick Note on Greenwashing

Greenwashing is the act of making false or misleading claims about the environmental benefits of a product, service, or company to promote it as environmentally friendly. This can take on various forms, like making exaggerated or unverified claims, using eco-friendly buzzwords and imagery, or highlighting a few green initiatives while blatantly ignoring other negative environmental impacts.

For example, a company might claim that its products are "eco-friendly" or "green" without providing specific information about how they were produced or what makes them environmentally friendly in the first place. The company might be hesitant to provide or refuse to disclose information about their environmental impact. You might also find them using confusing or ambiguous language or terms that have no standardized definition in their applied context, such as *all natural* or *nontoxic*. (How or why would a hairbrush be nontoxic?) Some companies might even use arbitrary certifications or labels with no regulatory oversight to give the impression that their practices are environmentally sound.

Greenwashing can be harmful because it can mislead well-intentioned consumers into thinking they're making environmentally responsible choices, and it can also divert attention and resources away from truly sustainable products and services.

In some cases, companies use green initiatives to camouflage their harmful practices. A classic example of this took place in 2000, when BP (formerly British Petroleum) launched a major advertising campaign with the slogan "Beyond Petroleum." The campaign promoted the company's commitment to the planet by reducing emissions, even as it continued to engage in oil drilling in ecologically sensitive areas. In 2010, BP was responsible for the Deepwater Horizon oil spill in the Gulf of Mexico, one of the largest environmental disasters in US history.

Social impact investing is not inherently a form of greenwashing. That said, it's important to carefully research and evaluate potential investments to ensure that they're both talking the talk and walking the walk. To avoid falling victim to greenwashing, look for companies with relevant certifications or labels that mean something, like the Energy Star label for energy-efficient appliances. Be wary of vague or unsubstantiated claims about a product or a company's environmental impact, and always look for specific details and evidence to back up any claims.

Pros

- **Positive impact:** Social impact investing allows you to align your investments with your values and contribute to positive social and environmental change. It offers an opportunity to support companies and projects that address important issues like climate change, affordable education, accessible health care, poverty alleviation, or gender equity and equality efforts.
- **Investor engagement:** Social impact investing often involves active engagement with companies, advocating for sustainable practices, transparency, and positive change. As

an investor, you can have a voice in shaping corporate behavior and driving social and environmental improvements.

Cons

- **Limited options:** The number of social impact investment opportunities might be more limited than your traditional investment options, which can make it challenging to achieve broad diversification or align investments with your specific impact goals.
- **Uncertain performance:** The performance of social impact investments can vary widely, and we don't have a ton of historical data on their overall performance. Some investments deliver strong financial returns alongside positive impact, while others might have lackluster returns. Kevin Starr, director of the Mulago Foundation, a foundation focused on using high-impact philanthropy to fight poverty, says this about impact investing: "Few solutions that meet the fundamental needs of the poor will get you your money back" and "The problem with impact investing is that there should be only one bottom line, impact."
- **Questionable credentials:** Assessing the social or environmental impact of any investment is not an exact science (yet). Measuring and evaluating the effectiveness of impact investments will require robust methodologies and data, and without clear metrics and standards at present, it can be challenging to determine the actual impact achieved (if there is any impact at all).

Social Impact Investments Might Be a Good Choice If

- You have a strong desire to make a positive difference, are willing to do some extra research to align your investments with your values, and are comfortable with the potential (but not for certain) trade-off between financial returns and the social or environmental impact generated by your investments.

Chapter 4

Your Investor Profile

The fundamentals of investing are pretty universal, but, as women, it's important to recognize that our investor *profile* is unique and should be tailored to our individual needs and goals. For starters, women tend to live longer than men, which means our investments may need to last longer to support a longer period of retirement or reduced income. Despite progress, the gender wage gap still exists, and earning less than men might impact our ability to save and invest at the same rate. On top of that, women are more likely to experience career interruptions due to maternity leave, ongoing caregiving responsibilities, or other family-related commitments.

Time is money, and all the time spent living longer, being paid less, and needing to take on more can really add up. Whether your goals are to save up for retirement or step down to part-time, purchase a home or find an amazing apartment, fund your child's education or travel the world kid-free, the investments you choose should align with what *you* want most in life. Everyone's investor profile is going to be different because people are different, and we each have our own financial goals, risk tolerance, time horizon, and resources. In this chapter, we'll break down the differences and consider these factors so that you can walk away putting your money where your values are.

Your Goals

The first step in building your investment portfolio is to determine your goals. Financial goals impact investment choices because different goals come with different levels of risk and return, time frames for investing, and corresponding investment strategies. Are you investing for retirement? What does your time horizon look like? What is your risk tolerance? What kind of income do you have at your investing disposal?

To keep it simple, we'll divide financial goals into three categories.

Short-Term Financial Goals

Short-term goals are the ones that you can reasonably accomplish within one to two years. Some examples of short-term financial goals might include:

- Saving for an emergency fund
- Paying off existing credit card debt
- Saving for childcare expenses while you continue working
- Saving for a down payment on a car
- Starting a wedding fund to save for your dream wedding

It's important to always keep your short-term financial goals in mind, even as you go about focusing on setting yourself up for the long-term ones. Checking short-term financial goals off your checklist can help you build confidence and momentum, as well as provide a sense of accomplishment and financial stability in the meantime.

Medium-Term Financial Goals

Medium-term goals—you guessed it—live in the middle between the short-term and long-term goals, so there's a little more gray area here. In general, we're looking at a time frame of around three to ten years. Examples of medium-term financial goals might include:

- Saving for a down payment on a house
- Paying off your student loans (this could be a long-term goal, depending on your balance)
- Saving to take time off to backpack across the world
- Preparing to take a career break to start a family
- Building an in-law apartment to care for your parents
- Saving for your child's college education

Long-Term Financial Goals

These are what I like to call the end game. These are the financial plays that you stick with for the long haul, the ones that you achieve more than ten years down the road. Examples of long-term financial goals might include:

- Saving for (a statistically longer) retirement
- Paying off a mortgage
- Building a successful business
- Establishing a legacy of philanthropy and giving
- Leaving an inheritance for loved ones

While investing can be a great way to reach many kinds of financial goals, it's especially great for the long-term ones. Because of the potential for much higher returns and the magic of compound interest, you have the ability to outpace inflation much more effectively by investing than you would with a low-interest savings account. As your investment gains generate earnings, those earnings can be reinvested to generate even more gains, and, over the long term, this compounding effect can significantly grow your wealth. And, of course, many long-term investment accounts offer tax advantages that allow your investments to compound on a tax-deferred (or even tax-free) basis, which can enhance the growth of your investments even further.

While investing always involves risk (especially in the short term), its potential for growth and compounding in the long term is a big part of what makes it such a powerful tool for achieving your financial end game.

Financial Goals in Action

We know it's important to figure out what our financial goals are, but actually doing this can be tricky, since figuring out what we want involves asking ourselves some pretty open-ended questions. To help visualize how to break down this thought process, here's an example featuring our hypothetical friend named Sarah.

Sarah is a career-driven data analyst who values financial freedom. She makes $120,000 a year, is currently renting an apartment in the city, and has around $55,000 in debt from credit cards and student loans combined. Her monthly expenses amount to $3,000. Aware at every waking moment that she is actively approaching thirty (thanks, society), Sarah is also starting to think about the future and is committed to building a strong financial foundation for herself over the coming years.

Personal Notes

- Needs: Rent, utilities, internet, cell phone bill, health insurance, groceries, minimum credit card and student loan payments
- Wants: Pacific Coast Highway road trip vacation, new shorts for summer, trying a new restaurant once a week
- Future: Standard savings account, no investments to speak of (yet)

Life Factors

What life factors might impact your ability to reach those goals? Do you plan to be working with one income or two? Do you have anyone who depends on you financially or plan to have anyone depend on you in the future?

Single, no plans on getting married any time soon (if ever), solo world traveler, foodie, willing to break bones to try new water sports

Life goals

Take two months off work to travel, pay off credit card and student loan debt, own a house near a lake, have a paid-off mortgage (eventually) and at least one dog that is not an off-leash escape artist

Short-Term Goals

- Pay off $8,000 in credit card debt within the next six months
- Save $10,000 for an emergency fund in a high-yield savings account within the next year
- Save $4,000 for a down payment on a used car within the next two years

Medium-Term Goals

- Save $60,000 for a down payment on a house within the next five years
- Pay off $45,000 in student loan debt within the next four years
- Save $6,000 for a California road trip within the next three years

Long-Term Goals

- Achieve $1,000,000 invested for retirement within the next thirty-five years
- Pay off mortgage on house within the next thirty years
- Leave an inheritance of $100,000 for loved ones within the next forty years

Worksheet: Outline Your Financial Goals

Now let's have you do the same thing. Create your own goal sheet before moving on to the next section. And don't worry—the goals you set here don't need to be permanent, and your answers to these questions can change over time. You can add as many or as few as you like, so don't feel pressured to write six goals just because you have a whole page to fill. Alternatively, if you feel as though you've been waiting your entire life to write these goals down and you need more lines than what I've allotted, feel free to make space elsewhere and write to your heart's desire.

Your Financial Goals

_____

_____

_____

_____

_____

_____

_____

_____

_____

_____

_____

_____

_____

_____

_____

_____

_____

_____

_____

_____

Personal Notes

Needs

• _____

• _____

• _____

• _____

• _____

Wants

• _____

• _____

• _____

• _____

• _____

Life Factors

What life factors might impact your ability to reach those goals? Do you plan to be working with one income or two? Do you have anyone who depends on you financially or plan to have anyone depend on you in the future?

_____

_____

_____

_____

Life Goals

_____

_____

_____

_____

_____

Short-term goals

- _____

- _____

- _____

- _____

- _____

Medium-term goals

- _____

- _____

- _____

- _____

- _____

Long-term goals

- _____

- _____

- _____

- _____

- _____

Your Time Horizon

Time horizon is the length of time that you expect to hold on to an investment before you sell it. It has a big impact on how much risk you can afford to make room for, and can help you decide the types of investments that might make the most sense for your timeline.

For example, if you're investing for a **short-term financial goal,** you'll have a short time horizon (one to two years). You'll likely need to be a lot more conservative in your investment choices to minimize the risk of loss in the near future, which might mean investing in relatively "safe" assets. Some examples of investments that might be appropriate for short-term financial goals include high-yield savings accounts (HYSAs), certificates of deposit (CDs), and short-term bonds. Each of these will generate modest but still noticeable returns without the risk of major losses, which is exactly what you're looking for if you plan to make a big purchase in the very near future.

Medium-term financial goals (three to ten years) tend to involve a moderate amount of risk. For medium-term goals, we're looking for not too hot, not too cold here; ideally, the investments you make to reach them should balance safety and growth potential. Some examples of investments that might make sense for medium-term financial goals include index funds or ETFs (if your goal is on the longer end of the spectrum), certificates of deposit (if your goal is on the shorter end of the spectrum), and maybe some medium-term bonds (for somewhere in between).

If you have a super-long time horizon and are reaching for **long-term financial goals** (ten-plus years), you can afford to remain unbothered by a higher level of risk, because your investments have more time to weather and recover from normal market fluctuations. (You'll find more on preparing for market fluctuations on page 194.) In fact, as long as the market ends up doing better than when you started, you'll still walk away profitable, no matter how many dips the market takes over the passing decades. For some people, working with a long time horizon might mean investing a larger portion of their portfolio into growth-focused index funds and ETFs, individual stocks, and other potentially "higher-risk" assets.

Of course, the exact investments you choose will depend greatly on the exact amount of time at play. For example, if you're saving to buy a home in two and a half years, it would not be fun to have all your money for the down payment stashed away in stocks, only for the stock market to tank right after you put an offer on your dream house. It might be better to just continue saving in your high-yield savings account, consider a CD that matures within your time frame for buying, or customize your perfect mix of all of the above.

Time Horizon in Action

Understanding our time horizon can help us tailor our investment choices to our itinerary. To get a better idea of how time horizon might influence our investing decisions, let's consider the financial goals of two sisters.

Hina is a thirty-five-year-old veterinarian who is saving for retirement. She has a time horizon of thirty years until she plans to retire at age sixty-five. Hina is comfortable with fluctuations in the market. She's not totally sure what she'd do if she saw her portfolio value drop dramatically overnight, but she's willing to find out for the chance at higher returns in the long run. Based on her long time horizon, Hina allocates a portion of her portfolio to index funds, stocks, and other alternative assets, like real estate investment trusts (REITs). Her ultimate goal is to maximize the potential for growth over the long term, while still maintaining an acceptable level of diversification to mitigate risk.

On the other hand, Hina's sister, Mahnoor, is a forty-five-year-old high school teacher who is saving for her daughter's education. She has a time horizon of seven years, which is when her daughter will be ready to go off to college. Mahnoor isn't comfortable with the potential for massive change in the value of her investments, and is well-prepared to trade gains for some added stability. Based on her medium-term time horizon, Mahnoor chooses to allocate a larger portion of her portfolio to safer, lower-risk assets, such as government bonds and CDs. Mahnoor's goal is to preserve capital and minimize the risk of loss, while still earning a modest return on her investments.

As shown here, Hina and Mahnoor have different time horizons, which impact the types of investments they choose, based on their individual needs and wants. Personalized investing rules.

Financial Goal	Time Horizon
College fund	7 years (medium-term)
Retirement	30 years (long-term)

Worksheet: Determine Your Time Horizon(s)

To determine the time horizon for each of your financial aspirations, think about how many years will pass until you'll need to access the money in your investments. Write down each of your goals in the first column. You can include goals with any time horizon, such as buying a house, saving for retirement, starting a business, or funding higher education. In the second column, estimate the approximate time it will take you to achieve each goal. Categorize them as short-term (within one to two years), medium-term (three to ten years), or long-term (ten years or more). You can use the table showing Hina's and Mahnoor's goals below to help you get started.

Financial Goal	Time Horizon

Your Risk Tolerance

All investments involve some level of risk, and some level of reward. In fairness, anything worth doing usually does. There is significant risk in starting a new business, because there's always a possibility of failure. Traveling to new and unfamiliar places can be risky, because navigating a new city in a new language is hard, and catching the wrong train might land you hours away from your hotel. Even learning a new hobby or developing a skill, like rock climbing or gymnastics, can be risky, because you might jump from the low bar to the high bar only to miss and fall flat on your face in front of *lots* of people and totally embarrass yourself. (What's that? Have I done this? No way, definitely not. Why do you ask?)

But what if your business doesn't fail, and it makes you more money than your nine-to-five? What if the road less traveled becomes your favorite road to travel, and you discover some of the most beautiful sights you've ever seen? What if your new skill or hobby becomes your passion? Risk is nothing to be *afraid* of, only something to be *aware* of as you move forward in creating an investment profile that makes you feel at home.

Knowing how you feel about risk starts by determining your risk tolerance. *Risk tolerance* is the level of risk that you personally are willing and able to accept when making investment decisions. It's important to give as much consideration to risk tolerance as to your personal goals and your time horizon, because it can influence the types of investments you feel comfortable in choosing and the overall asset allocation of your portfolio. For example, some people might be willing to take on a higher level of risk for the potential of earning higher returns, while others might prefer to play it safe and stick to lower-risk investments.

 TIP: Gains aren't everything (to everyone). While some people prefer to maximize returns, others prefer to maximize stability, and that's OK. As long as your strategy aligns with your overall money goals, you're on the right path for you.

Just as your financial goals can change over time, risk tolerance is fluid. Part of this will inevitably be influenced by your time horizon. For example, if you're someone who is younger and retirement still feels like it's light-years away, you might have a higher risk tolerance. Investors with higher risk tolerance understand and *accept* the potential for the value of their investments to fluctuate over time. They might be willing to invest a larger portion of their portfolio in stocks and other potentially higher-risk assets for the chance at higher returns in the long run.

On the other hand, someone who is mere months or years away

from retirement might understandably have a much lower risk toler-ance. They will need to access those funds in the near future and don't want any major dips or dents affecting their portfolio's value at the last minute. They might prefer to make more conservative investing choices, choosing to allocate a larger portion of their portfolio to safer, lower-risk assets, like government bonds and CDs, and they're willing to accept a lower return in order to minimize the risk of losing the money they have spent so many years working hard for.

Your risk tolerance can also change depending on the financial goal in question. For example, you might be more willing to take on a large amount of risk in exchange for the possibility of higher reward if your financial goal is a flexible want, like a dream car. For a less flexible need, like retirement savings, you might feel compelled to reel back the risk.

To visualize how changes in time horizon or necessity might affect your risk tolerance, let's revisit the table from page 148 and add a few new columns:

Financial Goal	Time Horizon	Risk Tolerance	Flexibility	Rationale
College fund	7 years (medium-term)	Moderate	Flexible	*7 years isn't super long, but my kid might not even want to go to college.*
Retirement	35 years (long-term)	Moderate to High	Strict	*30 years is plenty of time to take on added risk, but I want to make sure I don't suffer major losses in my retirement money.*
Dream vacation	4 years (medium-term)	High	Flexible	*4 years might not be much time, but precisely when I take this vacation isn't important to me, and I'd prefer more risk for the possibility of higher returns and a better vacation.*
Wedding fund	2 years (short-term)	Low to Moderate	Strict	*This wedding is right around the corner, so I need to make sure I don't have major losses.*

Women Aren't Afraid of Risk, We're Just Better at Recognizing It

There are other reasons—besides reaching the end of our time horizon or wanting to make sure we have enough money to cover our needs in retirement—that women sometimes lean more conservative in our investments. We often take our time researching our investments and making investment decisions, and, as a result, women sometimes get incorrectly branded as "risk-averse," when what we really are is "risk-aware." Women aren't afraid of risk; we just keep it on our radar. And that is not a bad thing—in fact, it can be very good! Thanks to our risk awareness, we are more calculated and remain calm even in the midst of turbulent market conditions. We tend *not* to make emotionally charged decisions, ahem, and this works out in our favor. Instead of solely chasing day-to-day returns, we find ways to look at the big picture of our money, how our lives can change with investing, and remain focused on reaching our long-term goals, even when things aren't going so hot in the short term.

Risk Tolerance in Action

Knowing our risk tolerance helps us make investment choices that keep us comfortable and maximize the outcomes that are most important to us. To see how risk tolerance affects the types of investments we tend to choose, let's take a look at Kate.

Kate is a forty-year-old marketing executive who's investing so that she can quit her job at sixty-five and move abroad. She has no idea where she's going yet, but she knows she has a time horizon of twenty-five years to figure it out. Kate would describe herself as having a high risk tolerance, and is comfortable with whatever rollercoaster ride the stock market decides to bring her on until she leaves the country. After that, she wants financial stability while she travels. Based on her personal time horizon and risk tolerance, Kate allocates a portion of her portfolio to index funds, stocks, and even a little bit of cryptocurrency for the added (but uncertain) possibility of additional gains, with a plan of eventually restructuring to include plenty of government bonds in retirement. Kate's ultimate goal is to maximize the potential for growth over the long term, while still maintaining a level of diversification (through index funds and a mix of assets) and eventual stability (in the form of bonds) after she reaches her goal of retiring abroad.

Risk Tolerance Quiz

Assigning yourself a risk tolerance is not an exact science, and these questions alone won't be able to dictate every investing move you make, but this quiz can give you a quick guideline about how comfortable you are with trading risk for reward.

1. When it comes to investing, how comfortable are you with the possibility that your portfolio value might significantly rise or fall in the short term?
   a. Very comfortable
   b. Somewhat comfortable
   c. Somewhat uncomfortable
   d. Very uncomfortable

2. How long do you have until you'll need to access the money you're investing?
   a. Less than 1 year
   b. 1–2 years
   c. 3–10 years
   d. More than 10 years

3. How do you feel about the possibility of losing some or all the money you're investing?
   a. Very comfortable
   b. Somewhat comfortable
   c. Somewhat uncomfortable
   d. Very uncomfortable

4. What is your primary goal for investing?
   a. Maximizing potential returns: Turn my existing money into as much money as humanly possible, no matter the cost
   b. Mostly growth, within reason: Significantly grow my wealth despite intermittent losses, so long as I net positive in the long run
   c. Balancing potential returns and risk: Moderately grow my wealth without losing significant portfolio value (and my sanity)
   d. Minimizing risk and potential losses: Maintain and slightly increase my wealth over time without noticeable setbacks

5. How much of a temporary dip in your investment value could you handle in the short term?

    a. I am comfortable with a 30–50 percent portfolio value loss in the short term.

    b. I am comfortable with a 20–30 percent portfolio value loss in the short term.

    c. I am somewhat comfortable with a 10–20 percent portfolio value loss in the short term.

    d. I am uncomfortable with any loss in the short term.

6. How much of a portfolio value loss could you tolerate in the long term?

    a. I am comfortable with a significant loss in the long term. If it means the chance at higher returns, it's a risk I'm willing to take!

    b. I am somewhat comfortable with a moderate loss in the long term. As long as it's not enough to negate my long-term goals, I'm okay with it.

    c. I am uncomfortable with a moderate loss in the long term, but I would be willing to tolerate a small loss.

    d. I am uncomfortable with any loss in the long term. My goal is to slightly increase my wealth or maintain it, not to lose anything.

7. How much risk are you willing to take on to achieve your financial goals?

    a. I'll do whatever it takes: I am willing to take on the highest level of risk to potentially earn the highest returns.

    b. Plenty of risk: I am willing to accept a moderately high level of risk in exchange for above-average returns.

   c. Just enough, but not too much risk: I am willing to take on a moderate level of risk to balance potential returns and risk.

   d. Barely any risk at all: I am not comfortable with risk and prefer to minimize risk at all costs.

8. How do you feel about the potential for long-term gains from investments with higher risk?

   a. I am willing to wait for potential long-term gains, and I prefer high-risk assets.

   b. I am willing to wait for potential long-term gains, and I'm not afraid of high-risk assets, but I wouldn't want them to make up my entire portfolio.

   c. I am somewhat willing to wait for potential long-term gains, and I can tolerate some high-risk assets, but I would prefer that they make up less than half my portfolio.

   d. I am not willing to take on any additional risk, even if it means potentially missing out on long-term gains.

9. How much time do you have (or want) to devote to managing your investments?

   a. I have a lot of time to devote to managing my investments, I enjoy doing it, and I'm comfortable making frequent decisions.

   b. I have some time to devote to managing my investments and am comfortable making occasional decisions, but it's not my favorite way to spend my free time.

   c. I don't have much time to devote to managing my
      investments, and I prefer a more hands-off approach.

   d. I have no time to manage my investments and no
      desire to make decisions about them.

If you answered mostly As for these questions, you might consider
your overall risk tolerance to be high. If you answered mostly Ds, you
might consider your overall risk tolerance to be low. And if you found
most of your answers somewhere in between, your overall risk tolerance may be moderate. Mostly Bs would place you somewhere in the
realm of moderately high, and mostly Cs moderately low, but risk
tolerance is a spectrum and you can land anywhere you'd like.

Think about your risk tolerance for each of the goals you listed on
your time horizon worksheet (page 148). Some goals might warrant
more conservative investment strategies, due to their shorter time horizons, while others might allow for more aggressive growth-oriented
investments.

Expand your table as we did on page 151. Consider how each of
your financial goals aligns with your risk tolerance and the flexibility
of that goal. Using this information, you'll be able to develop an investment strategy that reflects your preferences.

WORKSHEET: PUTTING IT ALL TOGETHER

Financial Goal	Time Horizon	Risk Tolerance	Flexibility	Rationale

Your Management Style

If you're feeling like you already have plenty of things to do and aren't exactly looking forward to adding "investment maintenance" to your daily checklist, I don't blame you. The good news is, investing can be as hands-on or hands-off as you want it to be.

You always have the option of individually adding, subtracting, or otherwise adjusting the investments in your portfolio on a regular basis to try to outperform a benchmark or the broader market. Of course, this would mean conducting regular and thorough market research, remembering to log in to your investment app or website, transferring the money from your bank account into your brokerage account, manually searching for your investments, and buying each of them individually based on your predictions. Oh, and then doing that again and again, visiting and revisiting your brokerage account periodically to make any adjustments. This is known as active management, and it's something I personally do not have the attention span, memory capacity, or time for. My to-do list is simply too long.

Alternatively, you can set all this to be done automatically so that you don't even have to think about it. This is known as passive management. The quintessential way of doing this involves buying index funds and ETFs that track the market passively, and subsequently "setting it and forgetting it." We'll talk more about passively managed portfolios in part II, but, for now, just know that hands-off investing isn't a bad thing: Research shows that the more hands-off you are, the better. An ongoing study comparing active investor returns to the broader market, Dalbar's Quantitative Analysis of Investor Behavior, has shown that between 1997 and 2017, the average active investor underperformed the S&P 500 by nearly 2 percent per year. With $100,000 invested over the same time period, the average active investor would have earned approximately $120,000 less than the hands-off, passive investor holding the S&P 500 alone.

Chapter 5

Create a Portfolio

Get ready to flex those financial muscles. You now have all the tools and knowledge you need to start investing. This chapter will show you exactly how to use them to open a brokerage account, choose a strategy, and construct a portfolio that is uniquely yours.

Opening a Brokerage Account

If you're going to start *investing*, you're going to need a safe place to put your investing money—and, spoiler alert, this can't be a bank. Nope, you need a different kind of financial institution, one that holds your money *and* lets you buy and sell investments: a brokerage firm.

A brokerage firm, also known as a brokerage, is a company that facilitates the buying and selling of securities, like stocks, bonds, and funds. It also holds your investing cash in the meantime. A brokerage firm acts as the intermediary between buyers and sellers so that all you have to do is click a button to buy or sell, and they take care of the rest.

There are two main types of brokerage firms: full-service and discount. Full-service brokerage firms offer a wide range of services in addition to their regularly scheduled bread and butter: trading and execution services. They might conduct research on specific investment opportunities, gauge the broader market sentiment, and even provide financial planning, portfolio management, and tax tips if you need them. They also tend to have their own array of financial products, like their own line of mutual funds, and their names tend to have the phrase "wealth management" in them (think Merrill Lynch Wealth Management or Morgan Stanley Wealth Management). They're like the first-class flight of investing, offering hands-off convenience with all the bells and whistles included.

But, of course, having a full-service brokerage do all your investing on your behalf will cost you, and it's not cheap. Full-service brokerage firms are known for charging pretty hefty fees or commissions for their services, and they're much higher than what you'll pay at a discount brokerage. The most common fee structure is a percentage of your assets under management (AUM), and the average fee can range from 1 percent to 2 percent. Some places might also charge an annual or quarterly fee, and some might charge a commission on each transaction. Either way, depending on the amount of money you've got invested, you could be paying thousands (or even tens of thousands) of dollars to have your account managed at one of these luxury firms, and some places won't even let you in before your assets hit six figures.

Discount brokerages, hence the name, come with a discount, but that doesn't mean you're sacrificing quality. These are the self-service options, the premium economy with extra leg room if you will (although I would argue that some of them feel more like business class). If you don't already have millions of dollars to your name, they're probably the investing brokerages you've heard of: Fidelity, Charles Schwab, Vanguard, E-Trade, etc. What do they all have in common? They charge low or no fees, and are usually totally commission-free.

They also typically offer their investing platforms online and in the form of an app to make sure you can trade from the comfort of your couch. Low or no fees means more earnings for you to keep, and you get to take the reins yourself. Plus, many discount brokerages offer pretty stellar customer support in case you get lost.

How Do I Choose the Right Firm?

The first decision you'll need to make when choosing a brokerage is whether to go with full-service or discount. If you're reading this book, you'd probably like to take your investments into your own hands, which means you'll likely be looking for a discount brokerage where you can manage your own investments. If I'm wrong, feel free to stop here, put down this book, and sign up for a full-service broker, which will take care of the rest for you. But if I'm right, let's keep going and learn how to choose the right discount brokerage for you. At the end of the day, many of the discount brokerages are *very* similar, and a lot of choosing which one is right for you comes down to personal preference.

- **Do they charge commission to trade stocks?** Because there are so many to choose from, all the discount brokerages you consider should charge no commissions to buy or sell, so if you find one that does, you can count it out immediately.
- **What kinds of investments does the brokerage offer?** For example, if there's a specific ETF or index fund that you want to invest in, make sure ahead of time that the brokerage in question offers it. Some brokerages offer certain index funds that can *only* be purchased through

their platform. If you have something you like, make sure you know where you need to be to get it. On the other hand, some brokerages tend not to offer their own branded products. Instead, they will sell ETFs that can be purchased from a variety of sources. For example, a very popular Vanguard ETF that tracks the S&P 500 (VOO) or the SPDR S&P (SPY) I mentioned earlier can be purchased on just about any platform.

- **Are the brokerage's trading platform and tools easy to use, and do they offer the features you need?** Make sure you find the interface user-friendly and you don't feel overwhelmed or dissuaded from using it altogether. Some brokerages are *known* for having a super simple (perhaps at times too simple) user experience. Others might be a little intimidating for a first-time investor. In the end, what you like is what you like, and what that looks like is up to you.

- **How is the brokerage's customer service?** It might sound obvious, but when you get an email that someone attempted to log in to your investment account and it wasn't you, you'd better believe you're going to want a brokerage whose representatives will pick up the phone as soon as you call. My best advice here? When in doubt, test it out. Make the phone call, see how long it takes them to pick up the phone, and when they do, see if a real human or a robot answers. Take notes, and choose accordingly.

- **Last but not least, what is the brokerage's reputation?** Some companies have been around forever and have earned themselves a solid reputation in the industry for all the right reasons: They offer solid products, with solid support, and minimal drama. Other companies have been around for less than half the amount of time and yet somehow their list of scandals looks longer than their list of assets. Check out reviews and ratings from other investors to see what they have to say about the brokerage's services and offerings, and read the news for any glaringly obvious pitfalls.

In the end, the most important piece is that you *pick one* and get started. Don't get too caught up in choosing the perfect brokerage, because they're all pretty similar. Whichever one you like the best and works for you, works for me.

Which Kind of Brokerage Account Should I Open First?

When you head online to create your first investment account, you'll likely encounter two main options: individual taxable brokerage accounts and tax-advantaged retirement accounts. In general, we prioritize tax-advantaged investment accounts first. These would include both traditional retirement accounts offered by an employer, like a 401(k) or a 403(b), and individual retirement accounts opened without an employer, like a traditional IRA or a Roth IRA. In practice, this typically means maxing out retirement accounts before moving on to your individual brokerage accounts.

Your Investing Order of Operations

If you're looking for an easy way to decide which tax-advantaged investment accounts to fund first, consider this order of operations:

1. Allocate enough money to your employer-sponsored 401(k) or 403(b), if you have one, to get the full employer match (hello, free money).
2. Max out either a traditional IRA or a Roth IRA—your choice.
3. Max out any other tax-advantaged accounts, like a health savings account (HSA), if you have one.
4. Max out your 401(k)/403(b).
5. Fund your individual taxable brokerage account.

The order of operations I've outlined here is just a suggestion, not a rule. What you choose to focus on will depend on your unique investor profile, including your time horizon, risk tolerance, and financial goals.

That said, retirement accounts also come with rules and even penalties on early withdrawals. So, once again, there is no single right answer here. If you prefer having more flexibility with your money, an individual brokerage account may suit your needs better. If you prefer tax advantages, you know what to do. Either way, it takes less than ten minutes to go on to any one of these brokerage websites, create an account, and sign up. So when you're ready, get set and go.

Do I Need a Financial Advisor?

The term *financial advisor* is very vague and can mean a lot of different things, but, generally speaking, it refers to a paid professional who provides financial guidance and advice to their clients. They help their clients create a financial game plan that aligns with their goals and objectives, and offer recommendations on investment products, insurance, retirement planning, and more.

Under that definition, a *lot* of different financial professionals might come to mind. Stockbrokers, financial planners, even insurance salespeople will fit the bill to some extent. In fact, unless they're selling securities, there is no need for a financial advisor to carry any specific licensure.

In general, if you sit down with a financial advisor, chances are you're going to go over a list of things. You'll create a financial outline, as you did in chapter 1, going in-depth on your net worth, income, and expenses. You'll figure out your saving habits and spending habits, as you've already done, create a game plan to manage your debts and maximize cash flow, as you've done, and set goals about what you'd like your money situation to look like in the future. The only difference is, instead of walking yourself through this process, you'll have someone else walking through it for you. And then, when that's done, you'll hand over the keys to your investments.

If you let your (licensed) advisor handle the asset management part, they'll be able to make your investment decisions for you. For me, a self-described control freak, that sounds like a living nightmare. But, for some people, it might be a dream come true.

As part of asset management, your advisor will create an investment plan for you, and manage, make updates to, and adjust that plan (according to your rules, supposedly) as time goes on. They'll buy and sell as needed, reinvest the profits, and make changes when necessary.

With so many different people calling themselves financial advisors, it can be hard to tell where their loyalty lies. Some people who take the title of financial advisor only operate under a *suitability* standard, which means their recommendation only needs to be *suitable* for the needs of their client rather than the *best* choice for their client. If an investment pays them a higher commission than another one that would be better for you, they technically *can* still sell it to you, and shrug it off by saying it's "suitable." Yikes.

Many financial advisors go one step further and adhere to a *fiduciary* standard. A fiduciary duty means that this person, by law, is supposed to put your financial interests ahead of their own and ride off into the sunset in good faith. Anyone you would ever want to work with should have this duty, and would be happy to tell you about it up front and in writing.

But even the fiduciary seal of approval is no guarantee of honesty. Not all financial advisors are bad, but the ones who are can persuade you to make unwise choices. For instance, some financial advisors also sell life insurance products. If they have been trained to believe whole life insurance is the best investment vehicle on earth (see page 110 to understand why it's not), what do you think they are going to recommend in your *best interest*?

At this point, after everything I've said, you might be asking yourself why anyone would *want* a financial advisor, but the truth is that the decision of whether or not to work with one is highly personal, and depends on your financial goals, risk tolerance, existing expertise, and desire to learn more. You might prefer the help that they offer and the knowledge they provide to bounce ideas off.

If you're looking for my opinion, I think that with a little legwork, most people are better off being their own financial advisor, if they want to be. That way, the power is in your hands. You'll know everything that's going on behind the scenes, save yourself lots of money, and never have to question whether you're secretly just a salesperson in disguise.

However, if you do choose to go with a financial advisor, it's important to determine *how* the advisor is paid. There are fee-based financial advisors and commission-based financial advisors, and if you're going to go with an advisor at all, please let them be fee-only. Fee-only financial advisors charge a fee for their services, which is typically a percentage of the assets under management or a flat fee.

Commission-based financial advisors, on the other hand, are paid through the commissions they earn on the financial products they sell, like mutual funds, stocks, or insurance policies. Remember that whole suitability standard versus fiduciary duty part? Yeah, this is where it starts to get a little hairy. As Warren Buffett once put it, "Never ask a barber if you need a haircut." Because commission-based advisors make money by selling you certain investments, they might be more inclined to sell some over others to earn a paycheck. There's no need to chance it on commission-based advisors, so save yourself the time and money, and don't.

While the fee-only assets under management model is relatively common, it can get expensive. The more money you have in your portfolio, the more money you pay them to advise you, so come up with a number for how much you'd be willing to pay someone each year, and stick to it. Even better, find a fee-only advisor that charges a flat fee for their services, which will make it even easier to stick to a number you're comfortable with.

As a final parting note, know that no financial advisor, no matter how much experience they have, how many credentials they've earned, or how seriously they take their fiduciary responsibility, can guarantee that they'll ever beat the market or even provide reliable returns. In the section on funds (page 97) we covered the evidence that professional asset managers and hedge funds *rarely* beat the market, and are actually more likely to lose against it. So if any financial advisor you meet tries to convince you otherwise, do not simply walk in the other direction—run.

What About a Robo-Advisor?

Have I scared you away from human advisors forever? If I have and you're still looking for someone (or some*thing*, beep-boop) to help you with investing, you should know that robot advisors, or "robo-advisors" for short, can offer assistance. They're programmed *without* the human features that sometimes make humans, well, less than great.

These digital financial advisors use algorithms and automation to provide investment advice and manage portfolios on behalf of clients. When you move money into your robo-advisor account, the robot invests the money for you.

Robo-advisors tend to use passive investment strategies, meaning that they typically aim to track the performance of a market index, rather than actively seeking out, selecting, and trading individual stocks or other securities. They all offer the opportunity to invest in a range of investment products, particularly index funds and exchange-traded funds (ETFs), and use algorithms to determine the optimal asset allocation for each client, based on the client's individual investment goals and risk tolerance. Most platforms typically ask you to take a quiz when you open your account (similar to the one you took in chapter 4), which gives the robot the information it needs to customize your portfolio to your preferences.

Much like a real live financial advisor, most robo-advisors also offer a range of other investment services and features, including automatic rebalancing (see page 190), tax-loss harvesting (strategically selling some investments at a loss to reduce the amount of taxes you have to pay on your overall investment gains), and goal-based investing. Plus, robots have no incentive to sell you certain products, and they don't charge commissions. Just like a good human advisor, most robo-advisors are fee-based, and typically operate on the assets under management model, but these fees are typically less than what you would pay a person to do the same thing.

If you've given up on humans but you're still looking for some guidance, a robo-advisor might be a good option for a passive investor for several reasons:

- **Cost:** Robo-advisors typically charge significantly lower fees than traditional financial advisors, saving you big money in the long run and making them a more cost-effective option overall.
- **Convenience:** Robo-advisors are typically fully automated and can be accessed both online and via an app, which can be pretty dang convenient for busy investors who might not have the time or inclination to meet with a financial advisor in person. (Do people still have meetings in person?)
- **Expertise:** Robo-advisors use algorithms and technology to analyze market data and track indexes, which we *already know* perform better than human guesswork. This can be especially helpful if you have no time or interest in doing any of the investment analysis yourself.
- **Diversification:** Robo-advisors typically offer a wide range of investment products, spreading your money across assets like index funds and exchange-traded funds (ETFs), which can help instantly diversify your portfolio and achieve long-term growth with less risk.

Investing for Kids: Custodial Accounts

If you've got your own investments covered, and you're looking to invest on behalf of your child (or grandchild, or your best friend's baby, or any non-adult you care about financially), you can do that with a custodial investment account. Anyone can contribute to it (think family, friends, not just the account owner), and there's no limit on how much can be contributed in a given year. When the child is old enough (between age eighteen and twenty-five, depending on your state), the account can be transferred to their name, where they can take their newfound generational wealth into their own hands.

Closing Checklist

Be real with me. Did you open a brokerage account yet? If not, stop what you're doing and let's go! To close out this section, fill out this checklist to put your knowledge into action:

☐ Researched three brokerage firms that fit my needs:

_____

☐ Chose the type of brokerage account I want (retirement, individual, etc): _____

☐ Opened my brokerage account!

Allocating Your Assets

Asset allocation—the process of dividing an investment portfolio among different asset categories, like stocks, bonds, and cash—is how we customize our investments. Think of it like creating your own personal wardrobe of financial products. The point of asset allocation is to create a portfolio that is well-diversified, balanced, and designed to meet your goals, time horizon, and risk tolerance. Some people might want more shoes in their wardrobe (stocks); other people are going to want more pants (bonds), or dresses (cash), or skirts (REITs). My garment of choice is a half-zip hoodie (index funds), but to each their own. Different asset classes have different levels of risk and return, and by allocating among the different categories, you can create a portfolio that is custom-tailored to your individual needs and objectives. In the pages that follow, we'll cover everything you need to know about precisely *how* to allocate your assets, so that by the time you reach the next chapter, you'll be ready to build a portfolio that is designed to serve *you*.

Step #1: Pick a Strategy

Before you start building your portfolio, it's important to have a strategy that you can fall back on and stick with when times get tough. This means that even when the market is doing poorly, you still have a game plan. There are many, possibly *infinite* strategies to choose from, but I've highlighted the main players—and the ones that are proven to work.

First, there are what I like to call the macro-strategies. These are umbrella terms that give you a zoomed-out, overarching picture about what you plan to do with your investments:

- **Short-term investing, aka day trading and swing trading:**
  If you're looking for some pointers with this strategy, you'll
  need to grab another book. I don't recommend this, and
  neither does the data. It's dangerous, and by now you know
  why. Let's move on.
- **Long-term investing, aka buy and hold:** The buy-and-
  hold strategy is exactly what it sounds like. You buy a
  selection of investments and resolve to hold on to them for
  dear life, regardless of how the market fluctuates in the
  meantime. Since, in the long run, the stock market *tends to
  go up*, the goal here is to earn returns through the
  appreciation of the assets over time. Of course, unless
  you're looking to invest a large sum of money one time and
  never do it again, you'll need to combine this strategy with
  another one that helps you decide how to *keep* investing as
  time goes on. To learn more about these strategies, keep
  reading.

Next, there are what I like to call the micro-strategies. These give
you a little bit more information about what *kinds* of investments you
are looking to buy with the strategy you've chosen above, and how to
buy them.

- **Dollar-cost averaging:** A fan favorite and for great reason,
  dollar-cost averaging involves investing a fixed amount of
  money at regular intervals, regardless of the price of the
  asset. The goal here is to average out the cost of the asset
  over time, through all the market's ups and downs, and
  reduce the inevitable impact of normal fluctuations. Like
  peanut butter and jelly, dollar-cost averaging makes a near-

perfect combination with its favorite macro-strategy, long-term investing (aka buy and hold).

- **Value investing:** As a strategy, value investing involves buying what the investor deems to be "undervalued" assets, with the expectation that they will greatly appreciate in value over time. Value investors typically look for companies that are trading at a discount in relation to their intrinsic value, using some of the tools we talked about previously in chapter 3, "Know Your Investments" (see page 85, "How Do I Pick the Right Stocks for Me?").

- **Growth investing:** Growth investing means buying assets that are expected to experience above-average growth, including stocks in companies with especially strong earnings, or funds that contain growth stocks within them. More recently, growth stocks have looked a lot like "tech stocks" (e.g., Amazon, Netflix, and Apple), but that isn't always the case. The industries with the most "growth" at any given moment can change over time.

- **Income investing:** In practice, the main focus of income investing becomes buying assets, such as dividend-paying stocks or bonds or bond funds, with the goal of generating a steady stream of income. The bulk of the portfolio goes toward choosing investments that generate money through regular payouts.

The investing strategy that you choose will depend on your personal financial situation and preferences. There is no right or wrong answer here. You can choose whichever investing strategy feels right for you, and, to be honest, you'll probably wind up using a combination of a few of them at any given time. (You'll see how each of these strategies play out in practice in part II with the sample portfolios provided.)

TIP: Pick a strategy and stick to it. In the beginning, while you're still getting used to the process of investing, I hope you will consider long-term investing a no-brainer, and dollar-cost averaging an easy way to get started. I also recommend picking at least one other micro-strategy here and sticking with it for what I will lovingly refer to as "a while." I'll admit, "a while" is *not* a precise time period, but it needs to be long enough. You have to give your portfolio "plenty of time" to do its thing so that you can determine whether or not you like your strategy and whether or not it's working. How much time "plenty" amounts to is entirely up to you. And, in case you're stuck between value investing, growth investing, and income investing, just know that the S&P 500, for example, lets you use all three.

Staying the
Course

A classic example of the importance of sticking with a strategy took place during the 2008 financial crisis. When many investors experienced significant losses as stock markets around the world tumbled into oblivion, those who stuck to their game plan, instead of panicking, saw a significant rebound in the following years. The trend lines of the S&P 500 during that time period speak volumes. From the peak in October 2007 to the bottom in March 2009, the S&P 500 lost more than 50 percent of its value. The entire world spiraled in panic, and many people chose to sell their stocks and move their money into cash or bonds out of sheer terror.

However, those who held on to their investments and stayed the course were ultimately rewarded. From the bottom in March 2009 to the end of 2019, the S&P 500 delivered an average annualized return of over 17 percent per year. A $10,000 investment in the S&P 500 in March 2009 would have grown to more than $50,000 by the end of 2019.

This example highlights the importance of staying invested and not letting short-term market fluctuations affect your long-term strategy. While it can be difficult to watch your investments decline in value, selling during a downturn can lock in losses and make it difficult to recover when the market rebounds. Instead, if you stick to your strategy and remain patient, you can benefit from the long-term growth potential of the broader market that we all know and love.

That's not to say you can't change your mind later, because you certainly can. I won't discount the importance of evaluating and reevaluating your portfolio and your strategy regularly, but it's just as important to be able to stick to your strategy when times get tough. Arguably, the most important strategy in investing is maintaining the mental fortitude to trust your process while the whole world panics. We'll talk about when to consider changing your strategy later in Conducting a Portfolio Tune-Up (see page 188).

Step #2: Transfer the Funds

The next step in allocating your assets is putting money into your brokerage account. If you're investing outside of your employer-sponsored investment accounts, one of the most important questions to ask yourself is *how much* money you can invest, and *how often* you're going to invest it.

For example, are you going to invest $100 once a month on the first of each month? Will you invest $50 every two weeks, after you receive each paycheck? Set an amount and frequency that is not only easily doable and achievable, but also sustainable. You want to choose an amount that you are guaranteed to receive each week, every two weeks, or however often you plan to invest so that you can fund your account consistently.

This number will be different for everyone. If you receive roughly the same amount of money every time you get paid, choose an amount that you can comfortably set aside each paycheck. If your income is different each week, one option would be to err on the side of caution and select a lower number that you're sure you will be able to meet no matter what. Alternatively, you could choose a percentage to invest from each paycheck. For example, you could commit to investing 10 percent of each paycheck, no matter what that actual number looks like each time.

You'll also want to make sure you don't forget to do it. (I'm speaking from my own personal experience here; trust me on this one.) For some people, this might mean setting up biweekly or monthly investing reminders on your phone. For others, this might mean setting up automatic transfers so that the money will automatically be drawn from your bank account and deposited into your investment account on a regular basis. Today, most brokerages offer some form of automated investing feature, which has personally changed my life. In the exact same way that I set up autopay for my credit cards so that I never miss a payment, I do the same thing with my investing so that I never miss an opportunity to pay myself first and build wealth.

Within your newly created brokerage account, you will be able to electronically connect your bank account to your investment account to provide a source of funds. In most cases you'll be connecting your checking account here, but you can also connect a savings account if you use it to set aside investing money. Linking your bank account is secure, it's fast, and it gets the money into your brokerage account as swiftly and efficiently as possible, eliminating the chance for any mishaps (like losing the check or, worse, your dog eating it) along the way.

The exact same process can be used for most investment accounts that you set up on your own, like your IRAs (Roth included) and your individual taxable brokerage accounts. However, with your employer-sponsored plan, like a 401(k), the process of moving money into your account is automatically done for you, in the flat amount—or more likely the percentage of your paycheck—that you choose to contribute. This can vary from employer to employer, so check with your benefits manager or HR department for more guidance on how to use their portal if you need some help. If your employer-sponsored plan is managed through a popular discount brokerage like Fidelity, as many are, their customer service department would also be happy to walk you through the process.

Step #3: Plan Your Asset Allocation

Just as it's important to go into investing with a strategy, it's also important to go into investing with a plan. Planning how you intend to divvy up your portfolio ahead of time makes picking assets much easier, because you already know where your money is going.

Now that you know everything you need to know about your investment options, risk tolerance, and time horizon, I suggest deciding what portion of your portfolio *you* would like to allocate to this starter pack of assets:

- Index funds, ETFs, or mutual funds (0 to 100 percent)
- Individual stocks (0 to 100 percent)
- Bonds (0 to 100 percent)

Yes, 0 percent *is* an option. As you can see, you can choose to allocate any amount into any of these categories, from no allocation at all to 100 percent. From there, you can then get more specific. For example, if you choose to allocate 10 percent of your portfolio toward individual stocks, you can then decide what those individual stocks are going to be. Also, remember that funds are simply baskets that *hold* assets. Some funds are made up entirely of stocks (like an S&P 500 fund), while others will hold bonds and a mix of other assets, so keep their contents in mind when choosing.

Once again, there are no right or wrong answers here. A young person with many years of investing on their side, a high risk tolerance, and no desire to choose their own investments may decide to allocate 100 percent of their portfolio to index funds that track the S&P 500—which is also to say that they've allocated 100 percent of their portfolio to stocks, albeit five hundred different ones. That person would be no more or less correct than another young person who is more risk-aware and prefers to allocate a portion of their portfolio to bonds for some added stability. Absolutely, their returns may differ, but not every investor is looking to maximize their returns at the expense of occasionally losing value. Your investment returns will always depend to some degree on factors you can control, like the investments that you choose, but also on many factors you can't, like the normal and expected fluctuations of the stock market, the broader market sentiment, and the state of the economy in general. (If you do figure out how to control those other things, let me know, and enjoy life as a gazillionaire.)

Since we already determined *how much* and *how often* you were going to invest in steps #1 and #2, we can use that as an example here. If you've decided to invest $200 a month, on the first of each month, and you allocated 100 percent of your investment to an index fund, you would then simply plan to purchase $200 worth of that index fund each and every month. If you wanted 90 percent of your portfolio to go toward index funds, and 10 percent of your portfolio to go toward individual stocks, you would plan to invest $180 into your index funds, and $20 into the individual stocks of your choice.

Step #4: Click the Button

Whether you fund your account every week or every month, the absolutely *critical* piece to understand here is that just because you put the money into your account, does *not necessarily* mean that it's invested. No matter how much money you put in, unless you tell your brokerage account where to invest it, your money will just sit there, exactly as it would in your bank account, doing nothing.

This, right here, is far and away the most important step: You have to actually click the button and make your purchase! Fine-tuning your investments can come later. If your favorite stock or index fund (or the first one you'll ever buy) has been sitting in your mental checkout cart for an extended period of time, now's your chance! Stop what you're doing, log in to your brokerage account, type in the ticker symbol, and buy it! It takes five minutes, and every day that you spend waiting is a day you miss out on potential returns and the opportunity to build wealth.

Study after study after study has shown that waiting around for the perfect market conditions before you start investing almost never beats the action of getting started as soon as possible, hence the saying, "Time in the market beats timing the market." Now that you've chosen a strategy, transferred your funds, and made a plan to allocate your money, all that's left to do is press go.

It's worth mentioning that when you do press go, you will have options. After typing your ETF or stock of choice into the brokerage search bar and selecting buy, you might be asked *how* you would like to buy. The two main options here are "market buy" and "limit buy."

A *market buy* means that when you hit go, you are purchasing at the market rate. Have you ever been to a seafood restaurant, and the price of the fish, or the lobster, or the crab on the menu just says "market rate"? It's the same exact concept. Whatever price that particular stock or ETF happens to be trading at, at that precise moment, is the price you'll pay when you buy it. Your order goes through essentially instantly. Since people are buying and selling stocks throughout the day during regular business hours—which, as a reminder are Monday through Friday, 9:30 a.m. to 4:00 p.m. Eastern time, no weekends, no holidays—the price will be fluctuating up and down in real time, and you will be able to see that reflected on your brokerage app or website. Choosing market buy means you are submitting your order in real time, for whatever the going rate is in that instant. So, if you're not worried about the going rate, either because it's already at a price you're comfortable with, or because as a long-term investor you only care about what the price is thirty years from now, a market buy will work just fine for you.

But what if you have a limit for how much you're willing to pay per share? Depending on the amount of market activity that day on your particular stock or ETF, the price could fluctuate cents or dollars in a matter of minutes. If, instead, you select *limit buy*, you can set a limit on the price you're willing to pay. For example, if you don't want to pay more than $150 per share of a stock, you can set your limit buy at $150. If the price is trading around $154 throughout the day, but at some point the price drops to $150 or lower, your order to buy the shares will go through, aka "execute." If the price remains above $150 throughout the day, you won't make the purchase. If the stock is already below your limit price, your order will execute right away. For most trades, the standard time in force (how long the order will attempt to execute before it expires) is automatically set to the end of the day, but you do have the option to extend the order indefinitely, known as good-'til-canceled (GTC). In that case, your order will attempt to execute every day continuously until it goes through, or you manually cancel it.

Whether or not you use limit buying or extend the time in force will depend on the investing strategy that you chose earlier. For example, if you're using the dollar-cost averaging strategy (page 173), the price on any given day doesn't matter, because the end goal is averaging net positive in the long run: A market buy that executes immediately will work just fine here. If you prefer value investing (page 174), you will want to use limit buy and perhaps adjust your order to good-'til-canceled, so that you can snag deals on stocks whenever they fall below your limit price, even if that's not today.

But How Do I Sell?

Now that you've learned how to buy investments, you might be wondering how to sell them. But don't get too far ahead of yourself. As a long-term investor, the most important part is getting into the market, not out of it. Handling the cashing out part can come (much) later.

That said, selling your investments is just as easy as buying them. You'll click sell, plug in the ticker symbol, the number of shares, your order type (market or limit), and select the time in force. The cash will then appear in your brokerage account. Easy peasy and nearly identical to the process of buying, minus a handful of potential tax implications.

When you sell your investments and make a profit, that profit is considered a capital gain, and it triggers a capital gains tax (unless you're selling investments in a retirement account). Likewise, when you sell your investments at a loss, that's considered a capital loss. Retirement accounts have a different set of rules, and investment gains there operate on a tax-deferred (or tax-free) basis.

As you can see, the tax implications of selling your investments can get a little nuanced, depending on your circumstances. So, in the far-distant future when you're looking to sell, chat with an accountant or another tax professional to make sure you'll have all your ducks in a row come tax season. Your brokerage will send you tax forms every year whether you make a sale or not, which you can hand over to your CPA, or your tax software, or yourself to plug in the numbers where prompted.

Closing Checklist

Time's a-wasting, and it's time to grow your money. To close out this section, fill out the checklist below to put your knowledge into action:

- ☐ Chose a macro-investing strategy: _____
- ☐ Chose at least one micro-investing strategy: _____
- ☐ Transferred money into my brokerage account

☐ Planned my asset allocation: _____

☐ Bought my very first investment(s)!

Understanding Your Investing Costs

Whoa, whoa, whoa, hold on. You thought we were just gonna catapult you into investing without so much as an afterthought? Not on my watch. YOLO-ing your life savings into oblivion is for the boys (kidding, sort of). In all seriousness, managing your investment expenses and understanding the fees at play are key parts of maximizing your returns *and* making sure you don't accidentally throw away everything you've worked so hard for.

As a brand-new investor, you might be used to bank accounts, like checking or savings accounts, that come with very few (if any) fees for their services. You can move money to and from your accounts, within limits, often without encountering any fees at all. If you do come across a banking fee, it's usually retroactive. For example, an overdraft fee that gets tacked on *after* you try to withdraw more money than what's left in your account, or a bank fee that fines you *after* using an out-of-network ATM. Investing fees are a little different because you can incur them *while* investing, which means they require a little more attention.

Ditch the Trading Fees (aka Commission)

A trading fee, more often referred to as a commission, is a fee that is charged by a brokerage firm when they buy or sell securities, like stocks, bonds, or mutual funds *after you click the button*. This could be a flat fee or a percentage of the value of the trade, and they might vary based on things like the type of security being traded or the size of the trade. Trading fees are used to cover the cost of executing the trade for you, plus maintaining the brokerage, and they can eat into your earnings (particularly for anyone who makes frequent trades and has a large portfolio).

The good news is this: Thanks to an industry-wide change over the last several years, trading fees for stocks and funds now almost exclusively exist in the realm of full-service brokerages (see page 160). By sticking to a commission-free broker, you can avoid them entirely.

Watch Your Expense Ratios

For most people using a commission-free brokerage, the expense ratio will be your primary concern when managing investment expenses and choosing which funds to invest in. Stocks don't have expense ratios, but funds do. The expense ratio acts like a fee that you pay to the fund in order to cover the basic costs of managing it, and is taken as a *percentage of the money you have invested in that fund.*

To know how much you're paying in expense ratio fees, you'll need to do some simple math. Let's say you're considering investing in a mutual fund with an expense ratio of 1 percent, and you're planning to invest $10,000. An expense ratio of 1 percent means that the mutual fund will charge you personally $100 per year in operating expenses, which is equal to 1 percent of your assets in that fund ($10,000 × 0.01). Since expense ratios are an *ongoing*, annual fee, you'll need to pay this fee every single year for as long as you keep your money in this mutual fund. The fee will be automatically deducted from your returns, which is how it can impact the overall return on your investments. It stands to reason, then, that *higher* expense ratios can result in lower returns, since a larger percentage of the fund's assets (and yours) are being used to cover expenses.

As a general rule, ETFs and index funds tend to have much lower expense ratios than mutual funds do (see page 107), but it's always best to check them on a case-by-case basis. It's easy enough to google [FUND NAME] EXPENSE RATIO for any fund you're interested in, or you can always pull it up through your app or brokerage website by typing the ticker symbol into the search bar, and it should tell you right there on the fund's overview page.

Personally, an expense ratio higher than 1 percent is excessive in my view, so I aim to invest in funds with a ratio of 0.5 percent or lower. In practice, as a long-term, primarily passive index fund investor myself, most of my funds have expense ratios much lower, usually less than 0.1 percent. You'll find that there are plenty of low-cost options to choose from.

Guard Against Fraud

There are many regulations in place to protect you as an investor. As long as you stick to the main roads with an established brokerage, a reliable strategy, and trusted investment products, outside of some of the less-traditional investing options we talked about earlier (see, for example, cryptocurrency, page 120), you're unlikely to encounter any trouble. But at the rate technology moves forward, new ways to trick beginner investors are born every day.

The inherently deceptive nature of investment fraud, the fact that it can be perpetrated by both individuals and groups, and the fact that it takes on so many different forms can make it difficult to detect. Some common red flags include:

- **Unsolicited offers:** If you receive an offer for an investment opportunity that you didn't ask for, this is an immediate red flag. Your brokerage, or any other legitimate investment group, would never solicit, offer, or persuade you to invest in any specific asset or investment product without an established fiduciary relationship. If a random guy from the internet sends you an email begging you to invest in his product, his motives are almost certainly not in your favor.

- **High returns with little or no risk:** You should become instantly concerned if presented with *any* investment opportunity that claims it offers high returns with little or no risk. By now you know that all investments carry some level of risk, that risk is not necessarily a bad thing, and that investing involves a trade-off between risk and reward. Anyone trying to tell you otherwise is hoping you don't know better. You can have impressive returns or you can have substantially reduced risk, but not both. Anyone who is unwilling or unable to provide adequate information on an offer's benefits *and* its risks (or tries to make it sound like there are none) can get lost.

- **Pressure to act quickly:** Fraudsters might try to pressure you into making a split-second decision, claiming that the opportunity is time-sensitive or that there are limited seats available and they're running out FAST! This is *never* the case, especially for long-term investors. Any investment worth your time and money will still be around the following month, year, or decade. This is not *Minute to Win It*; this is your life.

- **Complex or confusing terms:** Remember, investing is actually quite simple. If the terms of an investment are overly complex or difficult to understand, there's a good chance you want nothing to do with it. Scammy investment opportunists hire people to write contracts in purposefully difficult-to-understand language to hide the fact that the contract is *clearly in their favor.* Those offering a legitimate investment opportunity would *always* want you to have a clear understanding of what you're signing up for. There would be no need to trick you.

- **Lack of transparency:** Fraudsters might try to hide important information about the investment, like the granular details of the underlying assets or the company's overall financial health. A good investment can be read inside and out, front to back, like your favorite book (this one, perhaps?). There would be nothing to hide.

If you ever have any doubts or concerns about a product or service, especially if it displays any of these red flags, trust your gut. For starters, you can always ask another person, friend, or family member for a second opinion, but, ultimately, it's probably a good idea to seek the advice of a financial professional or the guidance of a regulatory agency.

Fortunately, or unfortunately since investment fraud happens at all, there are a few helpful resources (see page 301) if you fall victim to it. While I hope you never need to use them, they're good to know in the unlikely event that you or a loved one come across fraud during your investing journey.

In any case of possible or confirmed investment fraud, it's also a good idea to speak with an attorney. They can help you understand your legal rights and options, and do their best to assist you in recovering any losses.

Conducting a Portfolio Tune-Up

Every so often, it's a good idea to check in with your investments and make sure they're still on the track you want them to be on. Yes, this might feel tedious, but it's worthwhile, as long as it's done sparingly.

Remember my tip from step #1 (page 175)? You have to give your portfolio plenty of time to do its thing.

Review Regularly (but Not *Too* Regularly)

You don't want to be too zoomed in and hyperfixate on every little move in your portfolio to the point that you obsess over normal fluctuations. Worrying about the day-to-day market noise can lead to totally impulsive decisions, like selling perfectly viable investments at a loss in a moment of panic. Trends take time to develop, and you'll need more data points than just one bad day, week, or month to determine whether your investment will be profitable in the long run.

As a long-term investor, a good rule of thumb is to plan for possible adjustments no sooner than every six months to one year. This is for both your sanity and the overall well-being of your portfolio. Instead of waking up each morning and checking your portfolio balance, allow your mind to rest and wait until your designated checkpoint. Recognize that patience is part of the process. (Now, if you've already made some questionable investment choices and you're having second thoughts, you are welcome to make adjustments as needed. Nothing you decide on your journey through this book is set in stone.)

Once you reach your checkpoint, you can then decide if you need to move some money around. Checkpoints can also be a great time to decide whether you still like your investing strategy. While six months to a year is generally not enough time to pick up on any long-term trends, it's worth accounting for important milestones that might offer great opportunities to change your strategy and reassess your financial situation as a whole. For example, if you start a new job with a substantially higher paycheck, or score a hefty annual bonus, you might decide to start investing more money more often than you had previously decided. You can repeat this cycle over and over again to create and optimize an investment portfolio that will change and grow with you over the years.

Rebalance Regularly (but Not *Too* Regularly)

Over time, the value of different assets in your portfolio can change, which can cause the portfolio to become misaligned with your original goals. For example, let's say your goal is to hold a 60/40 mix of stocks and bonds. The price of your stocks (or the funds that hold your stocks) increases significantly to the point that they become 90 percent of the value of your overall portfolio. Your portfolio has now become more heavily weighted toward stocks than you wanted. This could increase the overall risk of the portfolio, and if you're not looking for that level of risk, you're going to want to make some changes by rebalancing.

Rebalancing is the process of adjusting the mix of assets in your portfolio to align or realign with your current investment goals and risk tolerance. In practice, this means making sure that your current asset allocation roughly lines up with the percentages you've designated to each investment type (see page 178 for step #3). You might need to sell some assets and purchase others to bring the portfolio back into that balance. For example, if you don't want the 90/10 situation that I described earlier, you could rebalance your portfolio by selling some of your stock positions (or the funds that hold them), or buying some additional bond positions, or both.

Someone who really enjoys active investing and the process of asset allocation might rebalance their portfolio on a monthly or quarterly basis. On the other hand, a more passive investor may only adjust their portfolio every six months to a year, or possibly even longer. In general, try to take a quick look at your portfolio at least every six months to make sure that you're still investing according to your preferences.

As with everything else, there's no need to time the market here, because chances are you won't beat it. Rebalance whenever it makes sense for you to do so, and don't worry about picking the right or wrong time. The most important thing is to make sure that your portfolio remains aligned with your goals and risk tolerance, especially if they've changed.

Of course, there's always the option to choose one of the more hands-off portfolios (you'll see some examples in part II). This might eliminate the need to rebalance often—or ever—at all.

Riding the Ups and Downs of the Market

During a down trend, the value of assets like stocks, bonds, and real estate will fall, and you'll probably see some red in your investment portfolio. (Some investing apps are kind enough to turn your entire home screen red with little icons—thanks for that.)

I've been lucky enough to invest before, during, and after a full-fledged stock market crash—*and* reap the rewards of maintaining my positions—so seeing red doesn't scare me anymore. And after reading this section, it won't scare you, either.

How Do You Define a Bull Market and a Bear Market?

When Wall Street veterans and financial newscasters talk about the general market sentiment, they sometimes use terms that make absolutely no sense when you first hear them. We've already covered a lot of financial lingo, but if you're going to talk it like you walk it, there are two more terms you'll need to know: bull market and bear market.

A bull market is a period when prices for securities are rising in financial markets. A hallmark sign of a bull market is a high level of investor confidence and optimism. A bear market is a period when prices in financial markets are generally declining. The opposite of a bull market, a bear market tends to carry a high level of market pessimism and investor fear. Both can occur in any financial market (including the real estate market, the bond market, etc.), but they're most commonly used to refer to the stock market. We generally define a bull market as one when stock prices have risen by 20 percent or more over an extended period of time, and a bear market as one when stock prices have fallen by more than 20 percent over an extended period of time.

The term *bull market* is rumored to have originated in the late 1800s, when Wall Street brokers would shout "bull" to signal that they were buying securities, as opposed to "bear," which indicated that they were selling them. The terms are thought to have come from the way that these animals attack their prey: A bull thrusts its horns upward when attacking, while a bear swipes its claws downward. Weird as they are, they've somehow stuck around to describe market trends ever since.

Bull markets can be caused by a variety of factors. In the best of times, this can include economic growth (lots of money in the economy), low unemployment (lots of people working and making money), and low interest rates (lots of people borrowing money). In the worst of times, they can also be fueled by investor overconfidence and temporary optimism. While bull markets can be great for investors and offer a fast way to make a lot of money, they can also be accompanied by irrationally high valuations and increased risk, and will, without fail, eventually give way to bear markets as part of the normal market cycle.

So what causes bear markets? Mostly the opposite of the things that cause bull markets. Think economic recessions (less money in the economy), high unemployment (fewer people working and making money), rising interest rates (fewer people borrowing money), and inflation (rising prices of goods and services). They can also be triggered by political or geopolitical events, like wars or natural disasters that create widespread stress and negative outlook on a global scale.

The more you look at historical stock charts and trends, the more you'll notice that what goes up does, indeed, come down. As of 2022, there have been twenty-seven bull markets on record, and there have also been twenty-seven bear markets on record. Truly a classic tale of yin and yang, day and night, or in *Star Wars* terms, the dark side and light side of the Force. (Some would argue the light side of the Force is simply the Force, but that's a conversation for another time.)

The point is, bear markets are nothing to be afraid of; they're a totally normal part of the stock market cycle. But to end on an especially positive note, bull markets measured by the performance of the S&P 500 have historically lasted more than three times as long as bear markets. In the last nearly one hundred years, the average bear market has lasted less than three hundred days, while the average bull market has lasted more than a thousand, explaining the age-old adage (and more recent internet meme) that, in the end, the stock market always goes up.

What Happens When Bubbles Burst?

Sometimes, bull markets can get a little out of hand. In the context of the stock market, a bubble can occur when prices increase rapidly and unsustainably due to investor optimism, herd mentality, sheer hubris, or excessive and unrealistic speculation about an asset's intrinsic value. When the bubble bursts, investors see a sudden and substantial drop in the prices of their overvalued assets, potentially resulting in a stock market crash in the blink of an eye.

No one really agrees as to what percent loss constitutes a stock market crash, but we generally decide to call it one when the S&P 500 declines by more than 10 percent in a single day. The key here is the speed at which it happens. Stock market crashes happen fast, with portfolios experiencing abrupt and dramatic loss in value. A full-on stock market crash happens roughly once every seven years: Since 1950, it's happened twelve times.

All bubbles will eventually burst, but not all bursting bubbles will cause a full-blown stock market crash. As I said before, what goes up must come down, but that doesn't mean it has to plummet through the floor. Sometimes, a stock market bubble will experience more of a slow leak: a noticeable but not entirely devastating pullback. This is called a correction. We tend to define a *correction* as a comparatively gradual decline in stock prices—usually more than 10 percent, but less than the 20 percent that constitutes a bear market. Corrections can last days, months, or even years—and while they might foreshadow a bear market, they won't always lead to one. And even if they do, it could take many more months, sometimes years, to do so.

How Can I Prepare for Normal Market Fluctuations?

Market downturns can be unsettling, particularly for those who are relying on their investments for retirement and are approaching it quickly. But there are two important things to remember.

First, market downturns are an entirely normal part of investing. Like a wave, the stock market has peaks and troughs, constantly moving up and down, always in search of its new baseline.

Second, market downturns can present an enormous opportunity for long-term growth. We'll take a deeper dive into this in the sidebar on page 196.

In the meantime, there are numerous ways to protect your portfolio against normal market fluctuations. Many of these strategies will sound familiar:

- **Diversify your portfolio:** One of the most effective ways to manage the risk of a downturn is to diversify your portfolio across different asset classes and sectors. This can help to minimize the impact of any one particular security or sector on your overall portfolio.
- **Practice dollar-cost averaging:** This investing strategy (see page 173) can help smooth out the impact of ups and downs in the market because you're investing a fixed amount of money at regular intervals, rather than trying to time the market. In the long run, you'll wind up buying more shares when prices are low and fewer shares when prices are high, bringing down your average cost per share and reducing the overall impact of short-term volatility.
- **Develop a long-term mindset:** If your time horizon is far out in the future—say, thirty years from now—the only thing that matters is that, thirty years from now, the final price of the stock or security is more than what you bought it for (and thus you'll net positive). From this perspective, the price today, tomorrow, next week, or next month doesn't matter.

**You Say Downturn,
I Say Clearance Sale**

During a market downturn, the prices of many investments are lower. In other words, they're basically on sale. If you buy them when they're cheap and the market goes back up, you can sometimes make a substantial profit when you go to sell them.

There are lots of ways to take advantage of a stock market sale, depending on your macro and micro investing strategies of choice:

1. Value investing: During a market downturn, you might have opportunities to buy already undervalued assets at an even deeper discount.

2. Dollar-cost averaging: If you're on board with dollar-cost averaging, a market downturn can potentially improve your long-term returns by lowering your average cost per share.

3. Long-term investing: Historically, market downturns have always been followed by periods of recovery and market upswings. Short of any unprecedented changes in this pattern, by investing during a downturn, you have the potential to reap the benefits of a market rebound and capture long-term gains as prices recover.

How Do You Know When to Buy, Sell, or Hold?

There aren't any hard-and-fast rules for determining when to buy, sell, or hold an investment, as long as you sell it for more than what you bought it for. If, or precisely when, that happens is wildly personal.

You should base your decision on your individual investment goals and risk tolerance, as well as your analysis of the market and the asset in question. Use these questions to help guide your decision-making:

- **What are the market conditions like?** If the overall market is experiencing a downturn, it may be a good idea to hold on to your securities and wait for conditions to improve, because you won't realize any losses unless you sell. In fact, if you feel strongly that the investment will improve in value when the market improves, it may be worth buying more at its discounted price.

- **Does holding a particular asset help you work toward your investment goals?** If a security no longer aligns with your goals, it might be time to sell it. For example, if you bought into the Dogecoin craze but have since decided the price will probably never return to what you bought it for (and you're tired of riding the hype train), you may consider selling, even though you'll lose some money in the process. Sometimes it makes more sense to cut your losses and move on, instead of leaving your money caught up in an investment you no longer believe in.

- **How has the security been performing?** When the market is down, most securities across the board will trend downward. However, if one security consistently and dramatically underperforms, compared to your expectations or to similar securities in its sector, it may be time to reconsider your position. On the other hand, if a particular security is outperforming most others in its category, you may want to consider adding to your position.

- **Is the security fairly valued?** Consider whether the security is fairly valued, based on its current price and its expected future performance. If it appears to be overvalued, meaning you think it's priced higher than what it's worth, it may be a good time to sell. If it appears undervalued, it may be a good opportunity to buy.

What Are the Long-Term Trends in the Stock Market?

The stock market has been around since well before you or I were even born, and that's a good thing. It means that we have years and years and years of data to help us understand what this roller coaster of a financial vehicle tends to do. While past performance can't predict the future, it can provide valuable insights and historical context that can help us make more informed choices, based on patterns, trends, and lessons learned from previous market cycles.

The stock market in the United States has had a long-term upward trend with some intermittent short-term fluctuations. Over the past century, the stock market has grown significantly, with the S&P 500 increasing by an average of around 10 percent per year since its inception in 1957. There are two main factors that have likely contributed to this long-term upward trend:

- **A thriving economy:** Over time, the US economy has generally experienced sustained growth, driven by technological advancements, innovation, and a favorable business environment, which has led to increased corporate profits and, in turn, higher stock prices in the long run.
- **Big companies making big money:** As companies grow and become more profitable, their stock prices tend to rise.

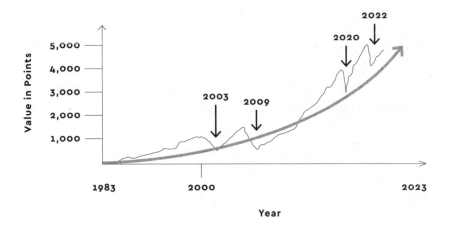

The United States is home to many corporate giants and companies that are household names, and those corporate earnings have boosted the stock market.

Most investors also tend to like the idea of making more money and often reach for opportunities to do that. When investors are optimistic about the prospects of the economy and the stock market, they tend to be more willing to buy stocks, which can drive prices higher. Inflation has contributed to the long-term upward trend as well. As the value of money decreases over time, stocks, which represent ownership in a company, can become more attractive as a long-term investment.

While the stock market has trended upward over the long term, it has also experienced periods of decline, and you should be prepared for both ups and downs. Market fluctuations are like the weather—sometimes sunny, sometimes stormy. But just as you need to go outside no matter what the forecast, it's important to stay invested in the markets, even during rough patches. Brighter market conditions have historically always appeared on the horizon . . . eventually!

Don't Stop Learning

In 1949, Lucky Strike ran a now infamous advertisement. The ad featured a group of physicians, all dressed in lab coats and looking very official, posing with packs of Lucky Strike cigarettes. Now, we look back at those old advertisements with a mix of amusement and horror—how could we have been so wrong? It just goes to show that what we think we know today may be totally different from what we discover tomorrow.

In pharmacy school, we're half-jokingly taught that most of the drugs we learn about will be irrelevant by the time we graduate. Everything we know, including our money knowledge, should come under scrutiny every once in a while. Rules, such as annual contribution limits and tax credits, change every so often, and so do the factors that shape us as consumers and investors.

Advances in technology have made it easier for us to access the information we need to make a solid purchase. The rise of online shopping has made it simple to price-match and find deals, while the growth of robo-advisors has made investing more accessible to the masses, even in times of economic uncertainty. With all this information at our fingertips, now is a better time than ever to level up our money game.

Women, who have historically been underrepresented in finance and investing, now have full access to the tools they need to take control of their financial future, something our ancestors would have only dreamed of. We can empower ourselves to make informed decisions about our money and our investments, and ultimately achieve greater financial security and independence than ever before. All we have to do is know where to look, and what to avoid.

Pay Attention to the News (but Not Too Much)

News can have a significant impact on market trends and individual stocks, so it's important to stay up-to-date on current events when investing. Being informed about what's happening in the world better equips you to make informed decisions about your investments and hopefully avoid costly mistakes, at least in the short term.

If a company announces a new product or a major partnership, this could cause its stock price to rise. On the other hand, if a company is hit with a major lawsuit or regulatory fine, this could cause its stock price to plummet. Even events that don't have a direct impact on the economy or individual companies can still impact market sentiment. For example, if there's a major geopolitical crisis or a natural disaster that causes significant damage to infrastructure, this could cause investors to become more risk-averse in a particular sector, leading to a drop in stock prices. Economic indicators like GDP growth, inflation, and unemployment rates can also influence the stock market. For example, if the unemployment rate is rising, this could signal that consumers will have less money to spend, which could lead to a drop in stock prices across the board.

To keep tabs on current events that might impact the market, it's a good idea to read a mix of general news sources and financial publications, such as the *Wall Street Journal*, *Barron's*, or *Morning Brew*. Many investment brokerages have launched online publications of their own that you can subscribe to receive by email. You can also consider setting up alerts for specific companies or topics, following relevant (and reliable) social media accounts, and participating in credible online forums or investment communities (think the opposite of r/Wallstreet Bets).

All that said, the news, the internet, and the media at large should be taken with a *major* grain of salt when it comes to your investment decisions. News can be a great source of information, but it's never advice. While it's important to stay informed about the day-to-day happenings, this information might not always be relevant if you're focused on holding investments for the long haul. The stock market can be incredibly volatile in the short term, with prices fluctuating wildly due to everything from economic indicators, to geopolitical events, to a billionaire's tweet history. Remember that many of these short-term fluctuations are often just noise, and they do not necessarily reflect the long-term value of the underlying companies. Long-term trends are more important, and that means looking at factors like a company's overall financial health, competitive advantage, and growth potential over a period of several years to even decades.

Keep Tabs on New Tech and Products

Every once in a while, there will be new products that break the mold. The Apple Macbook and the iPhone completely revolutionized laptops, smartphones, and, by proxy, the world as we know it. This is, in fact, the same company that started off with two guys named Steve mixing together computer parts in a garage. Today, Apple is the most valuable company in the world, with a market capitalization of more than $2 trillion. Not everyone could have seen that coming.

Years later, Amazon was formed, and completely revolutionized e-commerce and online shopping, replacing its small online bookstore with a trillion-dollar empire of its own. These companies—once no-names—became powerhouses, and there will be more like them to follow (women-owned next time, I hope). If you're interested in up-and-coming technology and are looking to invest in something at the ground level before it makes its big break, you can absolutely do so. Just know that timing the market and making accurate predictions about future stock prices is not as simple as it seems. While individual stock picking can seem fun at first glance, it's much riskier than a well-diversified fund, and is best reserved for only a small part of your portfolio.

Don't Believe the Hype

The late 1990s and early 2000s saw the emergence of what we now call the "dot-com" bubble. The internet was brand-new and quickly became the bee's knees. Everyone wanted a piece of it. Internet-based companies were popping up left and right, and investors were so excited about the seemingly endless possibilities they couldn't see straight.

Little did they know that many of these companies were flat broke and did not have a sustainable business model. But some investors were *convinced* that these companies were the future, the FOMO was real, and they were willing to pay top dollar for a piece of the action. Pets.com and Webvan became the celebrities of the stock market, with people buying shares frantically, sending prices "to the moon"— long before the moon meant anything in the context of investing.

Alas, what goes up must come down, and the hype couldn't last forever. The dot-com bubble eventually burst, and it burst *hard*. Many of these companies went bankrupt, and the starry-eyed investors who had offered up their hard-earned money lost it all. It was a tough lesson to learn, but it was an important one. It is *never* a good idea to buy into the hype and invest in something just because it's popular, and it's the fastest way to wind up broke. Investing is not just about making a quick profit, but about making smart, informed decisions that will stand the test of time.

As a long-term investor, the hype train is one locomotive I never want to be on. I am *immediately* wary of any new investment that claims to be the hot new thing. Nothing steers me away from an investment faster than hundreds of thousands of people talking about it on the internet. Investing is exciting, but it's not supposed to be *that kind* of exciting. Remember NFTs? Me, neither. Those were a blip on the radar in 2021, and we might not ever know what the future holds for them as assets.

It's not always possible to determine which up-and-coming investment will be the new Apple or Microsoft, but by sticking to a set of guiding principles, tried-and-true and averaged over time with an abundance of data, you can make decisions based on fact instead of fiction. And while the past is not always a perfect predictor of the future, since the market moves in cycles, the data we do have on past market performance is most assuredly more reliable than a self-proclaimed stock bro shouting out ticker symbols on TikTok.

Anything worth investing in will still be a sound investment long after social media has stopped talking about it. There is no need to rush.

Take What the Experts Say with a Grain of Salt

Publicly traded companies publicize quarterly earnings reports, and these are sure to get the professional stock analysts talking. After reading through each corporation's financial documents, experts will sound off one by one in all the major news outlets to publish their long-awaited recommendations to buy, sell, or hold.

But these price targets are rarely accurate. Even expert traders, known and recognized in their field, do *not* always make correct stock predictions. More and more studies come out every year to suggest that professional hedge fund managers, who are among the most sophisticated and experienced investors in the world, often struggle to outperform the S&P 500 index. From 2011 to 2020, the S&P 500 beat the average hedge fund's returns *every single year*—for seven of those ten years by a factor of two, and for four of those ten years by a factor of *three*! And because of this, billionaire Warren Buffett, one of the most successful investors of all time, has repeatedly argued that most individual investors would be better off investing in a low-cost index fund than trying to beat the market by paying for a professional fund manager.

Instead of relying on predictions and attempting to gauge credibility of individual expert opinion, consider a strategy that accounts for this risk by diversifying your investments. If your guesswork is as good as theirs, you might as well do your own.

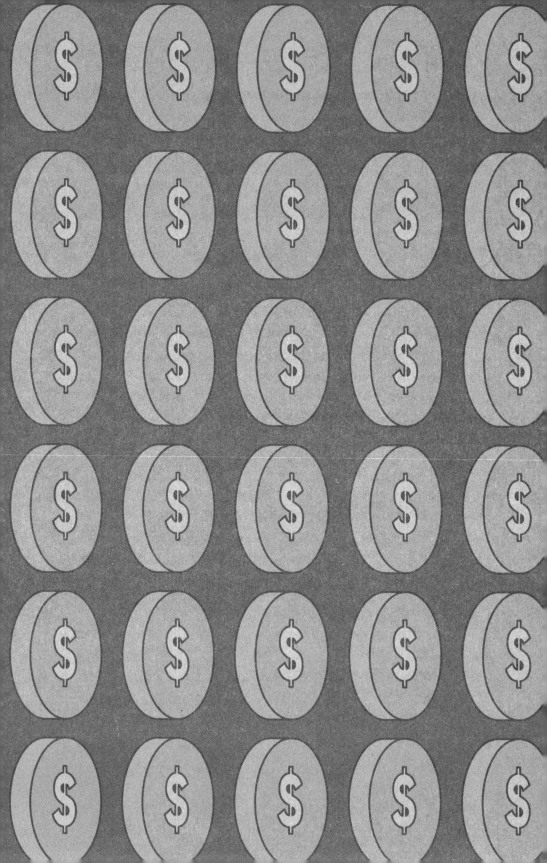

PART II

Building Experience & Wealth

Whew! We've come a long way from comparing investments to fruit salad, and I'm stoked that you've made it. By now, you're more than ready to start custom-building your own portfolio, but you might be feeling like your options are limitless—perhaps, a little *too* limitless. It's true—your portfolio can look however you want it to, and if you want to start entirely from scratch, go ahead and skip to chapter 12, "The Custom-Made" on page 291. But if you're looking for a jumping-off point, I'll introduce you to five sample portfolios that will help you start building your own in a jiffy. There's no shame in a shortcut.

Each sample portfolio will involve a different level of risk and a different degree of management, and you might find that some fit your goals better than others. If none of them match your style perfectly, that's okay, too. You can take what you need and leave the rest, and you'll have plenty of time (the rest of your life, even) to learn and adjust as you go. But before you dive in headfirst, there is one more thing I need you to know.

Designing the "perfect" investment portfolio is how I imagine it feels to be sucked into a black hole. The more you learn about investing, the greater the gravitational pull to try more elaborate investing maneuvers. You start to believe that the more complicated portfolio must be more profitable. So, to prevent you from falling into this notorious, bottomless pit of mind games (and reaching the point of no return), I'd like to introduce you to the Bogleheads.

Boglehead is a term lovingly used to describe an investor following the teachings of John Bogle. (He made an appearance in chapter 3, page 101.) Bogleheads believe that you don't need to be a stock market genius to invest successfully. Instead, they recommend investing in low-cost index funds and ETFs to build long-term wealth without unnecessary risk, and they'll defend their thesis in great detail on their popular internet forum if you want them to.

Their evidence? *Madsinger's Monthly Report*, which tracked the performance of a variety of passive investment portfolios for more than a decade, including a very simple portfolio made up of just one fund, and more complex ones made up of eight to ten. No matter how much tinkering you do or don't do—with asset classes and allocations, risk and reward—not one portfolio included in their report has performed more than a few percentage points better than another similar risk-adjusted portfolio in the last fifteen years. And while that 1–2 percent can translate to some pretty big numbers in the long run, it's nothing that can't be totally eradicated by panic-selling during a recession or paying commissions out the wazoo.

My point is, there are nearly infinite ways to end up with more money than you had in the first place. Investing can look however you want it to, and it doesn't have to be complicated. In the end, think of these portfolios as ideas for getting started. As long as you put the information that you've learned throughout this book into practice, it doesn't really matter which one you go with—as long as you just pick something and start investing. So decide what works best for you, adjust as needed, and have fun with it!

Chapter 6

The Full Autopilot

Your main financial goal is retirement, and you understand how investing can make sure you'll have enough money to stop working. *But!* You read this whole book, you understand the subject matter, and you still have absolutely no desire to choose your own investments. Listen, I hear you. I, too, am a busy woman, and I can appreciate the value in someone else doing the work for me. I know it's not because you *can't* do it, it's because you don't *want* to, and I respect that. Just because you don't want to be in the driver's seat now doesn't mean you don't want to *retire* in the driver's seat of a luxury vehicle later. The good news is, you still can, and I have options for you. A target date fund (TDF) might just be the perfect choice.

Portfolio Asset Allocation

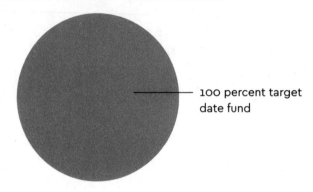

100 percent target date fund

How Does This Work?

So how do target date funds work, and what puts the *auto* in *autopilot*? The answer is twofold. First, they choose all your investments for you. Second, they balance and rebalance your portfolio for you. Target date funds are set for your target date, aka your projected retirement year, and for good reason. They're designed to *automatically* allocate your assets *and* rebalance your portfolio as you approach the end of your working years, going from "riskier" growth investments like index funds and stocks to earn you more money in your younger years, to more "stable" vehicles when you're older and closer to retirement, like government bonds. You don't want to lose all or most of your retirement money five years away from retirement, and, like a true friend, your target date fund does not want that life for you, either.

Target date funds are an option in just about any retirement account, including employer-sponsored retirement plans and self-directed retirement accounts, at any brokerage of your choosing, even without an employer.

Who Is This For?

The Full Autopilot Investor Profile

Time horizon	short-term, medium-term, or long-term (depending on how close you are to retirement)
Risk tolerance	low
Management style	passive

The Full Autopilot is for anyone who prefers their future car to be self-driving. Arguably, the most beautiful thing about the Full Auto-pilot portfolio is that you don't have to *do anything yourself*, except re-solve to invest your money in the first place. With each passing year, the target date fund will automatically move your money around, ac-cording to its own predetermined preferences, without requiring even so much as a nod of approval. If you love the idea of investing for re-tirement on autopilot, prefer to play it safe in the long run, and are totally comfortable with handing over full control to the fund, this portfolio lets you fully recline in your lie-flat seat, so feel free to take a nap and wake up in retirement.

Strategies Employed

Since the target date fund is choosing all your investments for you and they're usually found in an employer-sponsored retirement plan like a 401(k), there's a pretty good chance the money you're investing here is coming directly out of your paycheck in all its pre-tax glory. Whether you get paid weekly or biweekly, your investment account gets a por-tion of your paycheck. Then, the target date fund takes the money and allocates it where it wants to (which, if you've read this far, is just the way you like it).

Anything about this sound familiar? Setting up a recurring investment on a weekly or biweekly basis, having that money go directly into an investment account without lifting a finger, and then investing that set amount of money into a predetermined basket of investments, no matter what the price is on any given day? You guessed it. This is the dollar-cost averaging strategy (page 173) at its finest.

The Bad Stuff

Things *can* happen when we take our hands completely off the wheel and stop paying attention to the road in front of us. Any cool feature will come with trade-offs, and the wondrous life of stress-free investing comes with its own set.

Cruise Control (Usually) Isn't Free

You know how that self-driving car feature will run you an extra $10,000 or so in a brand-new electric vehicle? Yeah, there's something similar when it comes to target date funds.

The ability to sit back and relax while your fund manager does the work for you comes with a price tag, and that price tag can vary wildly from one fund to another. Target date funds are considered, thoughtfully, a fund of funds (FoF): a term used to describe a fund that invests in other funds, either mutual or exchange-traded funds. This means you're on the hook for paying the expense ratios of both the underlying funds and the fees of the target date fund itself. While the cost alone might not be enough to sway everyone from the stress-free approach to retirement investing, it does add up over time, and it will eat into your retirement earnings to a degree appreciable enough for me to write about it.

Take, for example, the ever-popular Fidelity Freedom Funds, Fidelity's target date fund products. At the time of this writing, they come with an expense ratio of around 0.75 percent. Looking closer at the asset allocation, for a target date thirty years in the future, it is roughly split into approximately 50 percent US equities, 42 percent international equities, and just about whatever is left over is put into a variety of bonds and debt products. It stands to reason, then, that you could design a similar—albeit not exactly the same—portfolio with only a handful of index funds instead:

- One index fund covering the total US stock market with an expense ratio of 0.02 percent
- One covering the total international stock market with an expense ratio of 0.06 percent
- And one covering US bonds with an expense ratio of 0.03 percent

Comparatively, the total expense ratio for a "copycat" portfolio consisting of those three funds would only amount to 0.11 percent. Investing with this self-constructed, cheaper portfolio over the course of your working years would save you a considerable amount of money in annual dues. By the time your retirement account reaches $100,000, an expense ratio of 0.75 percent means saying goodbye to at least $750 annually. If the same amount were invested into the funds with an expense ratio totaling only 0.11 percent, you would only be out around $110 bucks. As you can imagine, this cost savings can amount to thousands of dollars by the time you reach retirement.

Of course, choosing your own portfolio comes with the caveat that you would need to, you know, choose your own portfolio, and manage those funds yourself. Something tells me that if Full Autopilot is your kind of ball game, you don't mind paying the relatively small price for the comfiest seats in the stadium to sit back and truly enjoy the game.

Your Robot Is Less Fun Than You

It's possible that the "robot" driving your retirement choices is a more conservative investor than you are. And we do have some data to say that at one particular age, this might actually be the case.

A study conducted by researchers at the University of Illinois and MIT suggests that target date funds may actually become *too* conservative for most people at around age fifty. The authors noted that target date funds are good at owning stocks for a pretty long period of time, typically up to the age of fifty, allocating around 75 percent of investments in stocks at that age. However, the allocation of stocks drops sharply to 50 percent by the time of retirement and declines even further to between 30 percent and 40 percent in later years. Using a mathematical model, their research suggests that for a typical upper-middle-class couple with no family wealth, 80 percent of their portfolio should remain invested in stocks by age forty-five, with this proportion gradually decreasing to a more comfortable 60 percent by the time of and during retirement.

This is not to say that what a mathematical model determines to be most appropriate for most people is necessarily the most appropriate choice for *you*. Just know that choosing a target date fund means your portfolio will lean a little heavy on the bonds in retirement and a number of years beforehand. So, if you'd like to maintain more stocks before and during your well-earned retreat from the working world, you might want to consider rebalancing about three-quarters of the way there.

One-Size-Fits . . . Most?

Major employers tend to use only a handful of major asset managers for their employer-sponsored plans: Think big names like Charles

Schwab, Vanguard, or Fidelity. As a result, your choices are restricted to whatever funds those big names have to offer. Just like a one-size-fits-all clothing store, you can imagine how this can very quickly go from an easy-to-choose, minimalist shopping experience to a less-than-subtle way to say this is the optimal size, everyone should be this size, and if you don't fit in this size, you're out of luck. The fewer choices you have, the easier it might be to make one, but it might also make it less likely to fit your needs to the fullest.

An employee with a higher risk tolerance, making, say $90,000 a year will be offered the exact same investment choices as someone with a lower risk tolerance making $45,000 at the exact same company. An investor with a particular interest in sustainable investments or alternative assets will be offered the exact same choices as someone who prefers to stick to the road more traveled.

Why does this matter? It might not, but it may. The retirement needs for different people might be different (I know, shocking). Choosing a target date fund means losing the ability to individually select the things that make you unique, and your investor profile by proxy. That's the price of admission for investing on autopilot—hopefully not enough to outright stop you, but just enough to make you think about it.

The Good Stuff

I like to hear the bad news first and use the good news as a chaser. So now that we've gotten all of *that* out of the way, target date funds still have plenty of benefits. If you're the type of gal who would really prefer to just set it and forget it, but still fully intends to retire, here's why target date funds might be perfect for you.

They're Easy

Whether you're a seasoned veteran or a brand-new investor, the most you have to do here is pick the fund with the date closest to your retirement, and the fund will automatically take care of the rest for you. Not only will it choose all of your investments, it will also rebalance them for you toward more conservative choices as you approach your target date.

The target date fund essentially takes steps 2–5 of the portfolio-building process (see "Allocating Your Assets," page 172) completely out of your hands, if that's what you'd prefer. All you're responsible for is analyzing your financial situation and figuring out how much you'd like to allocate. Choosing your own investments can take as much or as little time as you want it to, and if you don't want it to take any time at all, target date funds might make a lot of sense.

They've Got Class(es) . . . and Lots of 'em

Just because target date funds take less time doesn't mean they have less substance. Target date funds are well-diversified, and I mean *well.* Despite serving as a one-stop shop, they still invest in a wide range of assets, so you don't have to feel like you're putting all your eggs in one basket, even though you're only choosing one fund. Close your eyes, spin around in circles, and choose any target date fund on the market— then take a peek at its asset allocation list. You'll see exactly what I mean. Within that one fund, your money is spread out over a large variety of stocks, bonds, funds, and more, all choices that you didn't have to make yourself.

A Win Is a Win

As a generalist catchall, the target date fund might not provide the *perfect something* for everyone, but it does provide *something* for everyone, and there's a lot to be said for that. Target date funds are not highly personal. In truth, they might not even cater to your specific investing goals and risk tolerance. But that's not really what they're there for. What TDFs lack in individualization, some would argue they do make up for in accessibility.

A Small Price to Pay

Even when you consider the variance in the expense ratios from one fund to another, it might still be worth the price, depending on how much you value your time and energy. If you have $20,000 invested for retirement, and the expense ratio for your target date fund is 0.75 percent, would you be willing to pay someone $150 to manage everything for you? Because that's what you'd be paying—essentially a convenience fee. For those who heavily value their time, and have no interest in choosing and re-choosing their investments for the next thirty years or so, the expense ratio might be a small price to pay to prevent what some might consider a headache.

How to Build It

If this all sounds good to you so far, I have even better news: Building a target date fund portfolio is even easier than maintaining it. All you need to do is log in to your brokerage account, select the target date fund that most closely matches your target retirement date, and allocate 100 percent of your contributions to it.

Because target date funds are geared directly toward retirement, they're a very popular option in employer-sponsored retirement plans, like your traditional 401(k) or 403(b) offered at work. In fact, because target date funds are so popular, they're often preloaded as your employer-sponsored retirement plan's default option. When you log in to your online employer portal, benefits page, or something similar, you might see target date funds listed in your 401(k) options as some-thing along the lines of "TGT DT 2050." The first part is denoting that it's a target date fund, and the second part is denoting your pro-jected retirement year, such as "2050" or "2060," which is when the fund expects you to start withdrawing money.

Alternatively, if your employer doesn't offer a 401(k)/403(b), or you don't qualify for the ones they do offer, you can easily find target date funds in any individual retirement account (IRA) of your choos-ing, including both traditional and Roth IRAs, by searching for target date funds in your online broker's search bar. Oh, and one last-minute important distinction: Not to be confused with a target date fund, "TGT" alone is the ticker symbol for Target stock, as in the big-box store with the red and white bull's-eye logo. If you're looking for a target date fund, make sure whatever "TGT" you're looking at has a date next to it.

Common Mistakes

To make sure running on autopilot doesn't accidentally turn into in-vesting indifference, it's important to at least be aware of your sur-roundings when choosing this portfolio option.

Apathy Syndrome

Target date funds can do just about everything for you, but they can't convince you to invest as much money as you possibly can. That part is up to you. Handing over complete control has the potential to cause indifference, and indifference is generally not a term we use to describe our desire to eventually stop working.

With any target date fund, especially if it lives in your 401(k)/ 403(b), you'll usually want to contribute *at least* enough to receive the maximum match amount from your employer, if that's something your employer offers. If you don't, you're leaving free money on the table. Contribute as much as you can reasonably afford, keeping those annual contribution limits in mind, and thank me later from your beach chair in Cabo.

Not Trusting the Process

So, your target date fund has chosen for you a variety of funds, all wrapped up into one cozy package for you to give your all to. Just *one* cozy package. Sounds scary, right? Putting all of your theoretical eggs in one basket? Committing to this *one* fund forever?

Don't let yourself fall into this mental mind trap. The final product might be wrapped up nice and neatly into one singular package, but beneath the surface are hundreds and hundreds of different investments. Your eggs are *not* all in one basket, unless it's like . . . a basket with lots of other baskets inside of it.

Panicking over an Account Balance

Come here for a minute, lean in. You chose this portfolio so that you could be totally hands-off, and it requires you to *remain* totally hands-off. You don't necessarily have to be hands-off forever; your goals and risk tolerance are bound to change, and that's fine. But you do need to stick to this when you log in nervously to check your account balance during your annual employer benefits renewal, especially when you find it bright red and subsequently begin to question every lack-of-investing decision you've ever made.

If you're going to relinquish control of your investments, you have to let the fund do its thing and recognize that it will still succumb to normal market fluctuations, like any other portfolio. You will have red days, and you will have green days, but worrying about your target date fund is like the investing equivalent of plugging your destination into Google Maps and then making your own right and left turns because you think it's steering you in the wrong direction. (Cue the passive-aggressive GPS robot calmly stating, "Turn around where possible.") If you want to sit back and relax, you'll need to *actually* sit back and relax.

The Modified Full Autopilot Portfolio: Robo Edition

If you're looking for a noticeably more personalized investing-for-retirement experience, but not so personal that you're looking to take the reins yourself, a robo-advisor is a great option to consider. When you choose to invest with a robo-advisor, it'll ask you a series of questions about what your existing retirement savings look like, how much you're contributing and how often, what your magic number is to live comfortably in retirement and when you expect that to be, and how you like to handle risk. Taking your responses into consideration (alongside some statistical and mathematical calculations on the back end, no doubt), the robo-advisor will spit out a plan to help you reach your retirement goals by your target date. If the robot thinks you're cutting it close, it can also recommend strategies and make portfolio adjustments to help you get back on track. And though their expense ratios and fees do tend to be a bit higher than those of your run-of-the-mill passively managed index fund or ETF, they do also tend to run substantially lower than a target date fund's, and almost certainly lower than an actively managed mutual fund's.

There are two important things to note about robo-advisors for retirement. First, most employer-sponsored retirement plans won't offer their services, so if you're going to use one, it would have to be in an individual retirement account outside of your employer, like a traditional IRA or Roth IRA. And, last, they've only been around for a short while (relatively speaking), so they haven't had much time to prove themselves with their long-term returns. In theory, the performance of the portfolios built by robo-advisors shouldn't look too different from a similarly allocated target date fund (or the underlying assets they're invested in), but without the thirty-some-odd years of data on their returns (which we do have for TDFs), your best guess is as good as mine. To revisit the earlier section on robo-advisors, head back to page 169.

Chapter 7

The Lazy Luxury

Simple at its finest means putting the smarter in "Think smarter not harder." In fact, as we've seen, letting your investments do their thing without unnecessary interference is one of the best things you can do as a long-term investor. At the same time, you might not want to hand over the wheel entirely. If you're going to be investing, you might feel like, at bare minimum, you want to be able to at least choose your own investments . . . even if you only choose one. And if you're only choosing one, you'll want to make sure your lone investment packs a punch and more than pulls its weight in profits.

Instead of spending a bunch of time trying to hand-select the perfect combination of investments, the Lazy Luxury investor just picks *a really good index fund,* and spends the bulk of their time trying to maximize their income and allocate more money to it. If this sounds boring to you, the wise Lazy Luxury investor would argue that the act of investing itself *should* be boring (see "Play the Long Game," page 76), but that doesn't mean your returns have to be. Instead of riding the ever-popular hype train, lazy investors win by relishing the less exciting but typically more successful act of putting their money into the same old, well-diversified, passively managed index fund over and over and over again.

Simple, right? Too simple? It depends who you ask. Take, for example, the decade-long bet that Warren Buffett, one of the most successful investors of all time, made with hedge fund manager Ted Seides. It began on January 1, 2008. Buffett wagered $1 million that over the course of ten years, a low-cost S&P 500 index fund would outperform a portfolio being actively managed by hedge funds—and that, over time, the professionals would underperform the returns of amateurs who invested passively.

By 2016, Buffett's S&P 500 index fund had already outperformed the hedge funds by a wide margin. The S&P 500 had generated an annual return of more than 7 percent over the course of the term, while the hedge funds had generated a return of only 2.2 percent. In fact, the index fund was so far ahead that Seides surrendered early, writing, "For all intents and purposes, the game is over. I lost." In the end, Buffett won $2.2 million and donated every dollar to Girl's Inc., a nonprofit that encourages girls to be "strong, smart, and bold" through direct service and advocacy.

Buffett's bet illustrates that low-cost, passive index funds *alone* can be a worthy portfolio in their own right, at least for some period of time. By investing in the S&P 500 or the overall stock market, you are essentially betting on the strength of the US economy and its largest publicly traded companies. And while past results can't guarantee the future, the historical performance of the S&P 500 and the stock market as a whole suggests that you *can* be both lazy in your investment choices and still reap luxurious outcomes.

Portfolio Asset Allocation

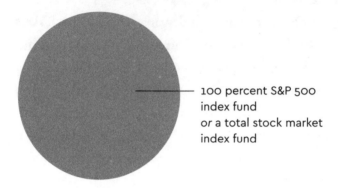

100 percent S&P 500
index fund
or a total stock market
index fund

How Does This Work?

When you invest in an index fund that tracks the S&P 500, you are effectively buying a small piece of each of the 500 companies in the index. This means that your investment is spread across different companies in different industries automatically, without you having to select any of them (lazy mode achieved).

While an S&P 500 index fund on its own will keep your portfolio pretty well-diversified, a total stock market index fund will help you diversify your portfolio even further. The S&P 500 contains large-cap companies only, which make up about 80 percent of the total stock market. A total stock market index fund is designed to capture the performance of the *entire* stock market, including the small-cap and mid-cap companies that may not be included in the S&P 500. In other words, investing in the total stock market guarantees that you are also investing in the S&P 500, but not the other way around. If you invest only in an S&P 500 index fund, you would be missing out on the performance of those smaller companies.

Some investors choose to invest in a total stock market index fund instead of the S&P 500 so that they can gain exposure to the entire US stock market, including smaller companies that might provide additional growth opportunities. But is one better than the other? Theoretically, the total stock market index could experience greater swings in performance, both positive and negative, than the S&P 500 because it includes small- and mid-cap companies that are just starting out and gaining their footing.

But, historically, in the long run, these temporary swings caused by fledgling companies haven't made much of a difference. The S&P 500 and the total stock market have produced *very* similar outcomes over the last thirty years. Both have experienced average annual returns of around 10 percent, and although there have been variations from year to year, the difference in average long-term returns between the two has been less than half a percentage point (0.5 percent). In fact, because the S&P 500 makes up such a large portion of the overall market, and the long-term performance of both the total stock market and the S&P 500 have been so similar, the S&P 500 alone is often used as a proxy for the overall direction of the market in general. Long story short, take your pick between the two. While their guts are 20 percent different, their returns have been very close to the same.

Who Is This For?

The Lazy Luxury Investor Profile

Time horizon	long-term
Risk tolerance	high
Management style	passive

If you're a member of the "work smarter, not harder" club, you may have met your match. The Lazy Luxury portfolio affords you the autonomy that a target date fund lacks, without bogging you down with an overwhelming number of decisions. Because both the S&P 500 and total stock market index funds perform almost exactly the same, you really can't go wrong. And unlike a target date fund, both an S&P 500 and a total stock market index fund come with the potential for higher returns. For many investors, especially those with a relatively high risk tolerance, a strong desire for growth, and little interest in making lots of decisions, this portfolio does more than enough to meet their needs until they are close to meeting their financial goals and decide to re-distribute their investments into something quite a bit more stable (like bonds).

Strategies Employed

There are two main strategies that Lazy Luxury investors will use. The first is buy and hold (see page 173). Holding as long as possible is what makes this portfolio both lazy and, ultimately, luxurious. As a lazy investor, you're looking for long-term growth without doing much work, so selling prematurely (or at any regular interval, really) would defeat this purpose. When you buy shares of an S&P 500 or a total stock market index fund, you are banking on holding them for a *long* period of time. I'm talking many, many years—ideally decades. You'll avoid trying to time the market by buying and selling often, which often leads to higher fees and lower returns.

Second, because it's possible to invest in either of these funds just about anywhere, including individual brokerage accounts and your standard retirement accounts like 401(k)s and IRAs, dollar-cost aver-aging (see page 173) can come into play as well. It *is* possible to man-ually choose either the S&P 500 or a total stock market index fund as your entire allocation for your retirement accounts instead of the stan-dard autopilot funds we talked about in the last chapter. You could use the same process outlined in the Full Autopilot portfolio: Your set amount of money would automatically come out of your paycheck pre-tax and make its way into your retirement accounts—but this time it would be 100 percent invested into either an S&P 500 or a total stock market index fund instead of a target date fund. You could also do the exact same thing in an individual brokerage account (albeit without the tax benefits) by choosing a set amount to invest in either of these funds at a set interval.

The Bad Stuff

So, what's the catch here? Choosing this ultra-straightforward option will guarantee that certain things will need to be left out (namely, everything outside of US stocks) and whether this works for you depends on whether you believe those things were necessary in the first place. Once working smarter and not harder becomes the name of the game, you'll also need to cut some corners, and there are a few things to keep in mind if you want to do it without sacrificing positive outcomes.

The Team USA Echo Chamber

"USA, USA!" Investing solely in the S&P 500 or the total stock market index means your money is stuck solely in the United States market. Traditional investors would argue that an excellent portfolio would *need* to include international funds to allow for maximum diversity and believe that international stocks tend to do better than US stocks when the S&P 500 is doing poorly. In other words, when your domestic investments aren't performing well, your international investments might be doing great. When you're only invested in companies from the good ol' US of A, you don't have the opportunity for international growth, if it takes place during your time horizon.

Big Name, Big Influence

The way an index is *weighted* determines how much influence each stock in the basket has on the overall performance of the index. The S&P 500 and most total stock market indexes are weighted based on market capitalization.

Market capitalization accounts for both the stock price and the number of shares currently held by shareholders. This means that if a bigwig company's stock price goes up or down substantially, it will have a *much* greater impact on the index than a smaller company whose stock price does the same thing. This is part of the reason that returns in the S&P 500 and the total stock market are so similar.

So why is this relevant? For you, a Lazy Luxury investor, when the major league companies aren't doing very well, neither will your port-folio. If you're going to embrace the simple route, you'll have to be okay with riding out the red. Which brings me to my next point . . .

Stability, Who?

I love a good growth portfolio, but for this approach, you're going to need a strong stomach to withstand the market conditions over the next thirty years or so, which inevitably come with ups and downs. If your portfolio is invested solely in the US stock market, there *will* be times when the US stock market isn't feeling so hot, and you might not be feeling so hot, either, after logging in to your brokerage account during a downturn. The good news is this: If history has anything to say about it, the market will recover, and so will your portfolio, but you *must* have either (a) the laziness or (b) the self-control to ride out these periods instead of selling at a loss.

The Need to Adjust . . . Eventually

Eventually, you'll need to adjust your portfolio, usually once you get closer to retirement. For most people, the Lazy Luxury will not be an investment portfolio that will last them their *entire* lifetime. In retirement, many investors will want to rebalance their portfolio and allocate 40 percent or more of it to assets that are much more stable, like government bonds, depending on your risk tolerance.

The Good Stuff

Being a lazy luxurious queen comes with its own set of downsides, but this portfolio can have serious returns if you stick to it, and being truly lazy makes that relatively easy to do. Cutting through the noise and skipping the fluff might be just your cup of tea.

The Grass Is Only Greener Sometimes

International funds might be missing you, but will you be missing them? While it's *sometimes* true that international funds may improve performance when the US market is doing poorly, data from more recent economic disasters suggest that this age-old adage is not always the case.

For example, in previous major market downturns, international stocks performed better than US stocks. In the early 2000s, the MSCI EAFE Index, which measures the performance of developed markets outside of the US and Canada, outperformed the S&P 500. However, during the onset of the global COVID-19 pandemic in 2020, the US stock market outperformed international stocks for much of the year. In short, when the US economy was suffering, the international markets fared better, but when *the entire world's* market was suffering, the US came out on top.

Zooming out even further, from January 1992 to January 2022, the S&P 500 had an average annualized return of about 10 percent, while the MSCI EAFE Index had an average annualized return of closer to 5 percent over the same thirty-year period. Sheesh.

This information alone is not enough to say that diversifying your portfolio into international markets is inherently pointless. But the Lazy Luxury investor would argue that it *might be* unnecessary. Going against conventional wisdom, a lazy investor might say that if the goal is to maximize long-term growth, it might be totally okay to leave out a usually underperforming asset with a long enough time horizon. It might even be more efficient that way.

The Price Is Right

If you love a good deal, this portfolio is a great one. S&P 500 and total stock market index funds can be relatively inexpensive, compared to other types of investments. In general, they tend to have lower fees and expenses, compared to actively managed funds. While actively managed funds are busy using more resources and research in a desperate attempt to outperform the market, index funds are just passively tracking it. And nine times out of ten, they still wind up ahead of their actively managed counterparts. Essentially, S&P 500 and total stock market index funds are a low-cost way to accomplish what most fund managers spend their entire careers trying (and failing) to do. Not bad.

What, Like It's Hard?

I hear you, target date funds are pretty dang easy, so it doesn't surprise me if they catch a Lazy Luxury investor's attention at first glance. But, luckily, to place emphasis on the *luxury* part, wanting higher returns than what TDFs have to offer doesn't mean your portfolio has to become more complicated. According to a comparison in *Barron's* between the returns from target date funds and the S&P 500, target date 2040 funds have "lagged [behind] the S&P 500 by a compounded annual average of 2.4 percent over the past 28 years, returning 750 percent in total over the time frame, versus 1,494 percent for the broader market." Historically speaking, by investing in an S&P 500 or total stock market index fund, you can be just as lazy and come out even more luxurious.

Not Forever, But Mostly

The Lazy Luxury portfolio might not be your forever and always, but it can be your forever and most days. You might find yourself looking to switch things up for some added stability eventually, but with returns like these—plus the added bonus of widespread accessibility, instant diversity, marked versatility, and very little effort—Lazy Luxury makes for an excellent companion for a very long time.

How to Build It

Building a portfolio that consists solely of either an S&P 500 index fund or a total stock market index fund is simple. The hardest part for you is choosing which one you want. Just about every brokerage in existence now offers their own version of either of these funds, so pick a brokerage that you like and check out what their funds in this category have to offer. You can search [BROKERAGE NAME] S&P 500 INDEX FUND or [BROKERAGE NAME] TOTAL STOCK MARKET INDEX FUND to see what I mean. For example, Fidelity will have its own version of these funds, just as Vanguard will have theirs.

There are also third-party S&P 500 and total stock market ETFs if you will: stand-alone funds that are offered across different brokerages and are not affiliated with any particular one. For example, the SPDR S&P 500 ETF Trust, also known as the SPY ETF (see page 104 for its backstory), is a very popular S&P 500 ETF that can be purchased through many different brokerage platforms.

When comparing S&P 500 and total stock market index funds across brokerages, they might have minute differences in returns and expense ratios, but, in general, they will all be pretty similar. They're all attempting to do the same thing, really, which is to track their respective indexes. Because they're all so similar, it usually makes sense to focus on choosing a fund that charges relatively low fees and has a proven track record.

If you're looking to invest in these funds in your employer-sponsored retirement account, like a 401(k)/403(b), you're at the mercy of whatever brokerage your employer has chosen. Regardless, just about every brokerage will have their own version of an S&P 500 or total stock market index fund to invest in. If your employer-sponsored account only offers one or the other, it sounds like they've made your decision for you.

As always, if your employer doesn't offer a 401(k)/403(b) or, for whatever reason, you don't qualify for whatever they do offer, that doesn't mean the Lazy Luxury portfolio is out of the question for you. You can easily find either of these funds in any IRA or taxable brokerage account of your choice.

Common Mistakes

When things get this simple, it can be easy to lose focus on the finer details. But fear not, my low-maintenance luxurious friend: These pitfalls take up such a small amount of mental real estate that all you have to do is remember to remember them, and you'll be good as gold.

Thinking More Is More

The longer we've been investing, the stronger the nagging feeling is that we should be doing *more* with our investments, and I get that. The more you know, the more it feels like you need to do. But what if more is actually less? S&P 500 and total stock market index funds have a long track record of providing sizable returns on their own, especially when averaged out over a thirty-year period. On the other hand, many people who try to time the market and roll the dice instead wind up with net losses. If you choose the Lazy Luxury path, don't fall victim to the idea that you're not doing enough. Being lazy, after all, is exactly what we're looking for here.

Being Unprepared for a Bumpy Ride

If choosing the Lazy Luxury portfolio were an amusement park ride, being able to tolerate unexpected twists and turns without tossing your cookies would supersede the standard height requirement. Many people love the simplicity of this portfolio, but they are (understandably) not able to handle the ups and downs that come with it. Trusting the performance of the S&P 500 or the total stock market alone means believing the end result will be positive in the long term, no matter what happens in the meantime. That means not selling all of your investments in a brief period of market upswing *or* when things take a sudden nosedive. You must be comfortable with everything that goes on between now and the time you retire, or whenever you antici-pate taking out the money. If you can't enjoy the ride, this may not be the portfolio for you.

Forgetting to Rebalance

Last, but certainly not least, in all of your lazy glory, you must remember one thing: to switch your money into something more stable *eventu-ally*. If you think that's disappointing, imagine watching your retire-ment savings drop dramatically on a whim, all because the S&P 500 decided to tank two weeks after your retirement party. To quote Uncle Ben from *Spider-Man*, remember that with great power comes great responsibility. When the desire for your investments to stay the same (due to fear of losing value) starts to outweigh the desire for more growth, it's probably time to make some adjustments.

Chapter 8

The Fun Money

Raise your hand if the last two chapters were totally boring. *Throwing all of your money into one thing? Have you ever heard of a little something called fun? What's the point of investing if you don't get to pick out some things you like every once in a while?* I hear your concerns, and they're valid. Sticking to the straight and narrow, while often profitable, can definitely get boring, especially if you like to branch out and try new things.

On the other hand, branching out and trying new things *all* the time might not end well. If you try a new meal at your favorite restaurant every time you go, you're bound to find something you don't like on that menu. Suddenly the restaurant that could do no wrong has, in fact, done something wrong. The occasional scathing one-star Google review begins to make sense. You start to question everything you know. Do you even *like* this restaurant?

The same can happen with your investment choices. Not every stock you think will be super successful will be spot-on, no matter how much *you* like that company. Even the restaurant's most popular menu item might not be the most critically acclaimed, according to the fancy Michelin star people.

So what if, instead of picking a new meal every time, you just changed up your sides? You get to keep your favorite dish, the one you know will taste good every single time, but if you opt for the asparagus and it's totally mushy and gross, no harm, no foul. The rest of your meal was still delicious. This is exactly what the Fun Money portfolio seeks to offer: a balance between novelty and consistency.

Portfolio Asset Allocation

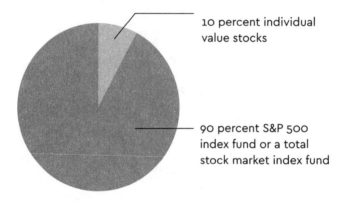

10 percent individual value stocks

90 percent S&P 500 index fund or a total stock market index fund

How Does This Work?

The Fun Money portfolio makes it possible to carve out a small, designated section of your portfolio for the investments you like, while still maintaining the majority in those that have historically proven to be successful, with an S&P 500 or total stock market index fund. Investing 90 percent of your money into this type of index fund will make sure you still benefit from a wide variety of top US companies that have a proven track record. That leaves you with 10 percent "fun money" to spend on companies that you deem worthy, by whatever criteria you feel is appropriate. The added fun (or risk, depending on your tolerance) gives your chosen stocks the chance to outperform the broader market. And, ideally, if you carefully select them based on strong growth prospects, competitive advantages, or compelling valuation, you might just earn yourself some even higher returns. (But, alas, if you're looking to YOLO 10 percent of your portfolio into something crazy, I'm not here to tell you how to spend your fun money.)

Who Is This For?

The Fun Money Investor Profile

Time horizon	long-term
Risk tolerance	highest
Management style	mostly passive

The Fun Money investor is the person who finds basic wooden roller coasters boring. They can do a lot more than just tolerate the regular ups and downs of the S&P 500 or the total stock market. With a higher risk tolerance than their Lazy Luxury or Full Autopilot counterparts, they actually *prefer* the added risk of buying a handful of individual stocks every once in a while. If they choose the right companies at the right price points, they have a very real possibility of some added upside, beyond just the returns of the overall market. If they choose wrong, they might have made more money sticking to the broader index funds alone, but that's a risk they are willing to take in exchange for the chance at higher returns. After all, what's life without the occasional loops and upside-down bits?

Strategies Employed

Value investing (page 174) has entered the chat. While the majority of your strategy here will rely on the fundamentals of growth investing (page 174), buy and hold (page 173), and typically dollar-cost averaging (page 173) as well, 10 percent of the Fun Money portfolio provides a great opportunity to make use of value investing, aka buying stocks that you believe are undervalued by the market. The basic idea is that you'll try to choose stocks that are trading at a price lower than their intrinsic value, making them "cheap" compared to their actual worth.

For the small chunk of portfolio dedicated to all things fun, Fun Money investors typically look for companies that have solid *fundamentals*, meaning they have strong financials, good management, and a competitive advantage. They also pay close attention to the stock's price-to-earnings (P/E) ratio, which is a measure of a company's stock price relative to its annual earnings per share. Ideally, the ultimate goal here is to buy undervalued stocks at a discount and hold on to them as their prices rise, while still primarily benefiting from the relatively predictable long-term upward trend of the S&P 500 or the total stock market.

The Bad Stuff

More fun doesn't always mean more profit. Taking on some added risk for the possibility of added gains also comes with the possibility of added losses. The better you understand the risks of the Fun Money portfolio, the easier it'll be to decide if this is the fun you want to have in the first place.

You Need Patience

We already know how to be successful when investing in the broader market, but value investing is its own ball game. You need to have patience and discipline. You need to be willing to wait for the last inning.

Let's say you've identified a new tech company that you believe is undervalued. After some digging, your hunch turns out to have some solid evidence: The company's balance sheet more than checks out, and its management team is filled with veterans from the industry. Even better, its product is novel, surpassing benchmarks, and is already being adopted by major market players, giving it an impressive competitive advantage.

You purchase shares of the company at what you believe is a discount on its intrinsic value, or what it's truly worth. However, much to your surprise, the stock price does not immediately go up as you had anticipated. In fact, the stock price *drops*, due to some unexpected spicy news about its brand-new CFO.

Profitable value investing is long-term investing, because it can take *years* for the market to reflect the true value of a company. Not to mention, during all those years of waiting, the stock price might not even move much at all, or even possibly decline. A Fun Money investor will need to be patient enough to hold on to their chosen stocks, even when the market is not immediately rewarding them, and diligent enough to remain confident that their prices will eventually rise. As Warren Buffett famously said, "Our favorite holding period is forever."

Fundamentals Aren't Foolproof

You can't judge a book by its cover or cash flow statements. Just because a stock has good fundamentals today doesn't mean it's guaranteed to do well in the long term or have strong financials, a solid business plan, and a great reputation forever. There are lots of factors that can affect how a company performs, like changes in the market, shifts in consumer preferences, or even new competitors entering the field. While strong fundamentals can be a great initial sign of long-term potential, you can't rely on that alone to predict its future success.

Take, for instance, General Electric. Once considered a blue-chip stock and known for its diversified business lines and strong balance sheet, it was a favorite among value investors. During the 1990s and early 2000s, GE's stock price steadily rose, and the company became one of the largest corporations in the world.

However, in the years following the 2008 financial crisis, the company's performance began to deteriorate. A series of missteps, including overexposure to the financial sector and a poorly timed (and very expensive) acquisition of a French power company, caused the company's earnings to decline sharply. Today, GE's stock price looks nothing like it used to. While the company is still considered a value stock by *some*, and a comeback isn't totally out of the realm of possibility, it's no longer the blue-chip all-star that it once was, and many investors have given up on its ability to generate strong returns altogether.

It's always possible to be wrong in your value stock pick, even if it seems strong on paper, for the time being. What's here today can be gone tomorrow. If you want to play with Fun Money, you have to embrace the element of chance.

The Crystal Ball Might Be Cloudy

The basic premise of value investing is that *the market* doesn't always accurately price stocks. If you believe this to be true, then that also means *you* might not accurately price stocks, either. Even the most rigorous analysis cannot predict the future with absolute certainty.

In the 1990s, Enron was a well-known energy company that appeared to be a strong investment opportunity. Its financial statements showed impressive growth, and it had a solid reputation. However, in 2001, it all came crashing down when it was revealed that Enron had been involved in massive accounting fraud, and the company ultimately filed for bankruptcy.

Enron's executives had created a complex accounting system that allowed them to hide the company's debts and losses from investors and the public. They fabricated financial records and inflated reports of company profits, all while secretly borrowing billions of dollars off the balance-sheet.

But it didn't stop there. Enron's executives also engaged in insider trading, where they used confidential information to trade their own stock and make a profit. They pressured their employees to buy Enron stock and discouraged them from selling it, even as the company's financial problems became more apparent.

Many value investors, at least in the beginning, had truly believed in Enron's success based on the company's supposed financial performance and reputation, but they weren't able to predict the fraud that was going on behind the scenes. It was the best they could do with the information that they had.

This is an extreme example of an uncommon situation, but the point still stands. Enron's collapse proves that even companies that appear strong, based on fundamentals, can still get knocked down by unexpected events that impact their overall performance. Successful value investors recognize that their analysis only offers a brief snapshot of the company's current situation and totally unpredictable events may require them to adjust accordingly. That's not to say you won't choose right, but it's also not to say you can't choose wrong.

The Good Stuff

Doom and gloom aside, there's still plenty of fun to be had with this portfolio. You can enhance your investing experience, win or lose, by embracing the risks and responsibilities that come along with choosing your own individual stocks. That's part of the fun! If you lose, you still have the reliable backbone of the broader market on your side. And if you win, you might just win big.

The Fun in Fun Money

It's easier to have fun making judgment calls on your portfolio when your wager isn't all or nothing. By allocating only 10 percent of your portfolio to individual value stocks of your choosing, you get to enjoy some creative freedom with a relatively small portion of your portfolio, allowing you to take on some additional risk and potential reward without putting a major dent in your overall returns.

For example, you can choose companies that you enjoy supporting in your everyday life (and that just so happen to also have strong financials), like the streaming service for your favorite TV show or the coffee chain where you always get your favorite latte. It could be, quite literally, putting your money where your interests are, and that's pretty nifty in my opinion. Supporting companies we already support anyway—by purchasing a tiny piece of them and thereby helping them gain traction—has the potential to be pretty magical under the right circumstances.

And even if your favorite company turns out *not* to be the greatest thing since sliced bread, your portfolio will still be relatively diversified and hopefully keep your returns steady in the long run, thanks to the unwavering support of an S&P 500 or total stock market index fund.

A Winning Combo

If you're like me at a diner and order the eggs and hash browns from the all-day breakfast menu only to, on first bite, immediately wish you also had a side of pancakes and syrup, you might love the two-for-one combo pack that the Fun Money portfolio has to offer. While your index funds will include both value- and growth-oriented companies, you can use your individual value stocks to hone in on your favorite companies with stable and consistent earnings, giving you added opportunity to practice value investing. And while growth stocks might experience more volatility but offer the potential for higher returns, value stocks may offer more stability in times of economic uncertainty.

Growth to Infinity and Beyond

The S&P 500 and the total stock market have historically provided strong returns over the long term. While past trends alone never predict the future with 100 percent certainty, it's not hard to imagine that this trend might continue when it has more than thirty years of solid data on its side. If you're feeling spicy, adding value stocks to your portfolio can potentially boost your returns even further, because in the long run, *some* individual stocks might go on to outperform even the broader market itself.

An example of a company that did just that is Monster Beverage Corporation. Yes, *that* Monster Beverage Corporation, the one that makes every middle school bully's favorite electric green energy drink. (Just my middle school bully? Weird.) For better or for worse, over the last twenty-seven years, Monster has generated a total return exceeding 200,000 percent, solidifying its rank as the best-performing S&P 500 stock of the past three decades. Since its inception in 1995, Monster shares have generated an average annual return of more than 30 percent.

Had you invested just $10,000 in MNST back when they first got started, your account value would look more like $20 million today.

(And here I thought my middle school bully was drinking battery acid in a can that would become largely irrelevant by the time we reached adulthood. I know what to call it when you regret buying something, but what do you call it when you regret *not* buying something?)

So, if you wind up choosing the next Monster in the early days before it takes off, you might give your own portfolio a pretty substantial boost.

How to Build It

If you're ready to party, getting started is simple. After you've decided how much money you intend to invest, the math is easy. You'll take 90 percent of that number (0.9 × your investment) and send it straight toward an S&P 500 or total stock market index fund or ETF. Then, you'll take the remaining 10 percent (0.1 × your investment) and put it toward your chosen value stocks.

Recognizing that your remaining 10 percent will not often be a nice, neat number, you may not have enough left over to buy a full share of stock each time. Luckily, most brokerages nowadays will allow you to purchase fractional shares (see page 88 for a refresher), so if you do decide to use this portfolio, make sure to double-check that your brokerage offers them. But if they don't, that's okay, too. The 90/10 doesn't have to be an exact science. You can adjust your ratios slightly more or less to fit your needs, but to avoid having too much fun, I would suggest rounding down on the amount you allocate for individual value stocks, not up.

It's worth noting that the Fun Money portfolio might work best in an individual taxable brokerage account, or your own personal retirement accounts. Most likely, you can't build this portfolio with your traditional employer-sponsored retirement plan. Most 401(k)/403(b) accounts will *not* allow you to use the Fun Money portfolio, because most employers are *not* fun. Just kidding (sort of). It's because most employer-sponsored accounts don't allow you to buy individual stocks.

Common Mistakes

Some people prefer to be here for a good time, not a long time. I prefer to be here for a good time *and* a long time, if possible. To make sure your fun is built for the long run, there are a handful of potential mishaps to cover.

Not Enough Sauce

One common mistake that Fun Money investors make is not doing enough research on the company they want to invest in. While value stocks may appear cheap, based on metrics like the price-to-earnings ratio, it's important to go beyond the surface-level numbers to determine if a company is a good investment for the long haul. This means looking at the company's financial statements, management team, industry trends, and potential risks.

For example, if you're considering investing in a retail company as a value stock, you would want to analyze metrics like same-store sales growth, inventory turnover, and online sales, along with broader industry trends like the rise of e-commerce and changes in consumer behavior. If you're just picking companies you like for fun, I won't judge you, but you might not be super successful in the returns department.

Holding Too Long?

While value stocks may take some time to pick up, it's important to have a clear exit strategy in mind and reevaluate the company's fundamentals on a regular basis. If a company's financial health deteriorates dramatically or the industry trends are looking mega scary, it may no longer be a good investment. In short, cheap shares aren't *always* a good thing.

Remember Blockbuster? Once a multibillion dollar company, as streaming services like Netflix, Hulu, and Amazon Prime gained popularity, Blockbuster's business model became outdated and the company ultimately went bankrupt (RIP). Intrinsic value reduced to effectively zero.

Investors who held on to Blockbuster stock for *too long* did not fare well in the end. Every once in a while, take the time to revisit whether something is still trading at a discount, or if it's on its way to becoming a total flop.

That Ship Has Sailed

Last but not least, some investors make the mistake of solely focusing on a value stock's past performance and not considering the company's current and *future* financial health and market position. A stock whose price has skyrocketed may have looked super cool when they were voted prom king, but what if they peaked in high school? No one has a crystal ball, and things can change.

Ideally, when choosing a value stock, aim for the up-and-coming, super-promising boats that haven't yet left the harbor. Even a seasoned, long-serving boat mid-journey can still make for a great buy. The problem comes when we choose a ship that has already sailed in its glory days, and now is only riddled with holes.

Chapter 9

The 50/50 Split

Are you a little indecisive? Do you get anxious choosing between tacos and pasta for dinner on date night? If so, you might be wondering how you'll confidently choose between the possibility of portfolio growth with boosted returns and the comfort of stability with fixed income. I have a portfolio that will do more than just meet you in the middle: It'll give you both. It's called the 50/50 Split.

If the idea of volatility by investing entirely in the stock market stresses you out, here, have some bonds! If the idea of monotony by investing entirely into the bond market stresses you out, here, have some stocks! We'll divide your portfolio between the two and call it even.

By now, you're probably starting to realize that stock portfolios tend to yield higher returns than their bond-only counterparts—but those returns come at a cost. And for some people, that cost might be their sanity. The stock market is prone to volatility, after all, which can lead to massive growth in the best of times or massive loss in the worst of times.

And guess what? *You don't have to like that.* Personal finance is personal, and this is exactly why we spend so much time mapping out our own preferences, like risk tolerance. If you'd prefer to take it down a notch, the bond market has plenty to offer, and what it lacks in gains it tends to make up for in security. If you prefer your serving of risk with an equal-sized portion of stability *and* fixed income, this might be the perfect portfolio for you.

Portfolio Asset Allocation

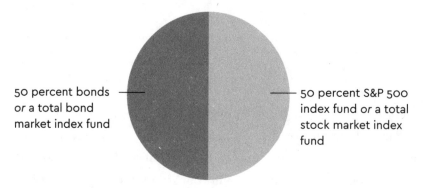

50 percent bonds *or* a total bond market index fund

50 percent S&P 500 index fund *or* a total stock market index fund

How Does This Work?

Having a healthy portion of bonds in your portfolio can help smooth out the bumps and make your overall ride more enjoyable. Instead of the jolting bursts of growth that you might see in a stock-heavy portfolio, bond-heavy portfolios take more of a slow-and-steady-gains approach. Whereas stocks alone might return something like 10 percent when averaged out over thirty years, bonds, on the other hand, might return more like 5 or 6 percent. By that logic, splitting your portfolio equally between the two should, in theory, land your returns somewhere in the middle.

Stock Portfolio Versus Bond Portfolio Growth over Time

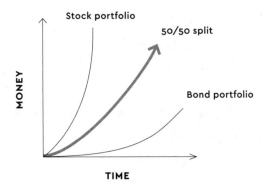

But smaller gains in exchange for added stability isn't the end of the story. As we learned on page 92, a big part of the stability that comes with bonds, comes from the fact that they offer a steady stream of income.

Who Is This For?

The 50/50 Split Investor Profile

Time horizon	short-term (only if your goal is retirement; if you have other short-term goals, revisit page 137), medium-term, long-term
Risk tolerance	low to moderate
Management style	mostly passive

The 50/50 Split offers a balance between growth and returns, and fixed income and stability. It's a Goldilocks portfolio, if you will: ideal for the investor who sits comfortably in the middle of the road in terms of risk tolerance—not ultra-conservative but not ultra-aggressive, either.

If you were looking to buy a plane ticket and you had two choices, a flight for $300 but very little turbulence, or a flight for $100 but the potential for lots of turbulence, which one would you choose? If you would prefer to choose the expensive flight with no turbulence over the cheap flight with lots of turbulence, you are probably starting to see the value in bonds. You'll have less money in the bank after the expensive flight, but, if you can afford it, maybe it's worth it for a comfy ride in the sky.

Including a significant portion of bonds in your portfolio might give you less dramatic growth in the long run, but, hypothetically, landing in the middle while preserving your mental health in the meantime might sound like the perfect compromise, especially if you can earn some extra cash along the way.

This portfolio might also make sense for you if you're at or approaching retirement. If you've already taken a long ride with another portfolio we've talked about here, and now you're looking to slow down and switch things up into a less risky option, the 50/50 Split might cover most of your bases. The income generated from bonds can be *especially* appealing if you're approaching the end of your career and need to generate some income to live on in retirement. Because bond interest payments are typically fixed, they provide a predictable income stream, an appreciable perk for anyone no longer working. See? The bond market isn't half bad! Get it . . . *half* bad? I'll see myself out.

Strategies Employed

As usual, we've got our typical long-term investor playbook here: dollar-cost averaging if you're investing a set amount into your portfolio at set intervals, the buy-and-hold lifestyle that will see you through the hard times and the good, and, of course, growth investing with the S&P 500 index fund or total stock market index fund portion of this portfolio.

When you introduce bonds into the mix, you also get to take advantage of income investing (page 174). Buying a bond is essentially lending out your money to *whomever*, be it a corporation or the government. In exchange for your loaned-out cash, the borrower will pay *you* interest until the date it matures—and this is where the income part comes in. When all's said and done, you trade in your bond, keep all the interest you earned in the meantime, *and* you get reimbursed for the original investment that you loaned out, also known as the principal.

The Bad Stuff

Investing half of your entire portfolio in bonds is not for everyone. For some people, allocating 50 percent of their portfolio to the relatively predictable, markedly stable, and overwhelmingly conservative nature of bonds might leave them feeling . . . unsatisfied. From a returns standpoint, that is.

The nature of bonds requires some serious understanding of an important distinction. There are some *major* differences between bonds and bond funds, up to and including their volatility. Bond funds are mutual funds or ETFs that contain bundles of bonds. Just as an S&P 500 index fund contains hundreds of underlying stocks, a bond fund contains dozens or hundreds of underlying bonds. And just as a total stock market index fund aims to track the stock market, a total bond market index fund aims to track the bond market.

Since we've already gone over the pros and cons of S&P 500 index funds and total stock market index funds in previous chapters, I'm going to venture that you've got that part of this portfolio all figured out. So, instead, let's take some time here to break down the good and bad in both bonds and bond funds so that you can decide what to do with your other half of the 50/50 Split. Starting with the bad, of course.

Not All Bonds are Predictable

One of the most noteworthy features of individual bonds is their commitment to pay out a predetermined, defined amount of income at regular payment periods, usually twice per year. This income is generally referred to as a "coupon" or a "coupon payment." Because bonds give you the ability to buy into a fixed coupon rate at the time of purchase, you can easily calculate your semiannual payments. The predictability of this income is part of what makes bonds often sought-after in retirement and explains why a hefty chunk of bonds is a wonderful addition to this portfolio. It's nice to have a reasonable idea about what you can expect to make at regular intervals, especially without a primary source of income, like a job.

Bond funds, on the other hand, are not so simple. They pool your money together with a bunch of other investors, and distribute it across various bonds accordingly. In this case, you're not lending your money directly to any one corporation or government entity, as you would a bond. You're lending your money to the fund itself, to do with it as it will. With bond funds, income payments are usually made on a monthly basis, and they have to reflect the entire mix within the fund, representing all the bonds and all their payment schedules. This means your monthly payment, in this case called your "distribution," can vary from month to month. Predictability over.

You're at the Mercy of the NAV

Unlike an individual bond that can be turned in at its maturity date, bond funds are constantly buying and selling individual bonds within the fund. The fund's prospectus can give you a weighted average maturity of all the bonds inside, but it's just an average. In this case, if you decide to sell your shares in a bond fund, you're at the mercy of the fund's net asset value (NAV) on any given day. The NAV isn't a promised principal amount; it's just a phrase for share price—which fluctuates. Long story short, unlike an individual bond that's held until maturity, it is possible to lose some or all of your initial investment investing in a bond fund, depending on what the share price looks like when you decide to sell, and that can certainly take away some of the stability you were looking forward to when dedicating half of your portfolio to bonds.

Some Bonds Are Pricey

If you're looking to create a super-diverse bond portfolio, investing in individual bonds will usually require a much larger initial investment than a bond fund will. This is mostly because if you're buying individual bonds with credit risk, like corporate bonds and municipal bonds, you're going to need to buy a bunch of different bonds at a bunch of different buy-in prices to create a reasonable amount of diversity in your portfolio.

The major brokerage Fidelity, for example, makes this recommendation on their website: "When investing in bonds that contain credit risk such as corporate bonds or municipal bonds, Fidelity recommends you have at least *several hundred thousand* dollars allocated to the fixed income portion of your portfolio, across multiple issuers, in order to diversify in the face of credit risk." Casual several hundred thousand dollars. No big deal.

Lions, Tigers, and Interest Rates . . . Oh My!

Bonds are often touted as one of the least risky investing options, but this doesn't mean they're totally immune to loss—especially if interest rates rise.

Interest rates and bond prices move in opposite directions. When interest rates rise, the coupon rate on new bonds increases, which makes existing bonds seem significantly less attractive. As a result, the market value of your existing bonds tends to decline.

For example, let's say you own a bond that pays a fixed coupon rate of 3 percent, and interest rates in the broader market rise to 4 percent. In this scenario, new bonds being issued might offer an even better coupon rate of 4 percent, which makes your bond look crummy in comparison. As a result, the *market value* of your bond may decline.

But market value hardly matters if you hold your bond until maturity and have no plans to sell it early. You'll cash it in for your initial investment, having spent years collecting your all-but-promised interest payments, and that's that.

Bond funds are a different story. When interest rates rise, the net asset value (share price) of the bond fund declines as the value of its underlying bonds decreases. This *can* result in a loss if you, in a state of panic, totally forget about the buy-and-hold strategy part and decide to sell your shares in the negative—or, for whatever reason, you have to.

Relatively Lackluster Returns

One thing bonds and bond funds do have in common is their less-than-stellar returns. To put some actual numbers to this, let's compare the performance of the S&P 500 index and the Bloomberg Barclays US Aggregate Bond Index, which is a benchmark of the US investment-grade bond market, over the past thirty years. From February 1991 to January 2022, the S&P 500 index delivered an average annual return of around 10 percent, while the Bloomberg Barclays US Aggregate Bond Index delivered an average annual return of around 5.8 percent. A noticeable difference, for sure.

To give you an idea of how investing $20,000 during that time period would have played out in the S&P 500 versus the bond market, let's consider two scenarios.

In scenario 1, you invested $20,000 in a fund that tracks the S&P 500 index. If you had invested $20,000 on February 1, 1991, and held that investment until January 31, 2022, your investment would have grown to nearly $400,000. This math assumes a perfect-world scenario, where you reinvested all dividends and capital gains, and there were no fees or taxes associated with your investment.

In scenario 2, you instead invested in a bond fund designed to track the Bloomberg Barclays US Aggregate Bond Index. If you had invested $20,000 on the same day, and held that investment for the same time, your investment would have grown to approximately $100,000. Once again, we're assuming the same perfect-world conditions. As you can imagine, with the 50/50 Split portfolio, your returns likely would've landed somewhere in the middle. While the income you received over the years would've undoubtedly been nice to have, the overall returns here could be considered lackluster, depending on what you compare them to.

Money on Fire

In 2021 and 2022, we all got a rude awakening about just how intense inflation can really get. Inflation doesn't just make everything from frozen pizza rolls to toilet paper more expensive; it also burns away our investment earnings. For every percentage of a step our money takes forward, inflation takes it some percentage of a step back.

Even though you may receive regular interest payments from a bond, the value of those payments may be eroded by inflation over time, reducing your "real" return. For example, if you purchase a bond with a yield of 3 percent, and inflation is running at 2 percent, then the real rate of return on your bond is only 1 percent after accounting for inflation.

When inflation is even higher, in the 6–7 percent range, you can see how this can begin to go south very quickly. Even though you're still receiving a regular income stream from your bond or bond fund, inflation is taking more than you can afford to give, and your overall purchasing power is actually *decreasing* over time. Your money just doesn't go as far when it's on fire, especially in the bond market.

The Good Stuff

So blah, blah, bonds and bond funds have downsides. In keeping with the theme of all things being good and evil, there should be no surprise there. Luckily, with this portfolio, you're not investing *all* your cash in either of their shortcomings, no matter which one you choose. And actually, bonds and bond funds have a lot going for them. The beauty of going halfsies is that you get to cash in on some of their positives without going all-in on their negatives. Some would call this a win-win.

You Get the Best of Both Worlds

Bonds and bond funds may curb your returns to some extent, but they do so for good reason. They're typically considered to be less volatile than stocks and provide the added benefit of income at regular intervals.

But that doesn't mean you have to FOMO over wishful stock market gains. With the 50/50 Split, you can benefit from both. During times of market turmoil, the bonds will do their best to keep your capital and cash flow *relatively* chill. And in a bull market, the stocks will pull their weight to boost your overall portfolio gains, picking up where the bonds left off.

For example, during the financial crisis in 2008 and 2009, the S&P 500 experienced a significant decline, falling by more than 50 percent from its peak in 2007. However, during the same period, bonds held up relatively well by comparison, as investors flocked to the safety of government bonds and other high-quality fixed income securities to feel, well, safe.

When the S&P 500 was down by more than 50 percent, the 50/50 Split investor would have been down by less, as the bonds would have helped to offset some of the losses in the stock market. They may have gotten lower returns in the long run, but they may have also felt considerably less stress in the interim.

As for the S&P 500 portion, we all know how that played out. In the end, there was nothing to worry about. After the financial crisis was over, in the years that followed, the S&P 500 soared higher than ever before.

It's the Principal

As long as you hold an individual bond all the way through until maturity, the bond's principal amount (aka your initial investment) will be returned to you. Unless your borrower goes bankrupt and defaults, or you decide to back out and sell early, you won't lose your initial buy-in.

If you've ever used the shopping carts at Aldi, the process is pretty similar. You put the quarter in, and it unlocks the cart from the storage rack, allowing you to use the shopping cart. For as long as you'd like, you are free to browse the store. Once you return the cart back to its rightful docking station, you get to remove your quarter from the cart, walking away with your initial investment intact. The only difference is, at Aldi, there's no one to pay you interest while you shop for groceries (if only).

The same can't be said for bond funds. But, as you'll learn, they've got plenty of benefits of their own.

Barrier of Entry

Creating a super-diverse bond portfolio can get pretty pricey, especially if you're branching out into corporate and municipal bonds and looking to bring down your overall credit risk. But buying bonds doesn't have to break the bank, and there are a couple of ways to lower the barrier of entry into the bond market.

For starters, you don't need to buy several hundred thousand dollars' worth of US Treasuries in order to diversify and reduce your credit risk, because US Treasuries have virtually zero credit risk to begin with. In the case of a US Treasury bond, you're lending your money to the US government, and they *guarantee* they will pay you back, plus interest. Without the need to obsessively diversify, the only minimum investment here is the amount needed to purchase the Treasury itself, and, in general, you can purchase US Treasuries for as little as $100. Your starting cost will usually land in the range of $1,000 to $10,000.

That might still be a considerable initial investment—I hear you. Which brings me back to bond funds. By creating a basket of a bunch of different bonds and then selling it to you at a relatively reasonable share price, the bond fund does all of the work of diversification for you, and you can make a smaller initial investment. This lets you generate a stream of income without doing any of the bond picking (or buying) yourself.

Cash Flow FTW

Having a reliable source of income is always important, but especially once we stop working altogether. Adding a significant chunk of bonds to your portfolio helps to make sure that you're taken care of on a regular basis once you reach retirement.

Let's say you invest $10,000 in a bond fund with a yield of 3 percent. This means that the fund estimates it'll generate around $300 in payments over the course of a year. If the fund pays out its distributions on a monthly basis, you would receive roughly $25 in dividend payments each month.

You can imagine how this might add up for someone who's been sending 50 percent of their investment portfolio into a total bond market fund over the course of thirty years or so. At $100,000 invested and the same yield, you're now looking at more like $3,000 a year. At $1 million, that's $30,000 a year in payments from your bond fund alone.

Plus, all of this is *before* we've taken into account the growth of our S&P 500 portion. With the two working together, you have the potential for a well-rounded portfolio that balances both cash flow and long-term growth.

A Portfolio for Life

Much like the Full Autopilot portfolio, the 50/50 Split *could* be your foreva-eva portfolio if you want it to be. Like, you can start with it at age eighteen and still have it work for you all the way into your eighties, if you want it to. If anything, traditional investment wisdom would likely argue that, overall, this portfolio may be a bit *too conservative* for a young person with a very long-time horizon and closer to the "perfect" mix for someone at or approaching retirement. But you know you better than any traditional investor does. If you like what this portfolio has to offer early on in life and sticking to a steady game plan forever makes you happy, this portfolio might just last you a lifetime.

How to Build It

Building your 50/50 Split portfolio only requires you to do exactly what the name says. Split your investment directly in half, with 50 percent of your money going toward an index fund or ETF that tracks the S&P 500 or the total stock market, and the other 50 percent going toward either a high-quality total bond market fund or any combination of high-quality individual bonds. If a bond fund is high-quality, they will have already chosen the high-quality bonds for you, but if you're picking your own, some options to consider include:

- US Treasuries: Issued by the US government and considered to be one of the safest investments in the world. They have a long history of timely payments and a very low risk of default.
- Investment-grade corporate bonds: Issued by large, financially strong corporations with an "acceptable" credit rating (for a refresher on AAA through BBB, see page 95).

- Municipal bonds: Issued by state and local governments and generally considered to be relatively low-risk investments. Some municipal bonds are backed by revenue from essential services, such as water or electricity, which provides additional security.

Common Mistakes

Up until this point, you might have thought your only options were high-risk, high-reward or low-risk, low-reward, and you just realized that you want both. This is a reasonable request. Nothing is totally off-limits when it comes to investing, but in a world of limitless options, it's a good idea to know what pitfalls might be waiting around the corner.

Thinking Biggest Yield Means Best Bond

Investing only in high-yield bonds is like eating only the frosting off your favorite piece of cake. It might *seem* like the most delicious part, but without the cake itself, it might leave you still hungry. High-yield bonds offer seemingly attractive returns, but relying solely on them can be risky and leave you vulnerable to losses in the long run, so much so that they've earned themselves a name: "junk bonds."

Investors often turn to high-yield bonds as a way to increase their returns, and that's not surprising. Some people want to earn as much as possible. However, you've got to keep in mind that bonds are more than just their payments. They also play a critical role in adding *stability* to a portfolio, by weathering market downturns in your other investments, like stocks. Not all bonds can do that, and junk bonds definitely can't. When the economy suffers and stocks take a hit, high-risk junk bonds are likely to suffer, too, and there's a chance that the issuer will never pay you back. On the other hand, investment-grade bonds tend to fare better during tough economic times and might even increase in value.

So don't be lured by the higher yields offered by bonds with lower credit ratings. Remember that yield is just one of *many* factors to consider when choosing a bond, and that higher yields come with higher risks. Keeping with the philosophy of the 50/50 Split, it's best to strike a balance between higher returns and protecting your portfolio from unnecessary nightmares.

Selling Before Maturity (and at the Wrong Time)

We know that as interest rates rise, bond prices fall, and vice versa. If you're buying bonds, you will experience fluctuations in interest rates and bond prices, just as you'll experience fluctuations with stocks. There is no way to stop this from happening; *c'est la vie*. But, unlike stocks, you can get all of your initial investment back—as long as you hold your bonds until maturity. If you do have to sell before the maturity date, know that you may do so at a loss if the interest rates (and bond prices, by proxy) are working against you.

Something similar can be said for bond funds. Since the NAV reflects the bond fund's going rate and bond funds don't have a set maturity date, they operate more like a stock in that regard. The possibility of selling at a loss is always there, no matter how long you hold it for.

Ignoring Inflation

A common mistake among brand-new bond investors is to take the "This is fine" approach, ignore the fact that inflation means they might be losing money, and move on with their life. But it doesn't have to be that way!

I bonds can offer a unique combination of inflation protection and a fixed rate of return. (See "A Quick Note on I Bonds," page 96, to learn more.)

There's also the I bond's not-so-distant cousin, TIPS (treasury inflation-protected securities). Unlike I bonds that have a variable component of their interest rate, the TIPS interest rate remains fixed. However, this time, it's the principal value that's adjusted, which also adjusts the interest payments to keep pace with inflation in their own way.

Since TIPS and I bonds are backed by the US government, they're considered super safe. They're also exempt from state and local income taxes just like other US Treasury securities (though you'll still pay federal income tax on your interest income, eventually).

To fight back against inflation, you can buy I bonds with as little as $25, or TIPS for as little as $100. And if you find yourself stuck between the two, it's never a bad idea to keep the spirit of this portfolio and have both.

Chapter 10

The Dividend Queen

Income investors face a never-ending quest for the investing holy grail: a way to produce stable income without excessive risk. If you amass the $1 million bond portfolio of your dreams, designed to pay you steady income with a 5 percent coupon rate, you might be able to walk away with $50,000 a year. That is, before we account for inflation. In 2022, 3 percent inflation felt like a pipe dream, but, hey, we made it happen eventually after enough rate hikes. Subtracting 3 percent for inflation, next year you're left with $48,500 in terms of "real" buying power. The year after that, $47,000. After twenty years, more like $20,000. How does that sound? Are you on board for this retirement plan?

The Dividend Queen says nay. Instead of lending your money to the government or otherwise, why not invest in a company that pays you a portion of their profits in the form of a dividend, and has some serious potential for growth in the long run? The Dividend Queen can't imagine anything better than having your retirement (or even just some extra pocket money) paid for at a major corporation's expense . . . except maybe having your retirement paid for at thirty-plus major corporations' expense. That sounds pretty nice, actually.

Portfolio Asset Allocation

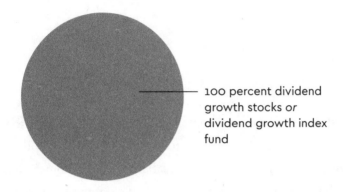

100 percent dividend growth stocks *or* dividend growth index fund

How Does This Work?

First, dividend stocks or dividend index funds provide you with a source of income by paying out dividends either monthly, quarterly, or annually.

Next, they can also provide you with *some* degree of security. Typically, companies that pay dividends have a strong track record of profits, and not only have they made their money, they also have enough left over to share.

And, last but not least, with dividend *growth* investing, specifically—where investors buy stocks of companies whose dividend payouts increase over time—you can receive regular income from your investments *and* enjoy the perks of stock prices appreciating in the long run.

Who Is This For?

The Dividend Queen Investor Profile

Time horizon	long-term
Risk tolerance	moderate to high
Management style	active or passive

This portfolio is for anyone who likes the regular income that bonds can offer but is looking for a little extra oomph. A Dividend Queen might be looking to supplement their regular income while they're still working, or they might ultimately be looking for a steady stream of income from their investments in retirement.

But, on top of that, the right dividend-paying stocks, if chosen with clear intention, can offer the potential for both growth *and* income. Imagine landing steady income *and* significant stock appreciation in the long run. We truly love to see it.

That said, because the allocation listed here is 100 percent into dividend growth stocks or a dividend growth stock index fund, key word here being *stocks*, there is a considerable amount of risk with this portfolio, compared to investing in, say, US Treasuries (though you'll soon see that some companies that pay dividends might be less risky than others). Overall, a Dividend Queen will need a high risk tolerance and a long time horizon to feel comfortable, in part because it takes a long time and a lot of money invested to generate substantial dividend payouts. Alternatively, if the full-on dividend stock life isn't for you, consider adding other income-generating assets, like bonds, to your portfolio to supplement where you see fit and adjust the allocation percentages accordingly.

Strategies Employed

If bonds feel boring, you're in luck. They aren't the only income providers. Dividend portfolios are another viable way to use an income investing strategy (page 174).

When a company creates a dividend, it can choose to pay out a percentage of its profits to its shareholders. For the companies that continue to *increase* their dividend payouts over time, they get the distinction of being "dividend growers," aka dividend growth stocks. Companies that consistently increase their dividends over time are generally considered stable, financially healthy companies. They may be less risky than other dividend investments since they have an established history of boosting payouts, which has the potential to boost stock prices over time, and they even get special names, like Dividend Aristocrats.

For that reason, investing in dividend-growing companies means more than just the regular income from the dividend payouts, which is already pretty great. It also means the potential for future increases in those payouts and their underlying share prices. This is what the Dividend Queen is ultimately looking for: a steady stream of income that *grows*, plus the prospect of capital appreciation in the long run.

The Bad Stuff

Dividends can be great, but that doesn't mean they're great for everyone. The Dividend Queen portfolio comes with its fair share of pitfalls, so if you're looking to dive headfirst into grandeur, you'll first need to read the royal manual.

Your Dividend May Be Aristocrap

Some companies can successfully maintain their business for many years, develop a standout product that becomes a household staple, steadily grow their profits and their payouts, and ride off into the sunset. If *all* companies were able to do that, dividend investing would probably be the talk of the town. The reality is that not every soda is the next Coca-Cola, and not all companies are able to consistently grow their dividends. If you're not sticking to the big names with an established track record of payouts, your dividend portfolio might look more like a gamble than a gambit.

Not to mention, even with the big names, dividends are *not* a guarantee. Unlike US Treasuries that you buy and hold to get your interest payments, there is technically no promise that even the most profitable companies will continue to pay dividends, even if they have always done so in the past. Things change, and factors like the current business environment, new competition, or general economic conditions can all impact a company's profitability and, as a result, their ability to pay dividends.

Boeing is a company that is well-known for producing some of the most iconic planes in history, and you needn't be an aviation buff to be familiar with the 747. However, in recent years, the company has faced challenges that have made it more difficult to maintain its coveted position, one of the largest being the grounding of its 737 MAX planes.

In 2018 and 2019, two separate crashes involving 737 MAX planes resulted in the deaths of hundreds of passengers and crew members. In response, regulators around the world grounded the planes and launched investigations into the safety of the aircraft. The company halted production of the planes, paid billions of dollars in fines, and set aside hundreds of millions of dollars more to compensate the families of the crash victims.

Right after that, the impact of COVID-19 on the aviation industry ran its course. With many countries implementing travel restrictions, and airlines cutting back on flights in general, demand for new planes declined sharply. Boeing was running out of money.

In response, Boeing did what it had to do to reduce costs and improve its financial position. In 2020, it suspended its dividend to help preserve cash and maintain financial stability during a period of major uncertainty.

In the end, Boeing made it through, and it remains a significant player in the aerospace and defense industry. The company has a long history of innovation, and there's no denying they revolutionized air travel. But what's that song that goes "Even the best fall down sometimes . . ."? Case in point.

You'll Need a High Cash Threshold

It takes big money invested to get to the point of considerable income with a dividend portfolio. For example, let's say you wanted to invest in a company like Coca-Cola, which is known for its consistent dividend payments. As of February 2023, Coca-Cola's stock price was around $60 per share, and its annual dividend yield was around 3 percent. This means that for every share of Coca-Cola you own, you would receive $1.68 in dividends each year ($60 × 0.03). To generate a reliable income stream from Coca-Cola dividends, you would need to own *thousands* of shares.

Assuming you wanted to generate $10,000 in annual dividend income from Coca-Cola, you would need to own roughly 5,952 shares of the stock ($10,000 ÷ $1.68). At the current price per share, this would require an initial investment of nearly $360,000 ($60 × 5,952). Woof. When I say *cash threshold*, this is what I mean. You need to have hundreds of thousands of dollars invested before dividends become an effective way of paying your bills. For that reason, dividend investing makes the most sense in the context of retirement, as most people only accumulate that kind of money in their retirement accounts (and because most people don't have six figures left over after investing in their retirement accounts, per the investing order of operations on page 165).

Of course, not everyone needs to generate $10,000 in annual dividend income if the end goal is just to have some extra cash on hand, and there are other companies with lower stock prices and higher dividend yields. Regardless, the point still stands: If you're trying to cover your expenses with dividends, you typically need to invest a significant amount up front.

Income May Not Be the Best Outcome

So here's the thing. You *can* live off the dividends from your investments, yes, if you invest enough. The spoiler alert here is that does *not* automatically make it the optimal retirement strategy. You might be better off focusing on maximizing your portfolio's total return than you would be chasing a high-dividend yield just for the sake of being able to say dividends replaced your income.

I understand that it's super satisfying to have your income paid for by corporations without working, believe me. The thing is, you can still live off your investment portfolio without scheduled dividend payments. What I'm saying is this: Whether you receive dividend payments at regular intervals or decide to sell some of your investments whenever you feel like it, you still get paid in the end.

To put it another way, if your portfolio has an overall return of 10 percent per year, does it really matter where that 10 percent comes from? If you sell some of your S&P 500 ETF shares every so often, as opposed to waiting for your dividends, is it any less convenient? Either way, you're making money, right?

Dividends Take the Wheel

Last but not least, shareholders get virtually no say in when they receive their dividends or how much they'll even receive, or when this information will be provided to you. If you're okay with handing over the wheel here, that might sound just fine. However, if you want to have more control over your income payments, you might be better off selling portions of your portfolio manually in the amount you choose at your own chosen intervals.

The Good Stuff

That said, there's still a lot of good things to say about dividends, especially when you're going for the dividend *growth* variety. What might seem like a downside at first glance can definitely work in your favor under the right circumstances.

The End Game

During a bull market, dividend growth stocks might look like they're lagging behind the traditional growth stocks. Give it time, though. Historical data paints a different picture when it comes to returns, and it changes the longer it goes on.

Let's say you invested $10,000 in two different stocks: One is a dividend growth stock, and the other is a plain old growth stock that does *not* pay dividends. Both stocks have an initial price of $100 per share, so you bought one hundred shares of each.

Over the next three years, the stock market experiences a strong bull market, and both stock prices rise significantly (as they tend to do during a bull market). The growth stock sees its price increase by an average of 20 percent per year, in typical growth stock fashion, while the dividend growth stock sees its price increase by an average of 10 percent per year. Meanwhile, the dividend growth stock also pays out regular dividends, which increase by an average of 5 percent per year.

After three years, here's how the two stocks compare:

- The growth stock: After three years, the growth stock's price has increased to $172 per share. If you sold your shares at this point, you would have made a profit of $7,200 ($17,200 – $10,000).
- The dividend growth stock: After three years, the dividend growth stock's price has increased to only $133 per share. But don't forget, you also received regular dividend payments amounting to $1,200 over those three years. If you sold your shares at this point, you would have made a profit of $4,500 ($13,300 – $10,000 + $1,200).

Uhh, so you're saying the growth stock outperformed the dividend growth stock? Sure, thanks to its price appreciation during the bull market.

But here's where things get interesting: Let's say the bull market eventually comes to an end (as they always do), and the stock market experiences a significant downturn (as it always does). Over the next three years, the growth stock's price declines by an average of 15 percent per year, while the dividend growth stock's price declines by an average of only 5 percent per year. All the while, the dividend growth stock continues to pay out regular dividends, which increase by an average of 5 percent per year.

Now, six years out from your initial investment, here's how the two stocks line up:

- The growth stock: After six years, the growth stock's price has declined to $105 per share. If you sold your shares at this point, you would have made a profit of $500 ($10,500 – $10,000).
- The dividend growth stock: After six years, the dividend growth stock's price has declined to only $114 per share. You also still received regular dividend payments totaling more than $2,600 over those six years. If you sold your shares at this point, you would have made a profit of $4,000 ($11,400 – $10,000 + $2,600).

Even though the dividend growth stock initially underperformed the growth stock during the bull market, the dividend growth stock ultimately provided a better return in the long run, in large part because the increasing dividend payments helped mitigate the impact of the downturn.

Now this is just one hypothetical scenario, and the actual performance of individual stocks and the broader market will vary, but under the right circumstances, there are potential benefits of investing in dividend growth stocks over the long term, even during a bear market.

An All-Weather Option

The ability of dividend growth stocks to help your portfolio withstand the inevitable fluctuations of the market makes them versatile in a unique way. You see, investing preferences tend to change with the seasons. When the markets are doing great, people tend to hop on growth stocks and trade readily. When the markets are doing not so great, people tend to search for more stable options, like bonds. The problem is, following the trends might mean missing the best parts. If you're only investing in growth when the market is at its peak, you may have already missed the ride.

Investing in dividend growth stocks or funds allows you to hang out in one spot for the long haul. Instead of heading to the beach in the summer and the slopes in the winter, you spend your time in a relatively temperate area all year long. While it would be nice to predict the future, like knowing when the market is about to take a tank versus skyrocket to the moon, most people can't do that successfully. So instead of trying to time the market, dividend growth investing allows you to harness some of the more conservative aspects while combining them with some of the more aggressive techniques. While it might not be *as* aggressive as an all-growth portfolio, it also gives you income to fall back on when things get less than exciting.

Dividend Growth Stocks Hang with the Greats

So dividend growth stocks sound pretty great. But can they truly hang with the greats? Can they beat, say, the S&P 500 in the long term?

According to a study by Hartford Funds that analyzed the performance of dividend-paying stocks from 1972 to 2016, dividend growers outperformed non-dividend payers *and* companies that maintained steady dividends, as well as the broader market. And by *broader market*, they mean the broader market as measured by the S&P 500. Oh, yeah, they went there. Similarly, between 1972 and 2020, the S&P 500 had an average annual return of 9.9 percent, while the S&P Dividend Aristocrats index—measuring the performance of S&P 500 companies that have increased dividends every year for twenty-five consecutive years—had an average annual return of 10.4 percent. This means that the Dividend Aristocrats index has actually, on average, *outper-*

formed the broader market over a long period. Not gonna lie, this statistic never gets less exciting.

It's worth noting that dividend growth stocks might not always win first place in the short term. For example, during periods of strong economic growth and bull markets, the reverse tends to be true: Growth stocks usually outperform dividend growth stocks. But if you're in it for the long haul, and if the future data turns out anything like the past, dividend growth investing can have serious rewards if you give it enough time to prove itself.

How to Build It

When choosing which dividend growth stocks to invest in, you need to look at what your goals are. If your main goal is income, it might be better to avoid the risk of a dividend cut. One way to measure a company's financial stability is by looking at its credit ratings. Aim for dividend growth stocks from companies with an "A" rating or higher.

It's also important to look for companies with modest payout ratios, which are dividends expressed as a percentage of the company's net income. A payout ratio of 50 percent or less is ideal, because it allows the company to have some wiggle room in case of unforeseen trouble, and, hopefully, still maintain its dividend payments. If a company is paying out *too* much of its profits, it raises questions about whether it can actually afford to do that and for how long. It's cool to give some money away, but probably not as cool to give *all* of it away. If a company wants to continue running its business, it's still going to need some money left over to, you know, run its business.

As for the dividend growers, these companies tend to continue their efforts to raise dividends, assuming their business continues to be healthy. The S&P Dividend Aristocrats list is a great place to start looking for companies with a history of raising dividends. To become a Dividend Aristocrat, a company must be in the S&P 500, have more than twenty-five consecutive years of dividend increases, and meet certain size and liquidity requirements. Think about that for a second: We're starting with a list of the top 500 companies in the United States, which we already know produce great returns, and then making that list even more exclusive and impressive by only including the ones that have continued to increase their dividend payouts for nearly three decades. With a roster like that, it's no wonder the Dividend Aristocrats have historically outperformed the overall stock market, which is pretty dang amazing.

Beyond that is the super-elite, ultra-VIP Dividend Kings list, which is also based on historical dividend increases. To call yourself a Dividend King, a company must have at least *fifty* consecutive years of dividend increases. (They missed a major opportunity to call this premier list the Dividend Queens, so, as you can see, I chose it for the name of this portfolio.)

It's best to diversify your dividend stocks to avoid the risk of a dividend cut in any one sector. The general rule of thumb is to invest in at least twenty different stocks across a variety of different industries.

If all of this sounds a little bit too time-consuming for your liking, you can always choose a dividend growth fund that will handle the diversification process for you. Using the exact same benchmarks, you can look for a dividend growth index fund or ETF that will take care of all the individual stock picking for you. For example, those Dividend Aristocrats we talked about? They have an index fund of their own, and it might be a good place to start. One of those will allow you to instantly invest across nearly every sector in sixty-plus companies that have all increased their dividend payments for at least twenty-five consecutive years.

Finally, reinvesting dividends can add a surprising amount of growth to your portfolio with minimal effort. If you start investing for income well in advance of when you'll actually need the money, consider reinvesting the dividends to maximize your portfolio's growth potential in the long run. Most brokerages will give you the option to do this automatically by setting up a dividend reinvestment plan—known as a DRIP—in your account settings right within their platform, and you can toggle this feature on or off at any time.

Common Mistakes

You might have noticed that this portfolio has the potential to be more active than some of the ones we've covered in chapters past (especially if you'll be choosing all twenty-some-odd dividend growth stocks all by yourself). More choice means more freedom, but it can also mean more room for error, unless you avoid doing the following.

Chasing High Yields

Just as some bond investors look a little bit too hard for the highest yield, some dividend investors do the same thing. It's an easy mistake to make. Higher yields are supposed to mean more money in your pocket, right? Not necessarily, and it might be a warning sign of an underlying issue, one that could possibly endanger your dividend payouts.

A company might throw out a ridiculously high dividend as a last-ditch effort to draw investors. This is a lot like filling a boat with water that already has holes in it. A suffering company is not going to last very long if they're hemorrhaging money by paying out dividends they can't reasonably afford to give. *But boy will they try.* This actually happens often enough that it has a name, and it's called a "yield trap." When a company offers an unsustainably high dividend yield to attract investors, but they're unable to maintain the dividend payout over time, the yield is just a trick to lure you in. When you fall for the trap of a super-high dividend yield, you might wind up losing money in the long run when the company is forced to reduce or eliminate its dividends, and its stock price plummets as a result.

Successful dividend growth investors tend to *avoid* stocks with the highest dividend yields, focusing instead on those that are reasonably priced and raise dividends consistently. Long story short, when investing in dividend stocks, you need to make sure that a company promising big payouts isn't unintentionally digging its own grave, too.

Ignoring the Need to Diversify

Diversification is key to any successful investment strategy, and dividend investing is no exception. Investing in just a few dividend stocks may lead to *concentration risk*, which means that your portfolio is heavily reliant on the performance of just a few companies.

To drive the point home here, let's take a look at a handful of classic dividend-paying companies during the COVID-19 pandemic. As you probably know, the pandemic had a huge impact on the global economy, and more than one sector was hit hard. Many companies in the business of travel and tourism saw their stock prices plummet, and some even had to cut their dividends to stay afloat.

Take ExxonMobil, for example, an oil company known for paying reliable dividends. In 2020, the company announced it would not raise its dividend for the first time in eighteen years. That same year, Walt Disney Company, the amusement park and entertainment powerhouse, admitted that it would have to pause its dividend altogether. Southwest Airlines, Delta Airlines, and American Airlines all suspended dividend payments as air travel plummeted. By the end of 2020, nearly 190 US companies stopped paying to save money.

So, imagine you're a dividend investor who had a bunch of energy and travel stocks in your portfolio, and you were relying on those sweet, sweet dividends and the reputation of historically predictable companies to pay your bills or fund your investment goals. Yeah, not great. The drop in the stock prices and dividends would have hit you hard.

If your portfolio were a little too concentrated, you would have been left with less income than you were counting on. Obviously, not ideal. By properly diversifying and spreading your money across plenty of different stocks and sectors, you can reduce the impact of any one company's performance on your overall portfolio.

If you find that hard to do, you don't feel like choosing your own, or you only feel like choosing some of your own, don't forget that you can always incorporate dividend growth ETFs and index funds, like one that tracks the Dividend Aristocrats Index, and the rest will be chosen for you.

Chapter 11

The Mega Mix

At every party, you'll find two sets of people. There are the ones who deliberately pick the pretzels out of the party mix to throw off the entire snack ratio for everyone else (If this is you, are you okay?), and then there are the people who eat a handful of everything. You might not love everything about any one of these portfolios on their own, but you might love *some* things about every single one of them. And you might feel that the perfect portfolio for you is somewhere in the mix.

So let's make one! No picking out the pretzels. The Mega Mix portfolio might just be your answer to the perfect portfolio mixture. Sometimes the result winds up being greater than the sum of its parts.

Portfolio Asset Allocation

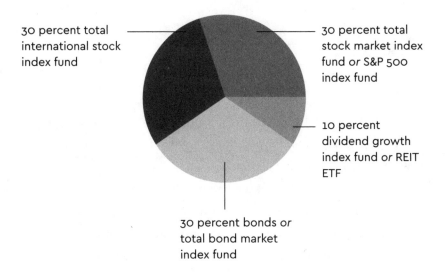

30 percent total international stock index fund

30 percent total stock market index fund *or* S&P 500 index fund

10 percent dividend growth index fund *or* REIT ETF

30 percent bonds *or* total bond market index fund

How Does This Work?

The Mega Mix portfolio focuses on, well, making a mega mix, in the form of portfolio diversification. It's broken into four components. First, you've got your total stock market index fund or your S&P 500 index fund, to hopefully live up to its impressive historical growth and returns. You've got your total international stock index fund to provide some overseas exposure and potentially capture growth for stellar companies outside of the United States. Next, you've got your bonds or bond fund to provide some protection and a regular income stream in times of volatility. And, last but not least, you've got your dividend growth index fund or, alternatively, REITs, to provide some added income, with the potential to drive your portfolio's overall returns even higher.

The idea behind this portfolio is to combine all these pieces so that they can work together to amplify the great parts and quiet the not-so-great parts.

Who Is This For?

The Mega Mix Investor Profile

Time horizon	medium-term, long-term
Risk tolerance	low to moderate
Management style	active or passive

This portfolio is for anyone who loves an everything bagel. Who likes to paint every room in their house a different color. Whose favorite appetizer is the sample platter.

The Mega Mix portfolio is for anyone who can appreciate variety—including all the pros and cons this variety brings with it. Most conventional investment advice would recommend a portfolio that looks something like this one, which includes a mix of different asset classes, provides a balance of growth potential and risk management, and helps you achieve your investment goals over the medium to long term.

Strategies Employed

You're getting a little bit of everything here, and the strategies you use will look like one big amalgamation of all the ones we've covered previously.

For starters, I'd like to draw your attention to the fact that this portfolio takes full advantage of a wide variety of funds available to you (see page 97). And what do we know about funds? They're wonderfully passive. They'll allow you to buy and hold (page 173), take advantage of some stellar growth investing (page 174), and strategize with dollar-cost averaging (page 173) with ease.

Of course, we've also got some bonds in here—either traditional bonds or bond funds, your choice—and with these, you'll be utilizing some good old-fashioned income investing (page 174). Same goes for your dividends and your REITs.

We've got plenty of diversity: Investing in a mix of different asset classes like stocks, bonds, and real estate means spreading out your investment risk and reducing the impact of market volatility on your portfolio. We've got international exposure: Investing in both domestic and international stocks means gaining exposure to different economies and industries, and potentially benefiting from growth opportunities in different regions of the world. Last but not least, we've got stability and risk management. Bonds or a total bond market index fund can help reduce the overall risk of your portfolio in the best of times and provide a buffer against market volatility in the worst of times.

Of course, by now you know that taking the benefits from a little bit of everything means you're taking the shortcomings from a little bit of everything as well. But, hey, not every snack in the snack mix is going to be your favorite on its own. It's all about the overall flavor of the final mix.

The Bad Stuff

I may have painted an awfully pretty picture thus far, but even the "perfect" mixture has its own set of setbacks. "Perfect" investing is an illusion. You can't say I didn't warn ya . . . how many pages ago was it that I told you about the black hole mental mind trap?

The More You Add, the More You Must Manage

I almost called this one the helicopter investor's portfolio, or the micromanager's portfolio, or the Virgo's portfolio (all of which are terms of endearment, I promise) because it requires serious maintenance. And serious maintenance requires serious time. If you don't like spending much time making sure things stay in balance, you might not love this portfolio. A Lazy Luxury investor would scoff at the mere thought of creating something like this. Yes, from a fund standpoint, most of these options are more or less hands-off once you buy them. But you do need to buy them, you will need to stay up-to-date on their happenings, and you will also need to rebalance them regularly to make sure all their percentages are lined up where you want them to be.

The Cost of Complexity

Holding a variety of asset classes means buying more things, and buying more things has the potential to involve higher costs. When you're purchasing multiple funds, each will come with its own set of fees, and if you've got enough of them, they can really add up. Some funds will have higher expense ratios than others, so it's a good idea to keep track of them so that you don't lose sight of your costs in the hubbub (see "Understanding Your Investing Costs" on page 184).

Jack-of-All-Trades, Master of None

The main downside to a portfolio with many different asset classes is that you will never be able to realize the full potential of any one class on its own. For example, if stocks are rallying up a storm, but you only allocated 30 percent of your portfolio to the total stock market, you won't experience as much growth as you would if your portfolio were 100 percent in the total stock market. In times like those, it would've paid better to be lazy (see chapter 7, "The Lazy Luxury").

Similarly, if stocks were really struggling, but the bond market was living its best life and you only had 30 percent allocated to bonds, you won't be partaking in those festivities, either. Your portfolio's overall performance will always be weighed down by the performance of its weakest member.

The Good Stuff

Maybe you love the idea of tinkering a bit more with your investments. Maybe you love staying organized with up-to-date information on market trends, economic indicators, and news affecting your investments. Maybe, just maybe, you even *love* making spreadsheets to keep tabs on your portfolio allocation in real time, ensuring a well-balanced and diversified mix of assets. Hey, not for me, but I love that for you. And if you love it, too, the pros of the Mega Mix might far outweigh the cons.

A Flexible Risk Cushion

If you love the idea of creating a portfolio that (a) provides you with the flexibility to make choices and (b) remains adaptable to a wide variety of market conditions, the Mega Mix might be your perfect match. By investing across a whole bunch of asset classes, industries, and geographic regions, you can take advantage of evolving economic trends and opportunities without feeling an enormous impact from a downturn in any one security or sector.

(Relatively) Smooth Sailing

This portfolio's greatest weakness is probably also its greatest strength. While the reduction in dramatic price swings also means no dramatic growth at the best of times, it also hopefully means no dramatic drops at the worst of times. Because your overall portfolio performance is the weighted average of its component parts, you still get to benefit from the highs and lows of each market's circumstances, without letting any one of these fluctuations on their own totally ruin you. There's a lot to be said for the stability this amount of diversity provides.

Outsmarting FOMO

If you invest in a little bit of everything, there's no way you can miss out on anything! A variety of assets improves your chances of capturing positive returns from all corners of the market, each with its own set of return drivers and performance cycles. By holding a diversified portfolio like this one, you can reap the benefits of all they have to offer.

How to Build It

For this portfolio, you'll want to split your investment into four parts, based on the asset allocation outlined on page 283.

For example, if you were investing $300 per month, here's what your portfolio would look like:

- $90 per month (0.3 × $300) in either a total stock market index fund or an S&P 500 index fund
- $90 per month in a total international stock index fund
- $90 per month in bonds or bond index funds
- $30 per month (0.1 × $300) in either a dividend growth index fund or a REIT ETF

As usual, these percentages are just a guideline. You do you, and I'll support it.

Common Mistakes

The beauty of a well-diversified portfolio is like savoring a gourmet meal—every ingredient is carefully combined to create a symphony of flavors. But even when it appears that the salmon is cooked perfectly, it's important to keep an eye out for fish bones.

Setting It and Forgetting It

If you're particular about your numbers, this portfolio will require regular maintenance and upkeep. With this many moving parts, it's only a matter of time until your percentages get out of whack. For example, if stocks have performed exceptionally well, their proportion in your portfolio might become disproportionately large, increasing your overall risk. If you don't check the status of your asset allocation every once in a while, you might find yourself with more eggs than you wanted in one particular basket.

Lack of Quality Control

Having more doesn't automatically make it good. A big-box variety pack of snacks is pointless if half the box contains expired cheese puffs. While diversification can be hugely beneficial, it's not a replacement for assessing the quality of individual investments within your portfolio. Holding poor-performing assets, even in the midst of a bunch of great ones, can still have a negative impact and drag down your overall returns. As always, carefully conduct your research and make sure anything you invest in is high-quality.

Paper Hands

Far and away, the major benefit of a diversified portfolio like this one is to provide a sense of *security* when the market starts doing poorly. In fact, it's a great option for people who get nervous and feel tempted to sell when things get bad. If you wind up selling anyway, you'll defeat the whole purpose of the portfolio. A growth portfolio might have given you more gains than this one, especially if you're young and you have time to let it ride out and withstand the bad stuff, so if you like the stability this portfolio has to offer, you need to stay put. Otherwise, you might've been better off accepting more risk from the get-go.

Chapter 12

The Custom-Made

If you're still here, first of all, congratulations. I get that a lot of this can be really daunting in the beginning, so I'm super proud of you for sticking it out. Your future bank account is even more proud of you, for the record, but it'll tell you that in a few years.

That said, if the reason you're still here is because none of the previous portfolios have resonated with you, I also understand. The truth is, your ideal investment portfolio might not be *any* of the ones I've listed.

That's the point of this book, right, and investing in general. You might need to make your own combination. I've lost count of how many times I've said it, but I'll say it again: Personal finance is personal. Everyone has their own preferences, risk tolerance, time horizon, and financial goals. My mom taught me first (and social media taught me second) that you can please some of the people all of the time, and all of the people some of the time, but you *cannot please all of the people all of the time*. This book can give you the tools you need to custom-craft and create your own, but it's up to you and you alone to execute. There is no perfect one-size-fits-all scenario.

Two hundred–plus pages of insight and my terribly punny sense of humor later, you now know that every investment portfolio comes with its own unique set of risks and benefits, pros and cons, good and evil. So, in this last chapter, I'll leave you with a template to help you custom-build your own. Think of this as an all-you-can-eat situation where you get to order à la carte off the menu of everything we've covered. Just keep in mind that the more you add, the more effort it might require to rebalance. You can take it or leave it with any one of these categories: None of them are absolutely necessary to include or exclude. You've got the knowledge at this point about what you like and what you don't. It's all up to you.

Don't mind me, I'll just be over here, cheering you on from the sidelines for all eternity. What's that? I'm not crying, you're crying.

Portfolio Asset Allocation

- _____ percent mutual funds, index funds, or ETFs
  - _____ percent total stock market funds
  - _____ percent S&P 500 funds
  - _____ percent total bond market funds
  - _____ percent dividend growth funds
  - _____ percent international stock funds
  - _____ percent REIT funds
- _____ percent individual stocks
  - _____ percent value stocks
  - _____ percent growth stocks
  - _____ percent dividend stocks
- _____ percent individual bonds
  - _____ percent US Treasuries
  - _____ percent municipal bonds
  - _____ percent corporate bonds
- _____ percent cryptocurrency
- _____ percent individual US REITs
- _____ percent social impact investments

Glossary

asset allocation: the process of distributing investments across different asset classes (e.g., stocks, bonds, real estate, cash).

asset class: a category of investments with similar characteristics, such as stocks, bonds, real estate, or commodities.

bear market: a prolonged period of declining stock prices in the financial markets, usually accompanied by pessimistic investors and often driven by economic uncertainty.

blue-chip stocks: shares of well-established, financially stable, and reputable companies with a long history of reliable performance; these companies are considered to be leaders in their industries and are often known for paying dividends to shareholders.

bond: a type of investment where an individual lends money to a company or government in exchange for regular interest payments and the return of the initial investment amount at a specified future date.

bond funds: investment funds that pool money from multiple investors to buy a diversified portfolio of bonds issued by companies, governments, or other entities; the aim is to provide regular income from interest payments and potential capital appreciation as the underlying bond prices fluctuate.

bull market: a prolonged period of rising stock prices in the financial markets, usually accompanied by optimistic investors and often driven by economic growth.

capital: the money or financial resources that a company or individual uses to invest in assets.

capital appreciation: the increase in value of an investment over time, meaning that the initial amount you invested has grown, leading to a higher overall value of your investment.

capital gains: the profit made from the difference between the selling price and the purchase price of an investment; the financial gain you earned from the investment when selling it.

capital gains tax: a tax imposed on the profit you make from selling your investments, such as stocks, real estate, or other assets, for a higher price than what you initially paid for them; the tax you may owe on the financial gain you earned through the sale of the investment (see related terms *short-term capital gains tax* and *long-term capital gains tax*).

compound interest: the process of accruing interest, not only on the initial amount invested, saved, or borrowed but also on the accumulated interest over time, leading to exponential growth.

distribution: the process of disbursing investment earnings or gains to investors, such as dividends from stocks or interest payments from bonds; a way for investors to receive a portion of the profits generated by their investments.

diversification: spreading investments across different asset classes, sectors, or geographic regions to reduce risk by avoiding overreliance on any single investment.

dividends: profits that a company shares with its shareholders in the form of payments.

exchange-traded fund (ETF): a type of investment fund that trades on stock exchanges; represents a basket of securities and offers diversification similar to a passively managed mutual fund.

401(k)/403(b): retirement savings plans offered by employers that allow employees to contribute a portion of their salary on a pre-tax basis, with employers potentially matching contributions.

growth investing: an investment strategy where investors focus on buying stocks of companies that are expected to experience above-average growth in the long run, with the goal of capitalizing on the company's future potential for higher stock prices, even if the current market valuation may seem relatively high.

high-yield savings account (HYSA): a type of bank account, typically online and without a physical location, that offers a higher interest rate compared to traditional savings accounts, allowing you to earn more on your savings while still keeping your money safe and easily accessible.

index fund: a type of mutual fund or ETF designed to mimic the performance of a specific market index, such as the S&P 500.

individual retirement account (IRA): a tax-advantaged investment account where contributions may be tax deductible.

inflation: an increase in the general level of prices for goods and services, eroding the purchasing power of money over time.

intrinsic value: in economics, the theory that all stocks have an underlying, fundamental value, independent of market fluctuations and emotions; typically based on objective measures, such as cash flow and the price-to-earnings ratio (P/E ratio).

large-cap: short for "large market capitalization"; refers to companies with a market capitalization value greater than $10 billion, typically consisting of well-established and widely recognized companies.

liquidity: the ease with which an investment can be converted into cash without a significant impact on its price.

long-term capital gains tax: the tax you pay on profits earned from selling investments that you've held for more than one year; typically lower than the rate for short-term gains, providing an incentive for investors to hold their investments for the long term.

market capitalization: also known as "market cap," this is the total value of a company's stock shares, calculated by multiplying the number of shares owned by shareholders by its current trading stock price (see related terms *large-cap*, *mid-cap*, and *small-cap*).

market index: a "scoreboard" that tracks the performance of a group of stocks or investments in a particular financial market; market indexes provide a snapshot of how a group of investments is collectively performing, allowing investors to assess the market's trends.

mid-cap: short for "middle market capitalization"; refers to companies with a moderate total value in the stock market, between $2 billion and $10 billion; smaller than large-cap companies but larger than small-cap companies.

mutual fund: an investment vehicle that pools money from multiple investors to invest in a diversified portfolio of stocks, bonds, or other securities.

net asset value (NAV): the value of all the assets (like stocks, bonds, and cash) held by an investment fund, minus any liabilities (like fees and expenses), divided by its total shares held by shareholders; representing the price per share of the fund.

net worth: the value obtained by subtracting an individual's liabilities (debts) from their assets, indicating their overall financial position.

portfolio: a collection of investments held by an individual or institution, including stocks, bonds, cash, and other asset classes.

public: as in "going public"; when a privately owned company decides to sell shares of its ownership to the general public through a stock exchange.

rebalancing: adjusting your portfolio to bring it back to its desired asset allocation; this involves selling some assets that have grown and buying more assets that have declined to maintain your target percentages.

risk tolerance: an individual's willingness and ability to bear potential losses or fluctuations in the value of their investments.

Roth IRA: an individual retirement account (IRA) that allows individuals to make after-tax contributions independent of an employer; qualified withdrawals in retirement are tax-free.

short-term capital gains tax: the tax you pay on profits earned from selling investments that you've held for one year or less; usually taxed at your ordinary income tax rate, which is typically higher than your long-term capital gains tax rate.

short-term investing: investing with the intention of profiting from rapid market fluctuations or short-lived opportunities; holding investments for one year or less, but typically days or months, before selling them for profit; examples include day trading and swing trading.

small-cap: short for "small market capitalization"; refers to companies with a relatively low total value in the stock market, $250 million to $2 billion, often consisting of smaller and less well-known companies.

stock: a share of ownership in a company that represents a claim on its assets and earnings proportional to how much stock is owned.

stock market: a place where people can buy and sell shares of stock, which physically or virtually exists in the form of a stock exchange (e.g., the New York Stock Exchange).

S&P 500: a stock market index that represents the performance of five hundred large and well-established companies listed on major US stock exchanges.

target date fund (TDF): a class of funds that will periodically and automatically rebalance your assets; designed to gradually shift to a more conservative portfolio as you approach your target date, which is usually retirement.

tax deduction: an item or expense that can be subtracted from an individual's taxable income, reducing the amount of tax they owe.

ticker symbol: a "nickname" assigned to a specific stock or security, usually consisting of a combination of three or four letters that uniquely identifies it; used in financial news and investment platforms; e.g., "AAPL" represents Apple Inc. on the stock exchange.

value investing: an investment strategy whereby investors look for stocks that they believe are currently priced lower than their intrinsic value, meaning the stock is potentially undervalued by the market; and an investing approach undergirded by the belief that all stocks will gravitate toward their intrinsic value over time as market fluctuations and short-term sentiment fade away.

volatility: the degree to which the price or value of an investment fluctuates over time.

yield: the income generated by an investment, typically expressed as a percentage of the investment's price or value.

Resources

Welcome to the Resources section, curated with care to help answer any lingering questions you might have. Here, you'll find a collection of valuable tools that I've personally found helpful, and that I believe would be well-suited to any reader. As always, remember to do your own due diligence before taking anyone's advice or engaging anyone's services, even the ones I list here.

Financial Literacy and Empowerment

Broke Black Girl (thebrokeblackgirl.com)
Dasha Kennedy's blog that focuses on financial activism and aims to bridge the gap between financial equity and education for Black women.

Clever Girl Finance (clevergirlfinance.com)
Founder Bola Sokunbi provides financial education and resources tailored to women, including articles and guides on investing.

Women Talk Money (fidelity.com/learning-center/women-talk -money)
While this resource is provided by Fidelity, it is not exclusively focused on their products. Women Talk Money offers articles, webinars, and tools to help women take control of their finances and investments.

Girls Who Invest (girlswhoinvest.org)
This nonprofit organization aims to increase the number of women in portfolio management and executive leadership roles in the asset management industry. They offer educational programs and resources for women interested in finance and investing.

Investopedia (investopedia.com)
Investopedia is a popular financial education website with a vast array of resources and information on personal finance, investing, trading, economics, and more, for beginners and experienced investors. Investopedia's "Diversity & Inclusion in Financial Services" section (https://www.investopedia.com/best-programs-improving -diversity-and-inclusion-in-financial-services-industry-5092350) includes insights for women and underrepresented investors looking to start a career in finance.

White Coat Investor (whitecoatinvestor.com)
Dr. James M. Dahle, a practicing emergency physician and personal finance enthusiast, provides financial education and guidance to medical professionals, particularly physicians, dentists, and other high-income earners in the health-care industry through this popular online platform.

WISE (Women Investing in Security and Education) (wiseinvestors.org/)
A philanthropic organization with a mission to provide opportunities and expertise for the financial education of women and girls.

Personal Finance Podcasts

Bad with Money
Author Gabe Dunn's money show for the "queerdos and weirdos." Gabe, a queer and trans writer and *New York Times* bestselling author, and their guests talk about money myths and discuss personal finance problems and how to solve them.

Brown Ambition
Hosts and personal finance experts Mandi Woodruff and Tiffany Aliche of the Budgetnista help you unapologetically build wealth by saving, investing, and making smart career choices.

The Financial Feminist
Hosted by Tori Dunlap of Her First 100K, this podcast explores financial and investing topics through a feminist lens.

Managing Medical Debt

Dollar For (dollarfor.org)
Dollar For is a national nonprofit that has crushed millions of dollars in medical bills by empowering patients and advocating on their behalf. Their work is entirely funded through philanthropic grants and donations and their services are completely free—no strings attached. I've met these people, and they're amazing.

HealthWell Foundation (healthwellfoundation.org)
The HealthWell Foundation is an independent nonprofit dedicated to improving access to health care for America's underinsured. When health insurance is not enough, they fill the gap by assisting with copays, premiums, deductibles, and out-of-pocket expenses. I've also met these people, and they're incredible.

Addressing Investing Fraud

Financial Industry Regulatory Authority (FINRA) (finra.org /investors/need-help)
FINRA is a self-regulatory organization that oversees the securities industry and investigates complaints against brokerage firms and their employees. You can file a complaint with FINRA through their website. If you're not sure what type of complaint you have and choose to file it with FINRA, they will evaluate the complaint and pass it on to the appropriate regulator if it is not within FINRA's jurisdiction.

North American Securities Administrators Association (nasaa.org /contact-your-regulator/)
Many states have their own securities regulators who can help investors who have fallen victim to investment fraud. You can find the contact information for your state's securities regulator through the North American Securities Administrators Association (NASAA) website.

Securities and Exchange Commission (SEC) (sec.gov/oiea /QuestionsAndComments.html)
The SEC is a federal agency that regulates the securities industry and works to protect investors from fraud. If you believe that you've been a victim of investment fraud, you can report it to the SEC through their website, by sending an email to help@sec.gov, or by contacting the SEC's Office of Investor Education and Advocacy (OIEA) at 1–800–732–0330.

Financial Abuse

National Domestic Violence Hotline (thehotline.org)
Twenty-four hours a day, 7 days a week, 365 days a year, the National Domestic Violence Hotline offers essential tools and support for victims of domestic abuse, including financial abuse. The service, which is free and confidential, includes compassionate support, crisis intervention information, education, and referral services in over two hundred languages. Please note: Internet usage can be monitored and is impossible to erase completely. You can always call the hotline at 800–799-SAFE (7233).

Office on Women's Health Financial Abuse Page (womenshealth .gov/relationships-and-safety/other-types/financial-abuse)
Financial abuse can be difficult to identify. This website defines abuse, describes what it might look like, and lists warning signs that can help you understand if you're experiencing it. It also offers advice on how to begin the process of leaving an abusive partner, and provides hands-on resources and a list of ways to implement a safety plan.

Women's Law (womenslaw.org)
Women's Law is part of the National Network to End Domestic Violence (nnedv.org/content/state-u-s-territory-coalitions/) and provides state-specific legal information and resources for victims of domestic violence, including a drop-down menu to find a list of local shelters, programs, support groups, crisis counseling, and safety planning assistance (womenslaw.org/find-help/advocates -and-shelters).

The Allstate Foundation (allstatefoundation.org/what-we-do/end -domestic-violence/resources)
Designed to help domestic violence survivors achieve financial independence and rebuild their lives, this curriculum covers budgeting, managing debt, and improving credit and has been proven to help survivors move from short-term safety to long-term security. It is available online for download in English, Spanish, French, and Vietnamese.

Help Guide Domestic Abuse Page (helpguide.org/articles/abuse /getting-out-of-an-abusive-relationship)
A detailed guideline of how to leave a financially abusive relationship, plus a walkthrough of common thought processes survivors might have before leaving, and how to overcome them.

Notes

Introduction

5   **less than 25 percent of high schools:** Carmen Reinicke, "Nearly 1 in 4 Students in the U.S. Has Access to Personal Finance Education This Year," CNBC, April 22, 2022, https://www.cnbc.com/2022/04 /22/nearly-25percent-of-us-students-have-access-to-personal -finance-education.html.

5   **Making 82 cents to every man's dollar:** "Highlights of Women's Earnings in 2020," U.S. Bureau of Labor Statistics, September 2021, https://www.bls.gov/opub/reports/womens-earnings/2020/home .htm.

6   **More than 80 percent of women between the ages of sixty and seventy-five:** The American College Center for Retirement Income, "Retirement Income Literacy Gender Differences Report," American College of Financial Services, 2017, https://retirement .theamericancollege.edu/sites/retirement/files/Gender_Differences _in_Retirement_Income_Literacy_Report.pdf.

6   **Families headed by women:** Ana Hernandez Kent and Lowell R. Rickets, "Gender Wealth Gap: Families Headed by Women Have Lower Wealth," Federal Reserve Bank of St. Louis, January 12, 2021, https://www.stlouisfed.org/publications/in-the-balance/2021 /gender-wealth-gap-families-women-lower-wealth.

7   **In Fidelity's 2021 Women and Investing Study:** "Fidelity Investments 2021 Women and Investing Study," Fidelity Investments, 2021,

https://www.fidelity.com/bin-public/060_www_fidelity_com
/documents/about-fidelity/FidelityInvestmentsWomen&
InvestingStudy2021.pdf.

Part I: Building a Solid Foundation

12   **Despite having far fewer years to accumulate it:** Anna Zakrzewski, Kedra Newsom Reeves, Michael Kahlich, Maximilian Klein, Andrea Real Mattar, and Stephan Knobel, "Managing the Next Decade of Women's Wealth," Boston Consulting Group, April 9, 2020, https:// www.bcg.com/publications/2020/managing-next-decade-women -wealth.

12   **Women-owned businesses generate $1.9 trillion:** "The 2019 State of Women-Owned Businesses Report," Ventureneer, 2019, https:// ventureneer.com/wp-content/uploads/2019/10/Final-2019-state -of-women-owned-businesses-report.pdf.

12   **during the 2008 financial crisis:** Pat Wechsler, "Women-Led Companies Perform Three Times Better Than the S&P 500," *Fortune*, March 3, 2015, https://fortune.com/2015/03/03/women -led-companies-perform-three-times-better-than-the-sp-500/.

12   **more than five million Fidelity customers:** "Fidelity Investments 2021 Women and Investing Study," Fidelity Investments, 2021, https://www.fidelity.com/bin-public/060_www_fidelity_com /documents/about-fidelity/FidelityInvestmentsWomen& InvestingStudy2021.pdf.

Chapter 1: Make Your Money Work for You

28   **the average credit card interest rate:** "Consumer Credit—G.19," Board of Governors of the Federal Reserve System, last updated July 10, 2023, https://www.federalreserve.gov/releases/g19/current/.

32   **He invested $1,700:** Justin Bandler and James Callahan, "Lord of the Roths: How Tech Mogul Peter Thiel Turned a Retirement Account for the Middle Class into a $5 Billion Tax-Free Piggy Bank," *ProPublica*, July 14, 2021, https://www.propublica.org /article/lord-of-the-roths-how-tech-mogul-peter-thiel-turned-a -retirement-account-for-the-middle-class-into-a-5-billion-dollar -tax-free-piggy-bank.

32   **Thiel's initial investment had grown:** Bandler and Callahan, "Lord of the Roths."

36   **In 2019, women hit a new milestone:** Richard Fry, "Women Now Outnumber Men in the U.S. College-Educated Labor Force," Pew Research Center, September 26, 2022, https://www.pewresearch .org/short-reads/2022/09/26/women-now-outnumber-men-in-the -u-s-college-educated-labor-force/.

37   **Today, women of all races earn:** "Highlights of Women's Earnings in 2020," US Bureau of Labor Statistics, September 2021, https:// www.bls.gov/opub/reports/womens-earnings/2020/home.htm.

37   **women who identified as either Hispanic or Latina:** "Highlights of Women's Earnings in 2020," US Bureau of Labor Statistics.

37   **Native American women earned only 50 cents:** "Highlights of Women's Earnings in 2020," US Bureau of Labor Statistics.

37   **Black women earned only 57 cents:** "Highlights of Women's Earnings in 2020," US Bureau of Labor Statistics.

37   **women who identified as Asian American:** "Highlights of Women's Earnings in 2020," US Bureau of Labor Statistics.

37   **while Indian American women earned:** "Highlights of Women's Earnings in 2020," US Bureau of Labor Statistics.

37   **Migrant women, in particular:** "Women and Men Migrant Workers: Moving towards Equal Rights and Opportunities," International Labour Organization, https://www.ilo.org/wcmsp5 /groups/public/@dgreports/@gender/documents/publication/wcms _101118.pdf.

37   **half of LGBTQI+ Americans reported:** Caroline Medina and Lindsay Mahowald, "Discrimination and Barriers to Well-Being: The State of the LGBTQI+ Community in 2022," Center for American Progress, January 12, 2023, https://www.americanprogress .org/article/discrimination-and-barriers-to-well-being-the-state-of -the-lgbtqi-community-in-2022/.

38   **when women have more information about opportunities outside of their current job:** Chabeli Carrazana, "Does Sharing Salaries in Job Postings Help Address the Gender Pay Gap?" PBS, March 16, 2022, https://www.pbs.org/newshour/economy/does-sharing -salaries-in-job-postings-help-address-the-gender-pay-gap.

41   **A Harvard study found that men were twice as likely:** Karin
          Hederos Eriksson and Anna Sandberg, "Gender Differences in
          Initiation of Negotiation: Does the Gender of the Negotiation
          Counterpart Matter?" *Negotiation Journal* 28, no. 4 (October 2012):
          407–428, https://gap.hks.harvard.edu/gender-differences-initiation
          -negotiation-does-gender-negotiation-counterpart-matter.

45   **In fact, the *Wall Street Journal* reported:** Sara Chaney Cambon and
          Ana Rivas, "Women are Winning the Biggest Pay Raises of U.S.
          Labor Boom," *Wall Street Journal*, March 21, 2022, https://www.wsj
          .com/articles/women-are-winning-the-biggest-pay-raises-from-u
          -s-labor-boom-11647864000?mod=hp_lead_pos10.

Chapter 2: Investing 101

61   **The average loaf of bread:** "Comparison of Prices over the Last 90
          Years," The People's History, accessed October 4, 2023, https://www
          .thepeoplehistory.com/70yearsofpricechange.html.

73   **The stock market has returned an average of roughly 10 percent:**
          Jeffrey Ptak, "What Beat the S&P 500 Over the Past Three
          Decades? Doing Nothing," Morningstar, April 17, 2023, https://
          www.morningstar.com/stocks/what-beat-sp-500-over-past-three
          -decades-doing-nothing.

78   **Bank of America found:** Pippa Stevens, "This Chart Shows Why
          Investors Should Never Try to Time the Stock Market," CNBC,
          March 24, 2021, https://www.cnbc.com/2021/03/24/this-chart
          -shows-why-investors-should-never-try-to-time-the-stock-market.
          html.

78   **A study published in the *Journal of Finance*:** Brad M. Barber and
          Terrance Odean, "Trading Is Hazardous to Your Wealth: The
          Common Stock Investment Performance of Individual Investors,"
          Journal of Finance 55, no. 2 (December 2002): 773–806, https://doi
          .org/10.1111/0022-1082.00226.

78   **The same study by Fidelity:** "Fidelity Investments 2021 Women
          and Investing Study," Fidelity Investments, 2021, https://www
          .fidelity.com/bin-public/060_www_fidelity_com/documents
          /about-fidelity/FidelityInvestmentsWomen&InvestingStudy2021
          .pdf.

79   **Research at Warwick Business School found:** Neil Stewart, "Are
          Women Better Investors Than Men?" Warwick Business School,

June 28, 2018, https://www.wbs.ac.uk/news/are-women-better
-investors-than-men.

79   **And a study by the University of California, Davis, in 2015:**
Brendan Boyd, "Women's Portfolios Often to Do Better Than
Men's," *Business Journals*, last updated January 20, 2003, https://
www.bizjournals.com/louisville/stories/2003/01/20/editorial5.html.

Chapter 3: Know Your Investments

81   **"securities that represent an ownership share in a company":** "What
Different Types of Securities Are Issued to Startup Investors?"
SEC.gov, accessed July 16, 2023, https://www.sec.gov/education
/capitalraising/building-blocks/startup-securities.

82   **Owning a stock meant earning proceeds:** Mark Smith, *A History of
the Global Stock Market: From Ancient Rome to Silicon Valley*
(Chicago: University of Chicago Press, 2004).

99   **"radiat[ing] total cool":** Barbara P. Barbash, "Remembering the
Past: Mutual Funds and the Lessons of the Wonder Years,"
SEC.gov, December 4, 1997, https://www.sec.gov/news/speech
/speecharchive/1997/spch199.txt.

99   **After reaching its peak in 1972, the market crashed:** Barbash,
"Remembering the Past."

99   **Account values dropped between 40 and 50 percent:** Barbash,
"Remembering the Past."

102   **A report by S&P Dow Jones Indices:** Berlinda Liu and Gaurav
Sinha, "SPIVA U.S. Scorecard." n.d., S&P Global, accessed July 16,
2023, https://www.spglobal.com/spdji/en/documents/spiva/spiva-us
-year-end-2020.pdf; "More Evidence That It's Really Hard to 'Beat
the Market' over Time, 95% of Finance Professionals Can't Do It,"
American Enterprise Institute, October 18, 2018, https://www.aei
.org/carpe-diem/more-evidence-that-its-really-hard-to-beat-the
-market-over-time-95-of-finance-professionals-cant-do-it/.

123   **the value of Bitcoin money lost:** Ahmed Oluwasanjo, "$24 Billion
Worth Bitcoin Lost to Forgotten Password: Report," *Peoples Gazette*,
January 19, 2023, https://gazettengr.com/24-billion-worth-bitcoin
-lost-to-forgotten-password-report.

128   **the MSCI EAFE Index:** "MSCI EAFE Index (USD)," MSCI,
June 30, 2023, https://www.msci.com/documents/10199/4753a237
-7f5a-4ef6-9f2b-9f46245402e6.

134   **"Few solutions that meet the fundamental needs"**: Kevin Starr, "The Trouble With Impact Investing," *Stanford Social Innovation Review*, January 24, 2012, https://ssir.org/articles/entry/the_trouble_with _impact_investing_part_1.

Chapter 4: Your Investor Profile

152   **incorrectly branded as "risk-averse"**: Kira Vermond, "Why 'Risk Aware' Is a Better Term for Women Investors Than 'Risk Averse,'" *Globe and Mail*, October 25, 2022, https://www.theglobeandmail .com/business/article-why-risk-aware-is-a-better-term-for-women -investors-than-risk-averse/.

159   **An ongoing study comparing active investor returns to the broader market:** James Chen, "Hands-off Investor," Investopedia, updated April 28, 2022, https://www.investopedia.com/terms/h /handsoffinvestor.asp.

Chapter 5: Create a Portfolio

176   **From the bottom in March 2009:** Michael Santoli, "10 Years Ago This Week, the Market Hit the Bottom of the Great Recession," CNBC, March 4, 2019, https://www.cnbc.com/2019/03/04/the -10th-anniversary-of-the-climactic-march-2009-market-bottom -arrives-this-week.Html.

193   **there have been twenty-seven bull markets:** "10 Things You Should Know About Bear Markets," Hartford Funds, accessed July 25, 2023, https://www.hartfordfunds.com/practice-management/client -conversations/managing-volatility/bear-markets.html.

193   **have historically lasted more than three times:** Malika Mitra, "How Long Do Bull Markets Last? Here's the Historical Data," *Money*, June 23, 2023, https://money.com/how-long-bull-markets-last.

198   **an average of around 10 percent per year since its inception in 1957:** "S&P 500® Data," S&P Global, https://www.officialdata.org/us /stocks/s-p-500/1957?amount=100&endYear=2022/.

205   **the S&P 500 beat the average hedge fund's returns:** Mark J. Perry, "The SP 500 Index Out-performed Hedge Funds over the Last 10 Years. And It Wasn't Even Close," American Enterprise Institute, January 7, 2021, https://www.aei.org/carpe-diem/the-sp-500-index -out-performed-hedge-funds-over-the-last-10-years-and-it-wasnt -even-close/.

Part II: Building Experience & Wealth

208   *Madsinger's Monthly Report*: Madsinger, "Madsinger's Monthly Report," Bogleheads.org, last updated 2020, https://www.bogleheads.org/forum/memberlist.php?mode=viewprofile&u=3530.

Chapter 6: The Full Autopilot

216   **A study conducted by researchers at the University of Illinois and MIT:** Taylor Tepper, "Target Date Fund Pros and Cons," *Forbes*, November 15, 2022, https://www.forbes.com/advisor/retirement/target-date-fund-pros-and-cons.

Chapter 7: The Lazy Luxury

225   **Buffett's S&P 500 index fund had already outperformed:** "Berkshire's Performance vs. the S&P 500," Berkshire Hathaway, accessed July 26, 2023, https://www.berkshirehathaway.com/letters/2016ltr.pdf.

225   **The S&P 500 had generated an annual return of more than 7 percent:** "Berkshire's Performance vs. the S&P 500."

225   **"For all intents and purposes":** Ruth Umoh, "Billionaire Warren Buffett won $2.2 million on a bet and gave it to this charity," CNBC, Februrary 16, 2018, https://www.cnbc.com/2018/02/16/warren-buffett-won-2-point-2-million-on-a-bet-and-gave-it-to-girls-inc.html.

227   **the difference in average long-term returns between the two:** Kent Thune, "Total Stock Market Index vs. S&P 500 Index," Balance Money, last updated October 17, 2022, https://www.thebalancemoney.com/total-stock-market-vs-sandp-500-2466403#:~:text=Market%20Index%20vs.-,S%26P%20500%20Index,indexes%20represent%20only%20U.S.%20stocks.

231   **in previous major market downturns:** "MSCI EAFE Index (USD)," accessed July 20, 2023, MSCI, https://www.msci.com/documents/10199/4753a237-7f5a-4ef6-9f2b-9f46245402e6.

232   **from January 1992 to January 2022:** "MSCI EAFE Index (USD)."

233   **"lagged [behind] the S&P 500":** Reshma Kapadia, "Target-Date Funds Have Mediocre Returns. It's Time to Take a Closer Look," *Barron's*, June 3, 2022, https://www.barrons.com/articles/target-date

-funds-are-popular-but-mediocre-returns-and-other-risks-warrant
-a-closer-look-51654277326.

245   **Monster has generated a total return:** Wayne Duggan, "10 Best-
Performing Stocks of the Past 30 Years," *US News and World Report*,
May 19, 2023, https://money.usnews.com/investing/stock-market
-news/slideshows/best-performing-stocks-of-the-past-30-years.

245   **Since its inception:** Brett Schafer, "This Is the Best-Performing
Stock Since 2000 (and No, It Isn't Apple)," Motley Fool, April 17,
2023, https://www.fool.com/investing/2023/04/17/the-best
-performing-stock-since-2000-and-not-apple/.

257   **From February 1991 to January 2022:** Michael Boyle, "Aggregate
Bond Index vs. Stock Index 1980-2021," Balance, last updated
March 5, 2022, https://www.thebalancemoney.com/stocks-and
-bonds-calendar-year-performance-417028.

Chapter 10: The Dividend Queen

276   **According to a study by Hartford Funds:** "The Power of Dividends:
Past, Present, and Future," Hartford Funds, accessed July 21, 2023,
https://www.hartfordfunds.com/insights/market-perspectives/equity
/the-power-of-dividends.html.

280   **In 2020, the company announced it would not raise:** Rich Duprey,
"ExxonMobil Fails to Raise Its Dividend for the First Time in
Years," Motley Fool, last updated October 29, 2020, https://www
.fool.com/investing/2020/10/29/exxonmobil-fails-to-raise-dividend
-for-first-time/.

280   **That same year:** Mark Maurer, "Some Companies Haven't Paid a
Dividend Since 2020. They Might Bring It Back as a Slowdown
Looms," *Wall Street Journal*, December 30, 2022, https://www.wsj
.com/articles/some-companies-havent-paid-a-dividend-since-2020
-they-might-bring-it-back-as-a-slowdown-looms-11661765401.

280   **all suspended dividend payments:** Lawrence C. Strauss, "Here Are
13 Stocks Whose Pandemic Dividend Suspensions Remain,"
Barron's, January 13, 2022, https://www.barrons.com/articles/here
-are-13-stocks-whose-pandemic-dividend-suspensions-remain
-51642091403.

280   **nearly 190 US companies stopped paying:** Maurer, "Some
Companies Haven't Paid a Dividend Since 2020."

Acknowledgments

Thank you to the many role model women in my life, who made me who I am today—this book would not have been possible without you. To, of course, my mom. To Aunt Shelley, Aunt Linda, and cousins Katie and Bridgitt. To my sister, Vicki. To my grandmothers, Maxine, Jacki, and Linda. To my mother- and grandmother-in-law, Christine and Valeria. To Miss Nancy, Aunt Des, and Kate. To my pharmacy mentors, Brianna and Shally. To my dear friends Hina and Lish.

Thank you to my dad, my biological dad, who taught me to have fun, and be silly, and that there is still so much left to live for, even after such profound loss.

Thank you to my dad, my chosen dad, who taught me how to re-place a great many things, to work hard *and* relax hard, and that any experience involving good food and family is always worth the money. You didn't have to be my dad, but you chose to be, and that means the world to me.

Thank you to my husband, who is in no way offended that I make more money than him. Likewise, I am in no way offended that he is, by far, the better cook. Take that, traditional gender roles.

Thank you to Elysia Liang, my editor, who believed in me to write this book in the first place, and believed in me to finish it, even when, at times, I didn't. Were it not for her exceptional ability to translate what I *said* into what I *meant to say*, I'd have surely embarrassed myself. Thank you to my entire behind-the-scenes team at Rodale Books and Penguin Random House, who, together, coordinated this effort into what you see today: Kim Suarez, Patricia Shaw, Diana Drew, Dustin Amick, and Odette Flemming.

And last, but certainly not least, thank you to you, reader. I now know for sure that it is much easier to invest from the comfort of my couch than it is to write a book about it. But for you, it was worth it.

Index

About the Author

Dr. Jessica Spangler is an award-winning money educator behind @ecommjess, emergency medicine clinical pharmacist, and online business owner. With more than a million followers across social media platforms, Jessica aims to make personal finance easy to understand and accessible to all. Her work has been featured on CNBC and Yahoo Finance and in *Insider*, among other publications and websites.